# PRAIRIE CROSSING

# PRAIRIE CROSSING

CREATING AN AMERICAN
CONSERVATION
COMMUNITY

JOHN SCOTT WATSON

UNIVERSITY OF ILLINOIS PRESS
URBANA, CHICAGO, AND SPRINGFIELD

Library of Congress Control Number: 2015954478
ISBN 978-0-252-03986-7 (hardcover)
ISBN 978-0-252-09797-3 (e-book)

The joy of the prairie lies in its subtlety. It is so easy—
too easy—to be swept away by mountain and ocean
vistas. A prairie, on the other hand, requests the favor
of your closer attention. It does not divulge itself to
mere passersby.

—Suzanne Winckler, 2004

The sea, the woods, the mountains, all suffer in comparison with the prairie. . . . The prairie has a stronger hold
on the senses. Its sublimity arises from its unbounded
extent, its barren monotony and desolation, its still,
unmoved, calm, stern, almost self-confident grandeur,
its strange power of deception, its want of echo, and,
in fine, its power of throwing a man back upon himself.

—Albert Pike, 1832

*For Daisy and Cheyenne*

# CONTENTS

# ILLUSTRATIONS

# ACKNOWLEDGMENTS

I owe a great debt of gratitude to my colleague Dennis Judd of the University of Illinois at Chicago. Over the years, he encouraged, challenged, and mentored me, and this book would not be possible without him. I would also like to thank three other colleagues at UIC, Dick Simpson, Evan McKenzie, and Andrew McFarland. Dick encouraged me to write the book and helped me navigate the waters of university publishing. Evan McKenzie helped me refine my ideas in the early stages of writing. Thanks also to Andy for providing constructive criticism of the first draft and occasionally tipping some beers at Blackie's.

I also want to acknowledge the efforts of many other people who helped shepherd me through graduate school: Marilyn Getzov, James Nell, Thomas Carsey, Barry Rundquist, Gerald Strom, Doris Graber, Kevin Lyles, Janet Smith, Ola Adeoye, Betty O'Shaughnessy, Bob McKee, and Patricia Mizrahi. Many thanks to friends and coworkers who over the years eased the struggles of earning a paycheck and attending university: Scott Peters, Ullica Segerstrale, Mary Withers, Wendy Clayton, Vito Caputo, Lance Michael Kopera, Chip Heinechen, Tim Heiser, Michelle McBroom, Phil Oshana, and Eric Watson. Thanks also to Tim Joyce of Wild Birds Unlimited of Glenview, who often acted as a sounding board for my ideas. I also want to acknowledge the role of several youngsters in my life who helped keep my childlike wonder for the world aflame: my nieces Samantha Watson and Morgan and Kendal Vette, my nephew Thomas Watson, and Steven Kopera, the gifted son of a friend and coworker.

In the course of writing this book, which is my first, I learned that it is much more a collaboration than the product of a sole individual. I am grateful for my acquisitions editor, Willis Regier, who guided me through the process of publication, and also for the efforts of the supporting staff at the University of Illinois Press, particularly Jennifer Comeau and Kevin Cunningham, and copyeditor Jane Lyle. I also would like to thank the two anonymous reviewers who took the time and care to provide academic criticism in a way that greatly improved my work. I am especially grateful to my wife and unofficial editor, Anne-Marie Cusac, for her criticism, editing, and infinite patience. Her experience in writing and journalism was invaluable. It is now my turn to help her with her next book project.

Special thanks also to George and Vicky Ranney, who over the years have been very generous with their time. The book would not have been possible without their efforts. Though I never met him, I would like to thank the late Gaylord Donnelley. In writing this book, I came to understand the immense impact he had on both people and places. He deserves to be remembered for his extraordinary efforts to make the world a better place. Many other people contributed to this project, including Michael Sands, Steve Apfelbaum, Mark Cusac, Frank Martin, Maryanne Natarajan, Linda Wiens, Maria Sanborn, John Breen, Jack Broughton, Erin Cummisford, Jennifer Miller, Sarah Surroz, and Brad Leibov. Thanks to all of you for making this book a reality. I also want to acknowledge the contributions of several organizations: Applied Ecological Services, Conserve Lake County, and the Liberty Prairie Foundation.

Thank you to my college friends and family, whose support made it possible to get through tough times and deadlines. Starting with the late Otto Karbusicky, my most inspiring high school teacher at Niles West in Skokie, Illinois, thanks for demanding my best work. At Western Kentucky University, where I did my undergraduate studies, thanks to David "Butch" Brewer, Jeff Cooper, David Mitchell, Jeff Moore, Larry Mountain, Joseph Hayden Pillow, Tim Porter, David Shannon, Michelle Shaw, Michael Wolfe, and Warren Wolfe for being good friends. Thanks also to WKU professor Jack McGregor, who urged me to go to graduate school. I took the scenic route, but I did it. I also want to remember the late WKU geology professor C. Ronald Seeger. Over the last twenty-five years, I have been fortunate to have the support of the Nelsons of Glenview, my adopted family of sorts. And I owe a debt of gratitude to the late Stephen Jay Gould, an intellectual mentor whom I never met. His writings invigorated my intellectual life during the gap between my undergraduate years and graduate school. Always the daring iconoclast, he taught me to challenge intellectual conformity.

I am grateful for the help my Wisconsin neighbors, Bob and Sue Glisczin-ski, gave us during the state's cold winter months. We couldn't ask for better neighbors. I also appreciate the support my mother- and father-in-law gave me throughout the project. Thank you, Joan and Irv Cusac. To my grandmother Elsa Emma Erbstoesser Broberg, affectionately known to all as "Alma," thanks for a lifetime of love. I wish I could have signed a book for you. And special thanks to my late uncle and godfather Leroy Olson, whose visits on my birthday to bring my gifts of savings bonds provided my first memories of hearing the word "college." I hope somewhere he is proud of me. Lastly, I want to thank my animal companions—my children, really. They have hearts of gold. Thanks to my dogs, Honey and Simba, for understanding that I had to cut their walks a little short as this book was going to press. I will make it up to them. They don't call them "man's best friend" for nothing. And thanks to Sundance, my kitty of eighteen years. She has been with me through it all. Her affection has kept me going during the years of hard work. For such a small creature, she has had a huge impact on my life.

# CHAPTER ONE

# SAVING THE LAND BY DEVELOPING IT

The goal of Prairie Crossing is to demonstrate how development can improve the environment.

—Michael Sands

Traveling outward from Chicago's downtown urban core, one traverses a landscape transformed first by the farmer's plow, later by America's industrial age. The extensive grasslands that once gave Illinois its familiar "Prairie State" nickname had been gone for nearly a century and a half when a novel experiment in urban public policy took root in Grayslake, a small community located in suburban Lake County. Conceived as one of the country's first conservation communities, Prairie Crossing is a common-interest housing development that opened for initial occupation in 1994 and consists of 359 single-family homes and 36 condominiums set near a town square.[1] Carved out of 677 acres of century-old farmland forty miles north of Chicago, the development clusters its Midwestern-style homes on 135 acres, preserving 69 percent of the total land area as open space. The open space, acres of ecologically restored wetlands and prairie grasslands, is permanently and legally protected through the management of private government—the Prairie Crossing Homeowners Association. Despite the re-creation and restoration of hundreds of acres of green space—a substantial public good—the $100 million project is a profit-making venture designed to compete in the marketplace with conventional housing developments.

Prairie Crossing is a for-profit derivative of the traditional land trust concept, a free-market attempt to preserve and restore environmentally sensitive land—

a secondary grassland remnant in a state that nineteenth-century agricultural practices and the twentieth-century automobile have substantially altered. The developers, George and Vicky Ranney, a husband-and-wife team, consciously sought to craft a new policy model to ameliorate many of the perceived problems commonly attributed to urban sprawl. The Ranneys were an unlikely pair to challenge the dominance of the urban-sprawl growth model, which is "strongly entrenched" in the American economy and way of life.[2] With no previous background in housing development, they planned on using the market to preserve and protect the environment from free-market excess. By employing the latest methods and practices in energy efficiency, ecological science, and private government, the Ranneys created a new developmental template—the conservation community—one that could be replicated and exported, and one that saves green open space through the real-estate value of the land itself.[3] In effect, and in stark contrast to conventional modes of housing construction, the Ranneys wanted to show that it was possible to *save* the land by *developing* it.

## Creative Policy Response to Urban Sprawl

In his 1971 bestselling book *The Closing Circle*, ecologist Barry Commoner argued that the primary cause of environmental degradation was that our economy had fallen out of sync with the laws of nature: "Human beings have broken out of the circle of life, driven not by biological need, but by the social organization which they have devised to 'conquer' nature: means of gaining wealth that are governed by requirements conflicting with those which govern nature."[4] By focusing solely on profits, Commoner wrote, America had disconnected from the natural world and degraded the environment through unsustainable practices in virtually every aspect of life. What was needed, he suggested, was a restructuring of the American economy—to change the way we do business, and to bring it back into balance with the ecosphere.

Postwar advances in technology and manufacturing transformed American life, including how and where we built our homes. Mass production of standardized tract housing significantly lowered costs and "revolutionized home building."[5] As homeownership became synonymous with the "American Dream," and America permanently transitioned to a mass-consumption economy, bulldozers began to arrive in the countryside, creating sprawling new suburban subdivisions.[6] The "principle of drive until you qualify put home ownership within the reach" of millions of people, who fled the decaying central cities and inner-ring suburbs to the cheap land on the suburban periphery.[7] Leapfrogging commercial development followed, with office parks, strip malls, and big-box retailing providing both employment and consumption opportunities. The end result of this sprawling development is a number of negative externalities, or external costs borne by society—including air and water pollution, long commutes, traffic gridlock, and obesity—that degrade both the natural environment and human culture.

The conservation community is a prescribed policy response to the social costs inherent in the urban-growth economic model. Conservation communities attempt to change the way we build neighborhoods and towns to bring back some measure of ecological balance to the economics of homebuilding. Using original research derived from the community's residents, this book examines the successes and failures of Prairie Crossing, one of the first conservation communities in the United States, and explores the ability of the conservation community concept to improve water quality, increase the diversity of plants and animals, contribute to residents' health and well-being, and encourage the use of public transportation, all while improving the aesthetic and environmental quality of the land.

## The Conservation Community:
## A New Kind of Living

"Now approaching Prairie Crossing," announces the conductor as the commuter train pulls into the station. I step off the Metra car into a brisk late-November day with steel-gray skies. Immediately I worry that I may have underdressed for the occasion. The purpose of my visit to the Prairie Crossing community this morning is to observe a somewhat unusual suburban "social" event, a prairie wetland burning.

Michael Sands, a Prairie Crossing resident and the environmental manager for the development, is leading a group of volunteer residents in burning acres of wetland and grassland habitat that border Lake Aldo Leopold. Armed with diesel-fuel drip torches, backpack water guns, rakes, and rubber swatter mats, Sands and his crew light the native prairie vegetation, which in some places is five or six feet tall. The dry vegetation burns quickly and intensely, with the flames occasionally reaching twenty feet or more in height. Residents come out for the burn and socialize while they watch the flames spread. Some snap photographs for distribution on the community email list. By now I realize that I have indeed underdressed for the weather, and I try to capture some of the warmth emanating from the burn, which creates a considerable amount of heat. Prairie burning is a technical enterprise, one fraught with the potential for trouble—the burns frequently take place in close proximity to the homes. And it is a sight to see, with walls of flame consuming dead and dying vegetation to make room for a rebirth of green growth the following spring. Prairie Crossing is not your typical suburban subdivision.

The Prairie Crossing grassland restoration is a valuable small-scale re-creation of a vastly diminished ecosystem that once dominated the region. But walking the grounds or living in the development is a long way from what nineteenth-century explorers observed when they crossed the intact Midwestern prairie grassland. Here is how George W. Ogden described the Illinois prairie not far from Prairie Crossing in the 1820s:

> The extensive valley, watered by the Illinois and its branches, is level or gently undulating. The prairies, on this river, are numerous, and many of them very large, extending further than the eye can reach; and some of them for sixty or seventy miles. These savannas or prairies . . . resemble large flat plains—here the traveller is struck with wonder and amazement—here he may, in many places, travel from the rising of the sun, until the going down of the same, without once having a hillock or a tree presented to his eye— nothing but grass of luxuriant growth, waving in the breeze.[8]

Even the large-scale prairie restorations at the Kansas and Midewin Tallgrass National Preserves, both of which exceed 10,000 acres, cannot replicate the "wonder and amazement" that Ogden and some of his contemporaries experienced. Many of them used the metaphor of an "ocean of grass" to describe a landscape so distinct from that of their European forebears. In walking the grounds at Prairie Crossing, however, it is possible to get a sense of what was lost when settlers plowed the tallgrass prairie under in pursuit of economic progress.

Hiking the miles of trails in Prairie Crossing and the Liberty Prairie Reserve awakens the botanical senses in a way that a stroll through most suburban communities cannot. "Plant blindness" is the term that biologists James Wandersee and Elisabeth Schussler coined to describe a seemingly pervasive perceptual deficit that Americans have in relation to the botanical world. Wandersee and Schussler define it as "the inability to see or notice the plants in one's own environment." The cause of the blindness, they argue, is "our misguided, anthropocentric ranking of plants as inferior to animals, leading to the erroneous conclusion that they are unworthy of human consideration."[9]

While grassland plants may not stir the twenty-first-century mind the way giant conifer trees do, they do seem to have invigorated the spirits of those nineteenth-century travelers who encountered them in their pristine state. William Cullen Bryant, Laura Ingalls Wilder, Walt Whitman, Willa Cather, and others wrote thrilling accounts of their travels among the Midwestern prairie grassland flora. And while those endless viewscapes are a thing of the distant past, Prairie Crossing has faithfully restored the colors, sounds, smells, textures, and movements of the indigenous grassland ecosystem. The extraordinary nature of many of the native prairie plants—be it their size, color, or sheer variety—makes Prairie Crossing a remedy for plant blindness. It is difficult to walk the property and not notice the riot of colors in season or the ten-foot-tall prairie dock plants with two-foot-tall basal leaves. The street names are constant reminders of what is out there: Blazing Star Road, Lupine Court, Coneflower Road, Penstemon Court.

The nature experience at Prairie Crossing varies with the season. Between late fall and early spring, the Homeowners Association burns the common-property vegetation in two-to-four-year rotations—burning different areas at different times in different years.[10] Because the homes are clustered within the natural areas, many of the burns border residents' private properties, and those residents who themselves have native flora on their property may also do their own burning. Frequent burning is a necessity to maintain the natural character and biodiversity of the prairie ecosystem. Fire suppresses tree and shrub growth, which otherwise would eventually overrun the landscape. Herbaceous prairie plants differ from woody plants in that their points of growth are either at the surface or down in the soil. New annual tree growth emerges from the stem tips. Prairie plants are dissimilar in that they generate fresh growth right beside last year's dead stems. The new shoots emerge from their surviving subsurface biomass. Burning the old, dead vegetation not only removes the dense grassy thatch, it also opens the soil to sunlight, suppresses both native trees and exotic invasive species, and returns nutrients to the soil for the next growing cycle.[11]

Big bluestem is the dominant grass within the development. Reaching heights of eight feet or more along many of the meandering hiking paths, the grass's trademark summer-season blue and purple stems take on a golden-brown color in late fall and early winter. Indian grass, switchgrass, little bluestem, Canada wild rye, and prairie dropseed compete with big bluestem for space and provide the bulk of the fuel for the burn.

On burn days, a half-dozen or more volunteer residents, led by Michael Sands, light the vegetation with a hand-held drip torch. Sands carefully selects burn days on the basis of favorable wind (5–15 mph) and weather. Volunteers control the burn by extinguishing flames with swatters (square rubber mats attached to a pole) and backpack water guns. The fire crackles as billows of gray smoke darken the sky. Left in the fire's wake is blackened earth. To the uninitiated, the land may look dead or badly scarred, but the fire has actually primed the prairie for the growing season. The group burns several acres at a time, providing residents with a vivid lesson in grassland ecology. Even casual observers notice the dramatic effect that burning has on plant growth the following spring.

Grayslake averages more than thirty-seven inches of snowfall per year, and the relatively large amount of open space at Prairie Crossing provides residents with opportunities to engage in a variety of winter sports and activities. Lake Leopold and Sanctuary Pond are often frozen three or four months out of the year, making ice-skating and hockey viable for much of the season. Cross-country skiing and snowshoeing are additional exercise activities on the development's trails; on average, one or more inches of snow covers Grayslake for fifty-four days a year. Winter has a different ambience at Prairie Crossing than it does in conventional suburban developments. The acres of open space preserve the freshness of the snow. In contrast, snow in many urban environments quickly loses its aesthetic appeal.

The melting of the spring snowpack offers residents an ecology lesson in the value of wetlands. The landscape at Prairie Crossing stores meltwater and run-off in many noticeable ways. Swales fill with meltwater and channel it into the prairies; the runoff then flows overland to the wetlands. The extensive root systems of the native flora help with the absorption process. Spring also reveals the ecological value of the prairie burns. The black scars on the land come alive with bright green shoots. In favorable conditions, the land visibly changes every few days. Exposure of new ground by the burn may open up an opportunity for a colonizing forb, such as black-eyed Susan or prairie ragwort, to take seed.

Spring also brings the return of migratory wildlife, particularly songbirds. Grassland nesting birds, such as sparrows, can suffer in the public consciousness because of their dull, inconspicuous coloring. In birding parlance, they are sometimes described as LBJs: "little brown jobbies." Often, it's only experienced birders who can distinguish LBJs by their distinct calls. However, their melodious voices reach anyone hiking the walking paths. The call of the red-winged blackbird can be heard from virtually any path in the development. The jet-black males sport epaulets of red and gold on both wings. A year-round resident, this songbird nests in the wet, marshy, and brushy habitats surrounding the lake and pond. If a resident or visitor is lucky—and I have never been so fortunate—one might see the distinctive black, white, and gold flash of a bobolink. The bobolink defies the grassland bird stereotype of dull indistinctness. An attractive, predominantly black bird with gold on the nape and white on the tail and wings, it is also acoustically unique, in that its voice sounds like the electronic warbling of R2-D2 from the *Star Wars* film franchise. The bobolink has been recorded on the property, though it tends to prefer more expansive habitat. It is common in the larger nearby Rollins Savanna preserve. Birds of prey, such as the northern harrier with its diagnostic white tail patch, also patrol the skies, sharing space with great blue herons traveling to and from the nearby rookery at Almond Marsh. Well over one hundred bird species have been recorded on the property, including the common loon, sandhill crane, and bald eagle.

Plant-centered management is practiced at Prairie Crossing to promote the growth of prairie vegetation. For example, mowing is sometimes used as a tool to suppress cool-season invasive grasses and foster growth of natives. However, the Homeowners Association does make some efforts to increase bird populations. Late March or early April brings the arrival of the eastern bluebird, a striking migrant with electric-blue plumage and a chestnut throat and breast. The bluebird is a cavity nester and covets the large rectangular nest boxes that rise above the prairie in many places throughout the development. Side compartments on the boxes permit humans to unobtrusively observe the grass-lined, cup-shaped nests and sky-blue eggs.

During the warmer months of the school year, one can occasionally encounter students from the Prairie Crossing Charter School sitting on mats along the pathways. Richard Louv, in his book *Last Child in the Woods*, has extensively documented the numerous benefits children receive from immersion in natural environments. The school uses the nearby open green space as a natural laboratory and incorporates the community outdoors directly into its curriculum. Many children ride their bikes to school, and the bike racks are usually full when the weather permits.

More than 130 species of prairie plants carpet the property. The plants have individual needs and grow differently by season. They can even vary in accordance with subtle differences in topography of just a few inches. Cool-season plants, such as Virginia wild rye, June grass, native fescues and sedges, and spring wildflowers, exhibit robust spring growth, bloom by early summer, and then taper their growth or go dormant during the summer heat.[12]

As late spring gives way to early summer, warm-season plants emerge from the Prairie Crossing grounds. These include the iconic grasses of the tallgrass prairie (big and little bluestem, Indian grass, switchgrass, prairie dropseed) and some of the spectacular large-stemmed forbs, such as sawtooth sunflower, prairie dock, compass plant, and cup plant. Big bluestem and Indian grasses make up the core of the biomass of the traditional tallgrass prairie, and they are ubiquitous throughout the Prairie Crossing development. Both exceed eight feet in height. These grasses are long-lived occupiers that have the resiliency to survive drought and extreme temperatures. Many nineteenth-century travelers and explorers described the original undisturbed prairie in terms of motion. Novelist Willa Cather wrote: "Everywhere, as far as the eye could reach, there was nothing but rough, shaggy, red grass, most of it as tall as I. . . . As I looked about me I felt that the grass was the country, as the water is the sea. The red of the grass made all the great prairie the colour of wine-stains. . . . And there was so much motion in it; the whole country seemed, somehow, to be running."[13] While it is still hard to imagine the seemingly endless expanses of golden wild grains, it is possible at Prairie Crossing to grasp the metaphor of the running oceans of grass by watching the movement of big bluestem, Indian grass, and prairie dropseed in the wind. In late spring, summer, and early fall, the presence of the tall grasses and forbs and the colors of the wildflowers, especially the yellows and purples, tend to dominate the natural experience.

Three tall forbs that are common within Prairie Crossing can impress even the casual visitor: compass plant, prairie dock, and cup plant. All three plants have disked yellow flowers and share the same genus, *Silphium*. Compass plant earns its name from its ability to align its large, deeply feathered (pinnatifid) leaves in a north-south direction to limit overhead sun exposure during the hottest parts of the day. Capable of reaching eight or more feet in height, and forming yellow composite flowers three to four inches across, it is one of the larger flowers in the Prairie Crossing community.

Prairie dock is perhaps the tallest of the development's forbs and commonly reaches heights of ten feet on the property, sometimes dominating the foreground of long-distance photographs of the homes. It is characterized by large basal leaves, disked yellow flowers, and spindly stems that tower over most other non-woody plants on the property. The leaves resemble elephant ears, feel rough like sandpaper, and like those of the compass plant often align in a north-south direction to limit sun exposure. Deep roots that can extend more than fourteen feet also cool the plant and allow it to endure long periods of drought and extreme heat. The roots make the leaves cool to the touch even in high summer temperatures.

Cup plant is the last of the tall *Silphium* plants within the development, and it is a common selection for homeowners on their private properties. Its name comes from the cuplike intersections of the leaves, which fill with rainwater or dew, an adaptation that helps keep the plant hydrated during periods of intense heat. This wildflower has recently made a comeback as an ornamental garden plant. Suburban homeowners have rediscovered many prairie natives, and in some Chicago suburbs they are using them to replace or augment the traditional bluegrass lawn. In Evanston, Illinois, cup plant and prairie dock are being utilized as lawn plants in many locations. All three *Silphium* plants at Prairie Crossing attract attention, and for some residents they help combat plant blindness by sparking botanical curiosity.

The trees at Prairie Crossing tend to cluster around the homes and along some of the walking paths, leaving relatively large expanses of open grassland space. The bur oak, with its wide-branching limbs, is the classic tree of the oak savanna ecosystem, and is present along with eastern cottonwood, American elm, black willow, box elder, and several other species. The cottonwoods, in particular, add visual and acoustic energy. The wind causes their spade-shaped leaves to shimmer independently in sunlight. These leaves also offer natural sounds that are often drowned out by mechanization in urban environments.

Invasive species are present, but one generally has to look for them. Glossy buckthorn is there, but not in large quantities. Three exotics—white sweet clover, Queen Anne's lace, and Canada goldenrod—have been measured in some numbers in the past and are suppressed through burning and mowing regimens. The property as a whole is heavily represented by natives and has the presence and feeling of a natural preserve just a short distance from the housing areas.

As the trails wind their way through the grasslands and wetlands, they lead to several organic farming operations on the northwestern fringe of the property. There, one can buy free-range eggs, honey, pears, and jam—paid for by cash or check with an "honor box" system. Horse stables and corrals permit owners to both house and ride their horses in the community, providing daily experiences for riders and path walkers that are not often encountered in urban America. Plots for personal gardening are available for homeowners to grow their own food.

The homes were designed according to New Urbanism principles—elegant nineteenth-century designs, front porch facades, and rear garage entries. They range in size from a modest 1,453 square feet to a spacious 3,240 square feet. All of the exteriors are wooden clapboard, and the color schemes are bright—reds, greens, yellows, browns, blues—but not repetitive. Many of the homes employ elements of Prairie School architecture, including American Foursquare. Sometimes referred to as the "Prairie Box," the Foursquare design was pioneered by Frank Lloyd Wright during the early years of the twentieth century, and is epitomized by its two-and-a-half-story cubic design with a sweeping front porch and wide staircase.[14] Prairie Crossing features an impressive red Foursquare near Lake Leopold that often appears reflecting off the water in photographs accompanying press articles on the development. The dominant horizontality of the Prairie School buildings echoes the wide, flat, treeless plains of the Midwestern prairie grassland. In addition to the Foursquare and Wright Prairie School homes are classic Midwestern farmhouse designs, modern variants of nineteenth-century homes still in use today in Lake County. Characterized by elegant gabled roofs, crisp lines, and wide front porches, variants of the Midwestern farmhouse are the most common design and help frame and project the community's country atmosphere.

The homes are clustered in small groups scattered throughout the green open space to help facilitate the residents' integration with nature. There are no sidewalks or curbs, only crushed limestone paths. The blacktop streets are curvilinear and snake through the development, generally on the periphery. The developers did utilize cul-de-sacs in several areas, and these can seem faintly reminiscent of conventional suburbia when homeowners employ bluegrass lawns as their primary landscaping. The Station Village and Square area consists of three yellow condominium buildings housing thirty-six individual units. Each unit in the complex has access to an outdoor balcony. Two of the three buildings have retail space below them. The retail units struggled with the recession, which occurred shortly after the completion of their construction. A nursery school, yoga center, tree-trimming business, and bakery are among the current tenants. A valid criticism of the Square is that most of the businesses are not community oriented, and on most days it lacks significant foot traffic. A mini-mart, grocery, or market store would have been helpful to allow people to pick up basic necessities without relying on the automobile, and much of the space seems geared toward tenants needing a business office rather than the arts, entertainment, or dining. Due to the recession, the rental units have experienced some turnover. However, as of fall 2014, the Square seems to be improving, and all but one unit is occupied.

As the accompanying photographs illustrate, the ecology of the prairie restoration and the Midwestern architecture combine to produce a fairly unique ambience for a primary home community in the shadow of the third-largest city in the country. Prairie Crossing revives the natural character of the native tallgrass ecosystem, providing residents with the opportunity to interact daily with nature in their own backyard. It is still possible for residents to return home from work, pull their cars into their garages, turn on cable TV, and never venture outside. However, the ever-changing seasonal ecology of Prairie Crossing can be enticing for anyone who is even slightly interested in exploring the natural world.

## Prairie Crossing's Conservation Impact

Among the most serious of the negative externalities associated with urban sprawl is environmental degradation, which affects most facets of the ecosphere, including air, water, climate, and biodiversity. The conservation community model provides policy remedies that mitigate these environmental problems. Prairie Crossing has been particularly successful in the areas of water quality and biodiversity.

Sprawl is characterized by low-density, often leapfrog development that expands out from central cities in a generally unplanned and uncoordinated manner—the result of individuals and municipalities seeking to maximize their own advantage. The government-subsidized arterial transportation network of highways and roads that feeds suburban sprawl both fragments and modifies the natural landscape. To accommodate the ubiquitous front lawn, the large-lot, low-density development has a big footprint, occupying a relatively large area per resident. To provide consumers with shopping opportunities, developers frequently turn to the shopping mall and big-box retailing with large expanses of asphalt parking. The extensive roadway network is needed to move the high volume of automobile traffic. Suburban sprawl thus develops very large tracts of land, leaving relatively little space for native flora and fauna. Ecologically speaking, suburbia can be analogized as a "sea" of human development that surrounds and isolates small "islands" of native natural landscape, a concept known as island biogeography.

The consequences of this eco-fragmentation, which will be discussed at greater length in chapter three, can be significant. Eco-fragmentation often decreases the diversity of habitats, making survival difficult for species that do not disseminate easily. For example, some species, such as frogs and dragonflies, rely on different habitats at different stages of their lifecycles. They depend on both aquatic and upland environments for survival.[15] Conventional suburban development frequently fragments, isolates, and eliminates these habitats, at great cost to such species. Fragmentation of habitat in general results in lower biodiversity as encroaching development reduces habitable space below the threshold of species survival, particularly for predators, which often play a vital regulatory role in ecosystem food chains.[16]

Prairie Crossing has been successful in preserving green open space and combating ecological fragmentation by reviving an old design concept, cluster housing. Prairie Crossing's homes are gathered in relatively small congregations interspersed throughout restored natural habitat while still embracing the low-density suburban philosophy.

Formerly a land of great biological abundance, the Prairie Crossing property changed significantly after its nineteenth-century settlement. An extensive tile system altered the natural drainage. Farmers tilled this soil for nearly 150 years, and in the years after World War II they applied herbicides and pesticides. The result was the near-total eradication of the native biological community species.[17]

The developers' ecological restoration returned 350 acres to something resembling their original natural condition; the land is now home to 130-plus prairie grassland species that are self-sustaining and indigenous to the Chicago region. Thirty-five acres of lake, pond, and wetlands restoration has helped to further restore ecological balance to a state that has lost more than 85 percent of its wetlands.[18] Furthermore, nearly 70 percent of the development is permanently protected green space. The restorations are ecologically rich and contain biologically sustainable communities, harboring stocked populations of endangered fish and 130 species of birds, 115 more than inhabited the property before development, and nearly 20 more than have been recorded at a nearby state preserve.

Prairie Crossing is not, however, just a postage-stamp grassland in a sea of degraded urban development. The remedy for ecological fragmentation is the creation of biotic corridors—ecological linkages between natural landscapes that provide for and facilitate the transfer of genetic material between populations. In restoring the property's wetlands, the developers created a corridor link with the Des Plaines River watershed. Prairie Crossing residents also created a local land trust and purchased an adjacent property to preserve and protect it from development. Though a roadway separates the community from a prairie reserve to the east that is part of the county forest preserve system, the two properties are connected by an underpass. Prairie Crossing forms the western boundary of the Liberty Prairie Reserve, a 5,770-acre public-private partnership designed to preserve and protect prairie grassland habitat and historical agricultural practices in Lake County.

The restoration of the Prairie Crossing wetlands is important. Sprawl often contributes to deteriorating water quality. Automobiles pollute water both directly and indirectly. Cars and trucks are non-point-source polluters. They directly leak numerous toxins, principally oil and antifreeze, onto roadway surfaces. Rain then flushes these pollutants into local watersheds. The leaking of underground fuel tanks at gas stations introduces additional toxins into watersheds. Urban application of salt as a roadway deicer significantly degrades water quality in northern climates.[19]

The American love affair with the suburban front lawn also threatens natural wetlands. While many think that "Kentucky" bluegrass is native to the southern state and the region, it is in fact an exotic invasive species that hitched a ride to North America on the hides of Eurasian cattle during European colonization in the seventeenth century. The United States has more than 150 million acres of lawn, and "the cumulative environmental impact is tremendous."[20] Homeowners treat their lawns with immense quantities of fertilizers, pesticides, and herbicides, all of which contribute to pollution of surface water and groundwater and degrade aquatic ecosystems. In an effort to "do right" by their neighbors—produce the greenest and best-manicured lawn possible—suburbanites often oversupply their lawns with fertilizer, applying up to five times the amount per unit area as in industrial agriculture.[21] Precipitation carries these excess chemicals into local streams and watersheds, with negative consequences for native plants and wildlife. Excess phosphorus creates algal blooms that deprive lakes and ponds of oxygen, suffocating native life, particularly the invertebrates that provide critical sustenance for organisms higher up the food chain. The chemical structures of pesticides can mimic natural hormones, interfering with the internal biological processes of amphibians. The impact of some of these chemicals can be felt around the world. Chlordane, a chemical used on home lawns and gardens, has been detected in seals and polar bears in the high Arctic, where it occurs in greater concentrations than in the cities where it was used.[22]

In contrast, the water quality at Prairie Crossing is one of the development's strongest environmental components. Wetlands restoration, including swales, deep-rooted native prairie grasses, and a 22-acre lake, provides the community with stormwater retention, biological treatment through the natural removal of pollutants, and solids settling, which results in water quality that exceeds the standards set by the Illinois Environmental Protection Agency in every category except chloride (a consequence of Grayslake's deicing practices). The development considered but did not institute a blanket ban on the use of lawn chemicals on private-property lots. The Homeowners Association instead encourages residents to adopt eco-friendly practices through an association-sponsored weed-management program, which is contracted out to a private company.

Suburbanization has a tendency to homogenize the natural environment, and in general, biodiversity declines with increasing urbanization.[23] Housing subdivisions in vastly different climates and environments often look the same and have the same lawns, trees, shrubs, and flower beds, irrespective of the native botanical communities and the fauna that depend on them. Urban environments often consist of monocultures—the overwhelming dominance of a single species. The bluegrass lawn is an obvious example, but single tree species also dominate many suburban neighborhoods, increasing their vulnerability to disease and parasitic infestation. Infestations of invasive insects, such as the Asian emerald ash borer, have devastated American tree canopies and neighborhood aesthetics. In some suburbs, such as Evanston, Illinois, a designated Arbor Day Foundation Tree City USA community, entire parkway blocks are treeless or nearly so, as city workers have cut down and removed thousands of ash trees to stem the infestation.[24] The homogenization of ecosystems, or what biologist Tim Low refers to as the "McDonaldization of ecology," is a problem not only because of the loss of biodiversity, but also because it affects suburbanites' view of the natural world. As scientists Julie Lockwood and Michael McKinney argue, "Perhaps the most troubling aspect of biological homogenization is how it could degrade the human perception of 'nature.' . . . People begin to care less about the species they see, as more and more of the things they *do* see are as 'common as dirt.' . . . Biological homogenization creates more than an impaired global environment, it creates a biologically indifferent culture."[25] What is needed to avoid homogenization is the integration of human communities into existing natural environments and ecosystems, precisely the goal of Prairie Crossing and other conservation communities. This human-nature integration benefits both human and ecological communities.

Prairie Crossing has been successful in reversing the biotic homogenization prevalent in the Greater Chicago area. The prairie and wetlands restoration re-created several hundred acres of the long-lost tallgrass prairie ecosystem, a biome that has been extirpated throughout most of the Midwest and Great Plains. Since the mid-nineteenth century, Chicago has lost more than 90 percent of its wetlands to agricultural and urban development, and only 2,000 scattered acres of native grasslands remain of the original 22-million-acre pre-Columbian prairie ecosystem that once dominated the state. To put this loss into perspective, if all virgin prairie in Illinois could be condensed into a single contiguous parcel of land, it would cover only one square mile.[26] In such a distorted landscape, regenerative efforts such as those at Prairie Crossing are of extraordinary importance.

And research has shown that restored prairies build "attachment to the natural world in a more grounded local way than a more diffuse embrace of nature in the abstract."[27]

Other positive benefits of ecological restoration include ecological learning opportunities. The most cost-effective way to preserve open space at Prairie Crossing would have been to cluster all the homes in one corner of the property. The developers rejected that mode of development because they wanted to integrate the residents into nature. Residents, the developers believed, should feel that they themselves are part of the environment. They can see the water-retention capabilities of the land because the stormwater treatment system is above ground and in plain view. The movement of water is readily apparent. Similarly, prairie burning by the Homeowners Association is a popular event that generates a high turnout of residents. Such experiences dramatically demonstrate the ability of fire and water to regenerate biological growth and reinforce the concept that the land is not static but a living, breathing entity.

Prairie Crossing achieved the preservation of open space and ecological restoration of the property. In developing it, however, George and Vicky Ranney sought to do more than simply return the prairie to its former glory. Through the built environment, they also wanted to foster greater civic participation and increase the socioeconomic and racial diversity of the community. Here they met with both success and failure.

## Changing the Culture of Sprawl

The central feature of Prairie Crossing's wetlands restoration is the 22-acre lake named for the famed ecologist and conservationist Aldo Leopold, whose *A Sand County Almanac* is a cornerstone of the modern environmental movement.[28] In the *Almanac* Leopold argues for the development of a land ethic, one that calls for a responsible and sensible relationship between people and the land where they reside. "The land ethic," Leopold explained, "simply enlarges the boundaries of the community to include soils, waters, plants, and animals, or collectively: the land."[29] Prairie Crossing builds on Leopold's principle and is premised on the idea that integrating citizens into nature has the potential to alter the social and political dynamics of the community, positively impact civic participation, and promote the common good.

With a land ethic, the sense of community begins with a strong attachment to the land. In this conceptual worldview, land has value beyond that of a resource that can be converted into dollars. Respect for and a feeling of responsibility to the land become the foundation for building a strong sense of human community and fostering greater civic engagement. The conservation community is more than a means to a better ecology; it is an economically viable alternative for many of the policy problems commonly associated with suburban sprawl. In creating a land ethic, Prairie Crossing's developers sought to, in the words of George Ranney, "change the culture" of their residents through a set of ten guiding principles consciously designed to remedy everything from traffic congestion to obesity to carbon emissions to architectural aesthetics.[30]

Prairie Crossing is a transit-oriented development that derives its name from the intersection of two passenger transport lines near the community. Two Metra rail lines offer transportation to both O'Hare International Airport and Chicago's Union Station, as well as stops in at least forty different communities. Nearly three hundred trains a week stop at the two stations, which are a short walking distance from every home in the development.[31] The trains run according to a regularly posted schedule and provide clean cars and restrooms for passengers. Shuttle buses take passengers to and from the terminals at the airport. Bicycle racks at the train station permit residents to shorten their trips there, which vary from two minutes to twenty minutes depending on the location of a residence. Bicycles are also permitted on the trains with some restrictions. The train stations provide indoor shelter to protect commuters from the elements.

The close proximity of the development to mass transit has had some impact. More than a third of residents reported using mass transit or carpooling to work. This number is more than six times the national rate (5 percent) and three times that of the Chicago metro area (11.5 percent).[32] Residents' use of mass transit not only reduces traffic congestion, it mitigates the development's impact on the environment. Fewer miles driven means a smaller carbon footprint and less air and water pollution.

One of Prairie Crossing's ten guiding principles is promoting "a healthy lifestyle." In addition to the fitness benefits afforded to train commuters who walk to and from the station, there is a ten-mile network of crushed-limestone walking paths that serpentine through the entire development and link the community to nearby forest preserves. The trails are available to walkers, bikers, and horseback riders, and nearly all the residents use them. The paths offer not only fitness opportunities but also immersion in the natural experience. They cut through 160 acres of undulating big bluestem prairie and the 35-acre wetlands complex. Both of these natural areas provide the opportunity to hear and see scores of songbirds and many species of native waterfowl. A strong body of scholarship suggests that walking the nature trails can strengthen not only the body but also the mind.[33] Direct exposure to nature may reduce the symptoms of ADHD and improve resistance to depression in children. Adults receive similar benefits. Interacting with natural settings "enhances the ability to recover from stress," and people also tend to be more positive and report higher levels of life satisfaction.

Another frequent criticism of suburban sprawl, one expressed by citizens and scholars alike, is that it lacks a sense of place.[34] It was the cookie-cutter "ugliness" of sprawl, that repetitive one-size-fits-all approach to building, that journalist James Kunstler memorably called "the geography of nowhere." That "nowhere" quality of suburbia is what originally prompted developer Vicky Ranney to study Frederick Law Olmsted's work on using the landscape to create better human environments. In Vicky's words, "landscape has the power to change people's lives."[35]

The Ranneys incorporated "a sense of place" as another of their guiding principles. To create a sense of place, the developers employed a diverse toolkit, including symbolism, color, local history, architecture, conservation, nature, and environmental psychology. Street and place names, for example, celebrate the cultural diversity of the regional human history—including the Native American inhabitants and early white settlers of the property—as well as the biodiversity of the local botanical species. The Ranneys also designed the physical structures that occupy the land with a sense of place in mind. The developers embraced New Urbanism, a relatively recent movement that revives and reinterprets traditional urban planning.[36] Historical structures from the past also provide a sense of place and a connection to the land. Two nineteenth-century buildings—the Wright Schoolhouse and the Byron Colby Barn—have found new life as a charter school and a community center where weddings, lectures, concerts, and events are held. A popular twenty-eight-member book club also meets in the barn. The organic farm and the horse stables further contribute to the community ambience. Resident surveys reveal very high levels of satisfaction with the community.

Related to a sense of place, yet distinct, is "a sense of community," another of Prairie Crossing's guiding principles. At its most basic, community consists of "participation in the social life of a place," and involves the communal sharing of social experiences, territory, traditions, institutions, common goals, and political or economic structures.[37] Prairie Crossing's developers actively sought to create a strong sense of community within the development by carefully designing the built environment to foster resident interaction, and also by encouraging engagement through a variety of community-sponsored activities and programs. The Ranneys appear to have been successful. Resident surveys reveal a community that is "more neighborly" than most other communities in which residents have previously lived, and the satisfaction with the Homeowners Association is much higher than in conventional common-interest developments. The absence of garage facades, the return of the front porch, a community center with regularly scheduled concerts, lectures, and other events, and a network of trails all create opportunities for residents to interact. The conservation agenda proved not to be divisive, and actually helped bring members of the community together in a common cause. Resident surveys strongly suggest that the many conservation amenities—gardens, organic farming, prairie burns, hiking trails, volunteer opportunities, a farmers' market—appear to have fostered bonds within the community.[38]

An important component of civic engagement is political participation. Political participation covers a range of activities, everything from voting in national presidential elections to involvement in the local private government of a homeowners association. Numerous scholars have noted in one form or another that Americans over the last several decades have been withdrawing from social and political participation.[39] One of the reasons George Ranney agreed to participate in this case study of Prairie Crossing was his interest in exploring the impact the community has had on political participation. George "suspect[ed]" that higher rates of political participation would result from the creation of community, but he had "no evidence" to support it.[40]

Increased political participation is not the only logical outcome of the policy model. The time required to maintain and manage the conservation of common-pool resources, in addition to maintaining and managing the traditional common-interest development infrastructure, could have resulted in less participation. How did the political participation of Prairie Crossing's residents compare to the participation of American voters at the national and local levels?

Analysis of voting records and resident survey data found that Prairie Crossing's residents tend to register and vote as expected based on the community's demographics (e.g., education, age, and income). Where they stand out relative to their peers is in non-mainstream political activity—contributing money to campaigns, attending meetings, displaying campaign messages, and pursuing additional campaign information.[41] Prairie Crossing's district has played a high-profile role in several congressional elections. Regarding participation in local elections, which in general tend to draw less voter interest, development residents vote much more frequently than their county peers. The conservation community agenda appears to provide positive feedback for political participation.

Prairie Crossing, however, was not successful in achieving all of its goals. The fifth guiding principle of the development is "economic and racial diversity." Communities need not employ physical barriers, such as gates and walls, to exclude other classes or segments of society. Wealth serves the same purpose, and often just as effectively. The ticket of entry into a particular housing development or neighborhood is a minimum level of income, below which purchase is simply not possible. The preservation of open space and the ecological restoration of degraded land is expensive, estimated at between 14 and 20 percent of the cost of developing the Prairie Crossing property.[42] The relatively high cost of the homes is likely the reason that the development failed to reach its goals of racial and economic diversity. Only 5 percent of the single-family homes were purchased by Hispanics or African Americans.[43] The median reported income of the residents of single-family homes is nearly three times higher at Prairie Crossing than in the nation and the state overall.[44] Prairie Crossing has experienced great success in many areas of social reform; however, it has fallen far short of its goal of racial and economic diversity.

## The Conservation Community: Creating Ecological Value through Development

Conventional economic wisdom holds that environmental degradation is the necessary price of "progress." The conservation community policy model provides a green alternative. The Prairie Crossing experiment shows that not only can development proceed in an eco-friendly manner, it can actually reclaim the environment, making it ecologically better than it was before construction. As Michael Sands explains, "The goal of Prairie Crossing is to demonstrate how development can improve the environment."[45]

Prairie Crossing and the conservation community policy model represent a new paradigm for real-estate development and community building. But they have their limits. A common question takes a variant of this form: "Can seven billion people live like this?" The answer is no. Seven billion people cannot live this lifestyle. But this criticism ignores the value of Prairie Crossing as a new exemplar of best practices. Seven billion people cannot live on Earth in any form without damaging the ecosphere, and that is the lesson of human development over the last century all over the globe. The conservation community model provides a template for how humans can live in greater concert with nature for the benefit of not only nature but people as well. And the opportunity to impact the environment is imminent. An estimated two-thirds of development expected to exist by 2050 has not yet been built.[46]

The conservation community concept can be employed in all types of environments and anywhere in the world. In the twenty-five years since Prairie Crossing's founding, more than a hundred conservation community developments have sprung up in thirty states from Maine to Montana and Florida to California. The conservation community has proven a profitable mode of development. A 2011 Colorado State University study revealed that conservation community homes sold for 29 percent more than homes in conventional rural residential developments. And though ecological restoration costs money, conservation developments are place specific. Not every development will require extensive restoration, and there are significant infrastructure savings to be found relative to conventional housing. Prairie Crossing's developers cut costs by narrowing the streets, eliminating curbs and sidewalks, and replacing storm sewers with natural stormwater management. As of 2011, 310,000 acres have been developed in the country as conservation communities.[47]

The chapters that follow reveal the results of my case study analysis of the Prairie Crossing development as a model for reform. Using both quantitative and qualitative research methods, including resident surveys, local, state, and national election data, and interviews with principal participants in the development and community, I focus on three main policy areas and their relationship to urban sprawl: conservation, community relations, and political participation. All three areas are of concern to urban planners, ecologists, and political scientists. The following chapter tells how two people with no background whatsoever in housing development managed to undertake a $100 million gamble on an untried idea to save the land by developing it.

# CHAPTER TWO

# GENESIS OF AN IDEA

We abuse land because we see it as
a commodity belonging to us. When
we see land as a community to which
we belong, we may begin to use it
with love and respect.

—Aldo Leopold

In crafting his land ethic, which would eventually provide a solid theoretical foundation for several of Prairie Crossing's guiding principles, Aldo Leopold argued, "If we are serious about restoring ecosystem health and ecological integrity, then we must first know what the land was like to begin with."[1] Following Leopold's cue, what was the nature of the Prairie Crossing land before the industrial and agricultural revolutions transformed it?

Eighteen thousand years ago, during a period of glacial maximum, ice of what Tim Flannery has described as "mind-numbing" proportions buried Prairie Crossing. The Laurentide ice sheet, one of several that gripped North America during the last ice age, piled two miles high over the region, a glacial event that dwarfs that in present-day Antarctica. The retreat of the ice twelve thousand years ago created the Great Lakes, the largest body of surface freshwater in the world, and opened up the land for a species new to the continent—*Homo sapiens*, the first Americans. Having recently crossed over from Asia along the West Coast, these first Native Americans would have a huge impact on the Midwestern ecosystem. By setting fire to the landscape, they suppressed tree growth to supply ample grassland forage for their prey, a mammalian megafauna that upon the initial arrival of humans exceeded that of contemporary Africa in both sheer numbers and range of biodiversity. The megafauna included many species now extinct: camel, ground sloth, sabertooth, lion, cheetah, mammoth, and mastodon, some of which occasionally turn up as fossils in Lake County backyards, in farm fields, and at construction sites. The hunting pressures of the first Americans likely contributed to the rapid extinction of these animals approximately ten thousand years ago.[2]

The Laurentide glacial advance bulldozed the Midwestern landscape, exerting on the land as much as ten thousand pounds of pressure per square inch. In retreat, the glaciers initially left behind oak and conifer forest, with prairie grassland species surviving in sunlit openings under the tree cover.[3] As the first Americans migrated eastward, they significantly altered the landscape through the masterful use of fire. Ecologists use the adjective "keystone" to characterize species that have a disproportionately large effect on their ecosystem and play a critical role in regulating and preserving the ecological structure of biological communities, and in the words of Charles Kay, Native Americans, particularly in the Midwest, were the "ultimate keystone species."[4] The fires they set "hindered the development of competitive grasses and invading woody species," and burning reduced dead and dying vegetation, which stimulated underground decomposition. Deep-rooted prairie species (with up to 80 percent of their biomass below the ground) can easily withstand high-temperature burning that others cannot. That competitive advantage helped the region evolve from a postglacial forest into a prairie grassland biome.[5]

By the time Europeans began colonizing the continent, fire ecology dominated Prairie Crossing and the Chicago area, covering the land in plants of the tallgrass prairie, some two hundred species of grasses, forbs, shrubs, sedges, and broad-leafed flowering plants. Most were uniquely adapted to the hot, dry summers and cold winters. Several species of high grasses would have been predominant, making up 90 percent of the living mass. Big bluestem, a tall grass with amber stalks topped by three-pronged bursts of grain, grew in lush abundance, thriving on the region's plentiful precipitation and productive soils. Big bluestem is capable of reaching nearly ten feet in height. Nineteenth-century explorers such as George Catlin were sometimes "obliged to stand erect in our stirrups, in order to look over the waving tops" of bluestem and cordgrass while traversing the prairie on horseback.[6] An individual big bluestem plant may hail from the time of Jefferson and Adams; the species has a lifespan that can last two centuries. More than 240 species of birds originally made a living off of the fertile prairie grassland ecosystem, many of them annually migrating to northern Illinois to breed, traveling thousands of miles from their wintering grounds in Central and South America.

This ocean of grass, which some observers described as seemingly extending "as far as the eye could see," provided sustenance for several Native American tribes in the years following the arrival of Europeans. Illini, Miami, Fox, and Potawatomi all occupied the region at various times, interacting first with French fur trappers, later with British colonizers, and lastly with American farmers. No single tribe permanently controlled the area. Living in small villages consisting of bark-covered domed wigwams located near waterways to facilitate trade and travel, the Potawatomi in the early 1800s subsisted on small-scale agriculture— mostly corn, squash, and beans—as well as the hunting of wild game. In 1826, four Potawatomi villages, ranging from two dozen to more than one hundred people, were located along the Des Plaines River not far from Prairie Crossing.[7] By 1833, all Native Americans were forced west of the Mississippi by the unfavorable terms of the second Treaty of Chicago, which granted approximately five million acres of Potawatomi land in northeastern Illinois and southeastern Wisconsin, including the Prairie Crossing property, to the United States government. Chicago, sitting fortuitously astride a divide between the two biggest watersheds east of the Rocky Mountains, was now poised to become the economic fulcrum for the taming of the continent.[8]

After the acquisition of the land in northern Illinois, technological developments facilitated the economic exploitation of much of the region. Chicago developed into the "city of the century," in the words of historian Donald Miller, and became an economic powerhouse.[9] By the 1850s, Chicago was home to the world's largest railroad hub, granary, stockyard, and lumberyard. Its Board of Trade developed the futures market, where grain "created a new form of money."[10] Chicago's pork "disassembly" lines would even provide the inspiration for Henry Ford's automobile assembly-line system. In less than a generation, the transformation of the region into the country's hottest urban market would make Prairie Crossing's bluestem grassland a highly sought-after agricultural commodity.

A one-square-yard plot of big bluestem contains twenty-five miles of roots, rootlets, and root hairs, which can extend below the surface to a depth exceeding nine feet. Early settlers found this tough prairie soil almost impossible to plow. In 1837, John Deere, a local blacksmith seeking a solution for the problem, invented the first commercially successful cast-steel plow in Ogle County, Illinois, not far from Prairie Crossing. Known as "the plow that broke the plains," it made large-scale farming of the tallgrass prairie possible.[11]

Having solved the "problem" of prairie-sod removal, Midwestern farmers turned to wetland modification. Chicago sits on a watery continental divide between two vital watersheds, the Mississippi River and the Great Lakes. The region's potential for transportation and commerce was recognized as far back as the late seventeenth century.[12] At high water it was possible to canoe from the East Coast via the Great Lakes to the Mississippi River without portage. The seasonal inundation of water, however, limited the area's agricultural potential. Twentieth-century corn and bean farmers on the Prairie Crossing site maximized their yields by creating an extensive tile drainage system that cut off the land from its hydrological linkage with the Upper Des Plaines River to the east and the Fox River system to the west. The destruction of those linkages resulted in serious ecological depletion.[13] The post–World War II petrochemical revolution further impoverished the Prairie Crossing land through the use of herbicides and pesticides. Only an estimated 15 common bird species out of an original assemblage of nearly 250, and a handful of native prairie grasses and forbs that survived the plow along fence lines, outlasted the agricultural assault on the natural character of the land. In less than a century, the grassland ecosystem that had once dominated the interior of the continent would be reduced to thousands of postage-stamp prairies, little ecological island remnants in a sea of urban and agricultural transformation. For the most part, the human inhabitants of the region would quickly forget what was lost.[14] Little more than the "prairie state" nickname would persist in the minds of most Chicagoans.

The final lasting consequence of the federal government's takeover of the northern Illinois region was the systematic campaign of predator eradication, which eliminated all of the remaining apex predators from the ecosystem. Hunters and habitat destruction forced the grizzly bear, originally a prairie and plains species, west into the mountains, where it currently clings to survival in several small populations totaling a few hundred individuals. Hunting and trapping extirpated the wolf entirely from the lower forty-eight states. Only recently has the species returned to a handful of northern and western states, stirring local and national political controversy. The loss of predators, which play a crucial role in regulating herbivores and second-tier predators such as coyotes and raccoons, helped create population explosions of those species and the resulting problems they often present for suburban communities.

By the end of World War II, Lake County and the Prairie Crossing area were still largely rural in character. Agriculture had fragmented much of the natural ecology, but pockets of oak savanna, grassland, fen, sedge meadow, and even a small amount of virgin prairie still existed. The interstate highway system was a decade away, but rail service made travel to downtown Chicago possible. In 1945, the mix of nature and small-farm agriculture appealed to two veterans seeking a bucolic existence to assuage their memories of wartime violence. They were George Ranney's father, George Sr., and his uncle, Gaylord Donnelley. These men offered the inspiration that five decades later would lead the Ranneys to create Prairie Crossing. Donnelley would provide the financial resources to turn inspiration into reality.

## The Influence of Family:
## A Conservation Legacy

In 1962, Rachel Carson launched the modern environmental movement with the publication of *Silent Spring*. Several other influential conservation publications followed soon after, including the republication of Aldo Leopold's *A Sand County Almanac*, *The Population Bomb* by Paul Ehrlich, *The Closing Circle* by Barry Commoner, and *Limits to Growth* by Dennis Meadows. The green movement gained momentum toward the end of the decade as a series of high-profile focusing events heightened public concern and awareness regarding pollution, conservation, and the environment.

In a preemptive move to beat the Soviets to the moon, Apollo 8 made history in 1968 by becoming the first occupied spacecraft to break the gravitational bonds of Earth. A photograph from that mission of the home planet rising above the surface of the moon—dubbed "Earthrise" by the media—generated immense public interest and altered the perspectives of many Americans. In the wake of Apollo, our planet seemed smaller, finite, and more fragile. As Stewart Brand, environmental activist and creator of the *Whole Earth Catalog*, explains, "Photographs of the Earth from space were a different kind of mirror than we had ever looked in before. It flips you from the world that we are in, to the planet we are on."[15] Underscoring that fragility, less than a year later the Cuyahoga River in Ohio caught fire, and an oil spill fouled the coastal beaches of California. And then in 1970, a decade of advocacy and activism culminated in the first Earth Day, the largest single-day demonstration in U.S. history. Washington got the message and passed an unprecedented package of comprehensive environmental legislation intended to protect endangered species and cleanse the nation's air and water. During the 1960s and early 1970s, the environmental movement significantly impacted public opinion.[16]

George and Vicky Ranney were young adults in their twenties during the sixties. While the environmental movement of the times undoubtedly affected their understanding of the world, it was not the emotional or intellectual inspiration for the conservation community policy model. The inspiration and driving force for Prairie Crossing came from their personal connection to the land and a family tradition of conservation and public service.

George Ranney's family has deep roots in the Chicago area. One of his great-great-grandfathers, Joseph Turner Ryerson, arrived in Chicago from Philadelphia in 1842—just nine years after the second Treaty of Chicago created opportunities for regional economic expansion. In 1864, Richard Robert Donnelley, a Canadian immigrant, founded a printing business in Chicago, one that still bears his name. Ryerson and Donnelley were skilled and tenacious entrepreneurs. Both lost their businesses in the Great Chicago Fire in 1871 and then rebuilt them into companies that would become economic powerhouses in their respective fields. J. T. Ryerson & Sons merged with Inland Steel in 1935. R. R. Donnelley & Sons today is a Fortune 500 company. Donnelley's grandson Gaylord Donnelley would marry Dorothy Ranney, George Sr.'s sister, and successfully manage the family printing business for twenty-three years.

The companies that Ryerson and Donnelley founded expanded over the generations and provided their respective families with wealth and security. Both sides of the family used some of that wealth to fund philanthropic causes, particularly in the areas of education and conservation. Joseph Ryerson's grandson Edward Ryerson Jr.—George Ranney's maternal grandfather—took over the family steel business in 1932 and was very active in Chicago's civic affairs. He was appointed chairman of Illinois's Public Aid Commission during the Depression, and served on the boards of several important city institutions, including the Chicago Historical Society, the Chicago Symphony Orchestra, and the Welfare Council of Chicago. In 1953 Ryerson was elected chairman of the Board of Trustees of the University of Chicago after thirty years of service as a board member. That same year he helped found the city's public television station, WTTW. "Long active in Republican politics," Edward Ryerson was a conservationist cast in the Teddy Roosevelt mold. In 1966 he donated 257 acres to the Lake County Forest Preserve system, which served as the core of the Edward L. Ryerson Conservation Area. Several other prominent families followed suit, and the Lake County Forest Preserve holding now encompasses 561 acres.[17]

Born in 1910, George Ranney's uncle Gaylord Donnelley served as a commander in the U.S. Navy during World War II aboard the aircraft carrier USS *Essex*. Upon returning from the war in 1945, he and George Sr., a Yale-educated lawyer who had also served in the war, elected to leave Chicago with their families for the tranquility of the country in suburban Lake County. Donnelley and Ranney commuted to and from downtown Chicago by commuter rail. They did so because of their love of nature and the strong sense of community they helped forge in the rural township. The strong community bond would later play a big role in both the development of Prairie Crossing and the preservation of the area's natural and agricultural heritage.

Gaylord Donnelley was a conservationist of considerable merit, though he is better known regionally than nationally. In an article published in 1990, two years before his death, the *Chicago Tribune* described his impact on conservation in Illinois: "After pioneers like Daniel Burnham, Jens Jensen and Dwight Perkins, he became this state's most powerful—yet subtle—sportsman/environmentalist."[18] An avid hunter and fisherman, Donnelley was ahead of his time in recognizing that "the most effective way to save wildfowl would be by enlisting voluntary support from the duck hunters themselves."[19] Gaylord began his lifelong support of Ducks Unlimited in 1938, one year after its founding. He served two terms as the national president of the organization in the mid-1970s, its period of greatest growth.[20] Ducks Unlimited has been criticized for its pro-hunting mission; however, its impact on wetland conservation is unchallenged. Highly active in the Prairie Pothole Region of the Dakotas, a critical flyway for waterfowl, the organization has conserved more than 13 million acres of wetlands in the United States since its founding.

In addition to his involvement with Ducks Unlimited, Gaylord and his wife, the former Dorothy Williams Ranney, had an impressive record of land conservation. Gaylord held numerous positions with environmental organizations, big and small. In Illinois he served as an advisor to the Illinois Department of Conservation, chaired the Nature of Illinois Foundation, and, as reported by the *Chicago Tribune*, "sat on the Illinois Nature Preserves Commission at a time when few people were interested in its work."[21] Nationally he served as a trustee of the North American Wildlife Foundation, the Conservation Foundation/World Wildlife U.S., and the National Wildlife Federation, one of the nation's largest conservation organizations. Dorothy was a distinguished environmentalist and philanthropist in her own right, a fact noted by the *Chicago Tribune* following her death in 2002.[22] In interviews she stated that she was driven by a desire to preserve the environment for future generations.[23]

The Donnelleys donated more than their time to conservation efforts. They created the Gaylord and Dorothy Donnelley Foundation, which "invests in land conservation, artistic vitality, and regionally significant collections in the Chicago region and Lowcountry of South Carolina" through a combination of grants, partnerships, and research.[24] The Donnelleys split their time between Chicago and South Carolina and made noteworthy contributions to environmental preservation in both regions. They gave 800 acres along the Illinois River to the state to serve as a refuge for waterfowl, which became the Donnelley-Depue Wildlife Area. A conservation easement near Prairie Crossing on land once owned by the Donnelleys preserves 300 acres, a mix of agricultural land, fen, and virgin prairie.[25] The Donnelleys' influence was "pivotal in creating the Illinois-Michigan Canal National Heritage Corridor, Illinois' unprecedented new federal greenbelt park."[26] The "crown jewel" of their life's work is the ACE Basin at the confluence of the Ashepoo, Combahee, and Edisto Rivers in South Carolina, which contains a number of protected areas, including the Ernest F. Hollings ACE Basin National Wildlife Refuge. Home to the endangered wood stork, ACE includes 117,000 acres of critical saltwater, brackish, and freshwater wetlands along the Atlantic seaboard. The Donnelleys donated 6,000 acres bordering the refuge, including five islands, to the Nature Conservancy and Ducks Unlimited, with an additional 19,000 family-owned acres under conservation easement.[27] The state of South Carolina established the Donnelley Wildlife Management Area to honor "the contributions they made to the ACE Basin Project and conservation across the continent."[28]

A strong interest in conservation and architecture was also present in Vicky Ranney's family.[29] Vicky grew up in Massachusetts near Walden Pond, which she visited frequently during her childhood. Her cousin, architect William Turnbull Jr., was one of the designers of the Sea Ranch, an innovative green community spanning ten miles of Highway 1 along the coast of northern California. Turnbull and his colleagues Richard Whitaker, Charles Moore, Joseph Esterick, Donlyn Lyndon, and Lawrence Halprin were guided by "a concept of dynamic conservation" or a philosophy of "living lightly on the land."[30] As Richard Whitaker, director of design review for the Sea Ranch Association, explained, "The concept has to do with an attitude that the environmental setting is more important than the building. The Sea Ranch is not about individual buildings, it's about ten miles of Pacific Ocean and the land adjacent to it. It has to do with developing a shared image [among residents]."[31] George and Vicky Ranney visited the Sea Ranch in 1968, and it immediately resonated with them. In George's words, "I think it's true that the first time the two of us really started talking and dreaming about [conservation development] was in 1968, when we visited the Sea Ranch in California, and saw what a development could do on the Pacific coast to blend into and protect the environment around it."[32] Rather than "bulldozing the countryside" and redesigning the urban landscape from scratch using exotic plantings, Vicky Ranney took away from the Sea Ranch visit the value of building in concert with the natural environment.[33] In her words, "people behave better in natural settings."[34] Levittown may have democratized homeownership by making it affordable to the masses, but it came at a cost: the repetitive ugliness of sprawl and the alienation of the residents from the healing power of the natural environment.

The Sea Ranch, however, was originally designed as a "second-home, vacation community," built long before modern-day electronic communication made telecommuting an economically viable option.[35] Today it has some full-time residents who are non-retirees. Prairie Crossing from the outset would build on some of the Sea Ranch's innovations but seek to be something new—a middle-class community of primary homes.

## A Personal Connection to the Land

The conservation legacy of the Ranneys was critically important in encouraging interests, channeling behavior, and creating expectations. But equally important was George Ranney's intense personal connection with the land. George's family moved to Lake County when he was five years old and settled on farmland one mile east of the Prairie Crossing property. The Ranneys and Donnelleys lived on adjacent properties and immersed themselves in an already tight-knit rural community. Seven decades later, George still has fond memories of his childhood growing up on the farm, where he rode horses, fed chickens, and hunted for pheasants and rabbits on neighboring properties, including the land that would eventually become Prairie Crossing. He has lived near Prairie Crossing on and off his whole life and currently owns a Civil War–era farmhouse outside of the development but within sight of it.

The land around Prairie Crossing was rural and relatively undeveloped until the early 1960s. Casey Road, the roadway the Donnelleys and Ranneys lived on, was gravel up to that point. In 1965 this "idyllic period," as George calls it, came to an end. Casey and nearby Almond Road were paved, bringing more traffic and development interests. Local concern over the impact of development spurred the community into action, as George explained: "When farms came up for sale, neighbors would actively seek out people with conservation interests to buy them. Over the years, the properties of well over five hundred acres changed hands in this way."[36] This personal connection to the land, not only for the Donnelleys and the Ranneys but also for their fellow neighbors, would drive the community's conviction to save the land when confronted with a threat of large-scale development.[37]

## Frederick Law Olmsted and the Restorative Power of the Landscape

When Frederick Law Olmsted was a young boy, his mother died unexpectedly. To deal with the grief, he spent hours and hours hiking and exploring in the hardwood forests of nineteenth-century Connecticut. In the process, he discovered the healing properties and restorative power of the natural world. It was a lesson he would apply years later in his work as a landscape architect.

Born in 1822 in New England, Olmsted lived during a time that encompassed the United States' transition from a primarily agricultural nation to an industrial world power. As the Industrial Revolution urbanized America, he understood the importance of saving nature, or at least re-creating it in a form that could coexist with the crowded new cities that were growing rapidly east of the Mississippi. Like his contemporary Herman Melville, Olmsted spent a year aboard a merchant vessel, and the experience had an impact. The hard work gave him empathy for the often difficult life of the common man. When he was appointed superintendent of New York City's Central Park in 1857, he drew from his life's experiences and sought to create a retreat where ordinary citizens could escape the stresses of every day life. He believed that immersion in nature would have positive and restorative effects for urban dwellers, who often lived in polluted conditions.

As a graduate student at the University of Chicago, Vicky Ranney studied the work of Olmsted and published a short composition on his projects in Chicago. Through the 1970s and 1980s she worked as an editor of his papers, which were being published in thirteen volumes by the Johns Hopkins University Press. Olmsted made a strong impression on Vicky, teaching her that the landscape could have "a controlling effect on man's behavior."[38] By democratizing access to nature in public parks, the landscape had the potential to bring people together, cleanse the body and mind of "morbid conditions," and exert a "moral influence" on citizens stressed by the unnatural environment of high-density urban living.[39] Olmsted taught Vicky that by integrating the citizen back into nature, it might be possible to create a more responsive, democratic, and civilized society. Far from urban window dressing, the natural surroundings of a neighborhood provided a foundation for the creation of a positive sense of place and community. People would simply act better toward one another in a more natural setting. Vicky summarized Olmsted's approach in her 1972 publication *Olmsted in Chicago*: "By bringing people in an industrial society into contact with nature and each other in a carefully planned environment, [Olmsted] felt he could increase their aesthetic sensitivity, their physical well-being, and their civilized appreciation of others. With a population so enlightened, he hoped, democracy might more easily prove a workable institution."[40] Olmsted's impact on Vicky's conceptual worldview was significant. Not only did it resonate with her personally, it provided in the early 1970s the mental scaffolding that prepared her to take advantage of a serendipitous opportunity—the sudden availability of the Prairie Crossing property—that was still more than fifteen years in the future.

## Riverside and Seaside

In interviews, Vicky Ranney repeatedly stressed the impact that both the Riverside, Illinois, and Seaside, Florida, communities had on her thought process. Olmsted designed and began building Riverside in 1869, nine miles west of State Street on 1,600 acres that stretched for three miles along the Des Plaines River. He conceived of the suburb "not as an escape from the city, but as a delicate synthesis of town and wilderness." He sought to build "close to nature" while still providing "a considerable share of urban conveniences."[41] The recent completion of a suburban station for the Chicago, Burlington and Quincy Railroad made the area an attractive location for a rural bedroom community, with a commute to the bustling city now possible.

Riverside is widely recognized as the first planned community and modern suburb in the United States, and in 1970 it was designated a national historic landmark. Following the lead of Alexander Jackson Davis in Llewellyn Park, New Jersey, Olmsted rejected as "too stiff and formal" the standard of laying out streets in the traditional grid pattern. Instead he selected a curvilinear pattern for the community, to "suggest and imply leisure, contemplativeness, and happy tranquility." He added trees to the street parkways "to break up the featureless prairie," and to retain a sense of open space he also set the homes thirty feet back from the roadway.[42] To further the development's nature theme, he named the streets after naturalists and landscape architects such as John James Audubon and Andrew Jackson Downing.[43] Along the river, Olmsted retained the natural wetlands. He planted trees in an irregular manner to mimic natural processes. And he built a village square around the train station to anchor the town.

The Ranneys incorporated many of Olmsted's design aspects into Prairie Crossing. His influence on Vicky Ranney is ubiquitous throughout the development. In creating Lake Leopold and Sanctuary Pond, she restored the natural hydrology to the property, which had been disrupted by agricultural drainage tiles. Narrow, curving streets slow down traffic and provide a prairie viewscape for contemplation of the local ecology. Vicky named the streets after local settlers, Native Americans, and native plants to ground the residents in the land and its history. The first guiding principle of the development is environmental protection and enhancement, which emphasizes Olmsted's concept of building close to nature.

In 1981, more than a century after Olmsted broke ground at Riverside, and half a continent away, Robert Davis hired a Miami-based architectural firm run by Andres Duany and Elizabeth Plater-Zyberk to help him build the "ideal" community on an eighty-acre parcel of land he had inherited on the Gulf Coast of Florida. Davis, known as something of a maverick, wanted to try something new, and the product of that effort, aptly named "Seaside," quickly became an "icon" for a movement—New Urbanism.[44] In preparation for the project, Duany and Plater-Zyberk toured the Southeast looking at the designs of old towns and searching for ways to re-create the yesteryear small-town charm of earlier generations.

The result was indeed something new. The lots in Seaside are small, density is high, and almost totally absent—except for a grassy public area that doubles as flood mitigation during storms—is the conventional suburban front lawn. Streets are brick-lined and deliberately narrow to slow down traffic. Cupolas, towers, tin roofs, front porches, and hidden garages create an inviting neighborly ambience. The towers on homes set back from the beach are staggered, providing many homes with property-enhancing views of the ocean. The core of the development is a town center with corner shops and stores. These buildings include live/work units that permit shop owners to live above their workplaces, all for the price of a single mortgage. The original beach property was somewhat unattractive, covered with brambles and other unruly vegetation, but the developers resisted the temptation to clothe the landscape in exotic nonnative plants. They stuck with the scrub oak vegetation that is native to the panhandle region of Florida. Unlike Riverside and Prairie Crossing, Seaside is built on a grid pattern, so all streets end at the beach and provide a view of the ocean. This orients residents and visitors to the water and invites people to the beach; it is a visual cue that the ocean is a shared amenity and not the sole province of the beachfront homes.

The most innovative aspect of the development, and the one that had the greatest impact on Vicky Ranney, was the creation of the Seaside Institute, a nonprofit organization. Created in 1982 by Robert Davis, the institute is dedicated to (1) "documenting the founding and development of the community of Seaside," (2) "educating public officials, students, professionals and the general public about the benefits and techniques of New Urbanism," and (3) "fostering education, cultural activities and the arts within Seaside and the surrounding area." The institute holds hands-on seminars on town planning, "educating other practitioners in the fields of planning, architecture and development." It also sponsors educational and cultural programming for residents and visitors, including workshops and classes, literary events, chamber music performances, dance recitals, and poetry readings. The scope of the institute has expanded over time; however, its mission has remained the same: "the restoration of civic life" and to make Seaside a better place to live.[45]

The Ranneys adapted the Seaside concept of a teaching and learning institute and created the Liberty Prairie Foundation. Its mission is to promote the integration of human communities and the ecosystems on which they depend. Much like Seaside's work on promoting and extending the principles of New Urbanism, Prairie Crossing's efforts center on their unique contribution to urban planning and design—the conservation community, sustainable agricultural practices, and the restoration and preservation of healthy ecosystems. Much of the foundation's work is local; however, its work is nationally recognized, and its ideas have been exported around the country.

The influence of Seaside on Prairie Crossing can be seen in many areas of the development. Seaside's absence of lawns and emphasis on the ocean find expression at Prairie Crossing through the emphasis on the prairie restoration and the significantly smaller number of bluegrass lawns relative to conventional developments. And like Seaside, Prairie Crossing incorporated its most significant natural feature into its name. More than a marketing ploy, the names are a constant reminder of the communities' place in nature. Seaside took a measure of risk in landscaping the development in the native scrub oak vegetation. When it was selected as the location set for the Hollywood film *The Truman Show*, the producers replaced the native vegetation with bluegrass lawns so that the community would appear more familiar to mainstream film watchers. Similarly, Prairie Crossing's landscaping can at times look "weedy" to those unfamiliar with the region's indigenous flora. Seaside's and Prairie Crossing's developers were taking something of a gamble in the 1980s by departing from the industry standard of reworking the landscape in conventional nonnatives.

Like Duany and Plater-Zyberk, who sought out graceful architecture in the Southeast before building Seaside, the Ranneys toured Lake County looking for elegant designs rooted in that region's past. As in Seaside, the homes in Prairie Crossing are lined around a village green, where residents engage in outdoor sports and other recreational activities. The Station Village and Square at Prairie Crossing was meant to attract small businesses and commerce, but it has struggled to some extent, unlike the town center at Seaside. The economic downturn in 2008, shortly after the completion of the Station Village, played a role in Prairie Crossing's difficulties. And comparing the two developments is somewhat unfair. Seaside is a second-home community in a state known for tourism. Homes there are routinely rented out to tourists, and the town received a significant economic bump from the advertising it received in *The Truman Show*. But it has to be acknowledged that Seaside's superior town center design, with its central location and live/work units, better encourages and facilitates commerce.

Lastly, the New Urbanism design of Seaside played a big role in influencing the design of Prairie Crossing. Though the design features of Prairie Crossing's homes—predominantly Midwestern and Prairie School—are very different, the Ranneys still employed many aspects of New Urbanism in their planning and architecture. Garages, for the most part, are accessed from the rear of the houses. Home facades are dominated by front porches, a throwback to nineteenth-century architecture, designed to get people out of the house where they can interact with the landscape and fellow residents. The outdoor orientation helps foster a greater commitment to the community than does spending extended time indoors. Prairie Crossing also adheres to two other tenets of New Urbanism: walkable neighborhoods and transit-oriented development. The Station Village and Square and the two train lines are a short walk from anywhere in the development. It does not currently offer a variety of shopping or dining, but the shopping plaza still has the potential for future improvement. And the train lines offer excellent service to many communities, O'Hare International Airport, and downtown Chicago.

Prairie Crossing's innovative contribution to urban planning and design is environmental enhancement—using the market to improve the environment. But many of the development's other successful design features were based on groundbreaking advancements first pioneered at Riverside, Seaside, and the Sea Ranch. It is the blending of conservation and open-space preservation with New Urbanism that has made Prairie Crossing a unique experiment in urban public policy.

## Prairie Crossing's Catalyst:
## The Heartland Development

For the Ranneys, the intellectual seeds for Prairie Crossing germinated in the 1960s and early 1970s. The Sea Ranch provided them with inspiration, ideas about what is possible using the power of the market, and Vicky's exposure to Olmsted taught her about the restorative power of nature and how it could channel human behavior. But it was a threat to George's childhood haunts that provided the catalyst for the conservation community concept.

In 1973, a proposal to put 3,000 nearly identical homes on what is now the Prairie Crossing property—to be known as the Heartland Development—triggered intense public and private community opposition. The Donnelleys and Ranneys were diehard members of the opposition, but not by any means the sole instigators. A battle ensued over the proposed development, and Heartland sued several public officials, including the mayor of Grayslake, for "conspiring to use the zoning process to stop development."[46] State courts awarded the Heartland developer $60 million in damages, an award that the U.S. Supreme Court ultimately overturned. In 1986, a compromise known as the Heartland Agreement resulted in a settlement of the lawsuit and the purchase of the Prairie Crossing land by a group led by Gaylord Donnelley. The group's lawyer for the settlement was George Ranney Jr., and Gaylord asked George and Vicky to help him develop the land in a way that would preserve its natural character while at the same time justifying the expense of the purchase. Gaylord again was thinking unconventionally, just as he had with Ducks Unlimited. With Ducks Unlimited, he was going to save waterfowl by enlisting hunters who killed them. With Prairie Crossing, he was going to save the land by developing it through profits generated in the free market. The Ranneys and the Donnelleys had the wealth, professional network, personal commitment, and experience to make it work.

## A Grand Vision: The Liberty Prairie Reserve

The tale of Prairie Crossing and the grander vision, what has become known as the Liberty Prairie Reserve, is one of a public-private partnership. Prairie Crossing and the reserve would not have been possible without the vision, leadership, commitment, and financial resources of the Donnelleys and the commitment of the Ranneys and other area landowners, including the Getz, Potter, Tieken, and Marshall Field families. The contribution of the public sector, however, cannot be discounted. The Village of Grayslake, the Libertyville Township Board, and the Lake County Forest Preserve District all embraced the open-space commitment. Libertyville Township Board political rivals Ralph Swank and Mike Graham set aside their differences and supported the township's acquisition of 714 acres in what was the state of Illinois's first open-space program in 1985. The executive director of the Lake County Forest Preserve District, Tom Hahn, and fellow board members Bonnie Thomson Carter, Jim LaBelle, Andrea Moore, and Betty Anne Moore also made significant contributions to the preservation effort.

Saving the land in central Lake County required a significant economic investment. Land has value, and preservation has costs. The development of Prairie Crossing would generate profits and bring an economic return. The vision for the area, however, was grander. A public-private partnership would seek to preserve the natural and agricultural character of the land on the scale of nearly 6,000 acres, all a short drive from the third-biggest market in the country.

The Liberty Prairie Reserve comprises 5,770 acres of land—3,383 of which have permanent legal protection—that includes Prairie Crossing, private land under conservation easement, individually owned land, and three substantial public landholdings: Almond Marsh, Independence Grove, and Oak Openings. The 3,383 preserved acres represent 80 separate acquisitions and conservation easements. The 2014 value of the public and private investments in the reserve exceeds $100 million, including $33 million in donated conservation easements.[47] Four municipalities, Libertyville, Grayslake, Gurnee, and Waukegan, contain portions of the Liberty Prairie Reserve, and nine government different bodies have jurisdiction in one form or another. Approximately 2,500 people live within the reserve, and several hundred people are employed there. The Liberty Prairie Reserve was established in 1991 through a comprehensive plan adopted by Libertyville Township, the Lake County Forest Preserve District, and private landowners in the reserve, including the Donnelleys and Ranneys. It represents a substantial public good; "Lake County is home to more endangered and threatened species than any other county in Illinois."[48] The preserved habitat includes graminoid fen, mesic prairie, sedge meadow, oak savanna, and a great blue heron rookery.

The name "Liberty Prairie Reserve" is a derivative of "Libertyville," the name of the nearby village and township. The Donnelleys and Ranneys originally coined the name "Liberty Prairie" for a unique prairie fen remnant on the Donnelleys' property just east of Prairie Crossing. In 1990, two years before his death, the township, the Lake County Forest Preserve District, and Gaylord Donnelley split the $100,000 cost for a scientific assessment of the area's flora and fauna. Jack

White, senior scientist at the Nature Conservancy, performed the review. The considerable cost for the assessment was controversial at the time, contested even by some committed environmentalists who felt the money might be better spent elsewhere. The review proved warranted. White discovered rare and threatened species on an undisturbed fragment of virgin prairie wetland, including slender bog arrow-grass, normally a polar species, suspected to be a holdover remnant from ice age glaciation.[49] White later recalled that upon being informed of the rare arrow-grass find, Gaylord "said it was one of his proudest moments."[50] That same year, Gaylord and Dorothy Donnelley were honored for their regional conservation efforts at the downtown Nikko Hotel, with a 950-seat black tie event that raised more than $400,000 for Chicago's Open Lands Project and the Upper Illinois Valley Association.[51] The Liberty Prairie Reserve got the publicity boost that it needed to take hold.

The entirety of the 5,770-acre reserve does not have an official legal distinction. Only 58 percent of the land within it is permanently protected from development. The remaining acreage remains in private hands. However, both public and private entities have embraced the name, the concept, and the symbolic vision, and the words "Liberty Prairie Reserve" regularly appear in print. In 2013, nearly a dozen of the region's agencies and several private landowners produced an updated "master plan" for future management of the reserve.[52] Its stated goal is to be "a model of exceptional land, water, and biodiversity health where public and private landowners manage their land in ways that sustain people, plants, and wildlife. The plan envisions people enjoying, enhancing, and restoring the reserve's rich array of natural areas. Additionally, the reserve's agricultural values and heritage will be celebrated and continued in ways that support clean water, healthy soils, and diverse agricultural products and foods." Specifically, the Liberty Prairie Reserve has six principal objectives: (1) "Expand core habitats," (2) "Support ecological management and restoration," (3) "Preserve more open space," (4) "Transition agriculture to sustainable and 'biologically-based' practices," (5) "Improve public access and movement through and around the Reserve," and (6) "Establish a Planning Council for Stakeholders."[53]

The coalition of forces that represent the Liberty Prairie Reserve have largely been successful. In addition to continually adding to the legally protected acreage, their influence helped modify a proposal to expand Illinois Route 53/120, which borders the northern boundary of the reserve, into an environmentally sensitive road. The Route 53/120 issue illustrates the organization's pragmatism. Realizing that an expansion was inevitable due to the traffic needs of the surrounding region, Liberty Prairie Reserve forces sought to mitigate environmental harm without creating opposition to the institution's core values. Several organizations affiliated with the reserve actively pursue its objectives. Conserve Lake County and the Liberty Prairie Foundation have created specific programs to support ecological management and transition agriculture to sustainable practices. Conserve Lake County offers on-site consultations to encourage homeowners to plant native species on their private properties with its Conservation@Home program, which will be discussed in detail in chapter five. And the Liberty Prairie Foundation, an organization created with seed money from the Prairie Crossing development, mentors budding organic farmers on five-acre plots on the Prairie Crossing Farm.

## Regional Planning

The Liberty Prairie Reserve is an example of something relatively rare in American public policy: voluntary, comprehensive regional planning involving a viable public and private partnership. Other examples of regional planning in the United States do exist, most notably the urban growth boundary system in Oregon and the urban-rural demarcation line policy in Baltimore County, Maryland. How does the Liberty Prairie Reserve compare to these initiatives?

Portland, Oregon, was a hotbed of green activism during the late 1960s and early 1970s.[54] Two visionary politicians from that time, the state's governor, Tom McCall, and the city's mayor, Neil Goldschmidt, understood the value of protecting the state's natural resources—the wetlands, woodlands, watersheds, wildlife habitat, and farmland. In 1973, capitalizing on the political energy of the first Earth Day and the environmental movement, McCall and Goldschmidt helped pass landmark legislation: the nation's first urban growth boundary. The law required every city and county to draft long-range plans addressing future growth according to local and statewide criteria, and created an "agency with teeth" (the Metropolitan Service District, or "Metro") to enforce the law.[55]

Because nearly half of the state's residents resided in and around Portland, the growth boundary had its greatest impact on that city. Essentially, the law draws a line around the metropolitan area, outside of which commercial, retail, and housing development are not permitted. In practice, however, that line has not remained fixed; Metro has moved it to permit additional development more than thirty times since 1973. The boundary was then, and continues to be, controversial. The most obvious consequence of a growth boundary is that it artificially increases land costs inside the line and lowers them considerably outside the line. The result in Oregon was a significant loss in housing affordability. By 2000, only three states had worse housing affordability than Oregon.[56]

The growth boundary has drawn both criticism and praise. Andres Duany, whose New Urbanism designs helped inspire the Ranneys, has criticized the policy on two grounds: it has not stopped sprawl, and it has "increase[d] the cost of housing by creating scarcity."[57] As Duany stated in 2000, nearly three decades after the law's enactment, "Portland's growth boundary does not deserve to be accepted uncritically as an unqualified success. It was originally drawn not at the edge of urbanization but at a distance many miles out, anticipating and effectively sanctioning twenty years of bad growth. . . . [T]he growth boundary contains *within it* thousands of acres of the most mundane sprawl."[58] As an alternative to the urban growth boundary, Duany prefers the countryside preserve, which "sets aside multiple parcels of conservation land independent of their relationship to the center city" and bases their preservation on "objective environmental criteria."[59]

In contrast, James Kunstler, author of *The Geography of Nowhere*, praises Oregonians for "setting an example in regional land-use policy that the rest of the nation would do well to heed."[60] Kunstler viewed the growth boundary as an opportunity for Oregonians to find new ways to build community, including urban infill, consolidation, and densification. The urban growth boundary has helped generate all of these results, to some degree; however, it has also generated opposition.

While Oregon voters do not view the urban growth boundary as an unmitigated success, they are not willing to jettison it. In 2004, the voters overwhelmingly passed Ballot Measure 37 with 61 percent of the vote. Measure 37 required state or local governments to compensate private property owners whose properties were devalued by environmental or land-use regulations. As a result, government entities lacking in funding were unable to protect environmentally sensitive lands from being developed. Three years later, a vote with a nearly identical margin brought in Measure 49, which restricted some of the damaging environmental effects of the original 2004 law. The new legislation permitted an "express" option for small claimants to build between three and ten homes but restricted huge, sprawling developments on valued farmland and wetland and riparian areas.

More than four decades after its enactment, the verdict on the urban growth boundary is mixed. The boundary lines are readily recognizable from the air, and the effects are dramatic—on one side is dense development, on the other nature or farmland. The boundary has saved precious natural resources from development. Ninety-five percent of the state is currently located outside urban growth boundaries. The practice has not, however, stopped the spread of sprawl inside the boundaries, and studies have found that the boundaries have increased the cost of housing.[61] The urban growth boundary system has also proved to be politically contentious, with numerous unsuccessful attempts over the last few decades to overturn it or gut it. Approaching fifty years of experimentation with urban growth boundaries, Oregon has undoubtedly saved many acres of valuable farmland and native landscape while at the same time permitting the spread of the same monotonous sprawl that mars most other U.S. cities.

Baltimore County, Maryland, surrounds the city of Baltimore on three sides, and is located within the Chesapeake Bay watershed. The county's urban-rural demarcation line predates Oregon's urban growth boundary by several years, having been established in 1967 by the county planning board. Its purpose is to "maximiz[e] the efficiency of county revenues on infrastructure in urban areas and preserve important natural and agricultural resources in rural areas."[62] The demarcation line differs somewhat from an urban growth boundary. Property on the urban side of the demarcation line is permitted to have public water and sewer infrastructure; development on the rural side must supply its own water and sewer through well and septic systems, and those systems are subject to strict county standards. Development on the rural side is not prohibited; it is merely discouraged by the requirement for private water and sewer infrastructure. This particularly limits commercial and large-scale residential development, and helps preserve the land's agricultural and natural areas. Beginning in 1972, the Baltimore County Council began issuing a series of master plans to guide future development. Bruce Seeley, the county's master plan coordinator, argues that the urban-rural demarcation line has been effective: "About 90 percent of our population lives inside the URDL. There is considerable support for maintaining the URDL well into the future. Master Plan 2020 proposes to continue protecting the rural area by encouraging new development and redevelopment in higher density, mixed-use, walkable communities inside the URDL."[63] In addition to the urban-rural demarcation line, Baltimore County preserves valuable land through two other means. The county offers a government-sponsored land preservation program, which encourages the adoption of conservation easements on private property. The program provides tax credits for those who enroll, and approximately 58,000 acres are presently under permanent protection. Regulatory zoning is another method used to protect land outside the demarcation line. The most restrictive form is resource conservation 2, or RC2. Under RC2, property lots smaller than 2 acres cannot be subdivided. Lots exceeding 100 acres can only be subdivided in 50-acre increments. More than 139,000 acres are currently zoned under the RC2 standard.[64]

Environmentalists, pro-development advocates, and even farmers have all criticized the effectiveness of Baltimore County Master Plan 2020 (adopted on November 15, 2010). Environmentalists argue that it lacks clout. "While the master plan may state things as requirements, it has generally been determined that it is just a guideline and that local jurisdictions are not actually bound to what it says," says Mike Pierce, president of North County Preservation, a community nonprofit committed to land preservation in northern Baltimore County. Long-time resident and environmental activist Lynne Jones strongly concurs: "Unfortunately our master plans do not have the teeth they need in order to make any difference when it comes to developments being built out here. Our government is a big rubber stamp for development."[65]

In contrast, Wade Kach, former Republican delegate for Baltimore County District 5B, is concerned that the success of the plan's land preservation program has greatly decreased the number of developable building lots: "At one time there were approximately 10,000 building lots in northern Baltimore County. There have been focused efforts to purchase land and development rights through land preservation programs and willing people volunteering to put their land in preservation. It is estimated there are just under 4,000 building lots remaining in northern Baltimore County as a result of such efforts and willing individuals."[66]

Farmers in Baltimore County also have problems with land preservation outside the demarcation line. Some see the limitations on farm development within the zone as too restrictive and have concerns that farming is losing its appeal as a profession: "One of the challenges is that we are preserving land for agriculture, but if there is no one to farm it, then what? The farm operators are aging, and there is a shortage of the next-generation farmers. It's not seen as a viable career," said Pierce. County farmer David Smith says that his neighbors' opposition to the construction of a farm store on his property, on a site where a barn was previously located, has made it difficult for him to maintain a viable business. Due to master plan building restrictions, Smith is forced to sell eggs, dairy, poultry, meats, and ice cream out of his garage: "[Some residents] are just not willing to accept that a farmer should be allowed to be successful. They and much of the population of this country expect to see farmers dirt poor and be forced to sell what they raise at a price barely sufficient to meet costs."[67]

Like Oregon's urban growth boundary, Baltimore County's urban-rural demarcation line has achieved its goal of preserving valuable conservation land. Most of the development follows the region's arterial roadways and surrounds the city of Baltimore, focusing 90 percent of growth in the southern third of the county and leaving just 10 percent of the population in the northern two-thirds. While this pattern saves relatively large amounts of territory, it does not permit the establishment of biotic corridors for flora and wildlife, which facilitate the flow of animals and genetic material across regional habitats (to be discussed at greater length in chapter three). The county's master plan has a green building program, which promotes energy efficiency and sustainable buildings by offering tax credits, low-interest loans, and grants. The plan does not, however, promote large-scale restoration or incorporation of existing natural areas into the urban fabric of the development, as is true of the Prairie Crossing conservation community model. Though Baltimore County's urban-rural demarcation line permits—and to some degree facilitates—suburban sprawl, it is still a progressive regional model of considerable merit.

The Liberty Prairie Reserve differs from the urban growth boundary and demarcation line models in several ways. At 5,800 acres, the scale is local rather than statewide or regional. The reserve also places perhaps a greater emphasis on the private element of the public-private partnership. And Prairie Crossing (which in many respects is the showcase development and cornerstone of the reserve) is unique in that it has used market forces for restoration and preservation in ways that the city of Portland and Baltimore County have not. Much of Portland's development inside the urban growth boundary has been "mundane sprawl," growth that degrades the environment. Oregon—and, to a lesser extent, Baltimore County—achieved success in preserving natural and agricultural lands by taming market forces through government regulation.

In contrast, the Liberty Prairie Reserve and Prairie Crossing have partnered with government, developed policy initiatives, and employed markets wherever practical. For example, the Liberty Prairie Foundation has helped train the next generation of farmers, placing a strong emphasis on sustainable methods. Baltimore County has experienced problems in supporting community agriculture, and the Chesapeake Bay watershed has also suffered severe environmental degradation due to unsustainable agricultural practices.[68] By actively seeking a balance between business and conservation, Prairie Crossing and the Liberty Prairie Reserve have demonstrated that green development can be profitable. Nature and economics are not incompatible.

Prairie Crossing's true value lies in the potential for mass replication of the model. Its integrated approach—market emphasis, land preservation and restoration, creation of a sense of place and community, and focus on its residents' bond with nature—has the potential to lessen the impact of future development and foster a greater respect and empathy for the natural world. This bottom-up approach may be essential to protecting the country's biological heritage, as ecologist Doug Tallamy argues: "My central message is that unless we restore native plants to our suburban ecosystems, the future of biodiversity in the United States is dim."[69] The future of conservation in America is not in the national park but in the suburban backyard.

## Prairie Crossing's Guiding Principles

The idea of using a set of principles to guide a business venture predates their use at Prairie Crossing by fifteen years. In the late 1970s, while an executive for Inland Steel, George Ranney worked with the late Clifford McIntosh, a management consultant for the Quetico Centre in Ontario, Canada. McIntosh, who eventually became a close family friend of the Ranneys, developed the concept of using formal written principles for business units to provide direction, measure progress, and improve performance. Prairie Crossing's guiding principles are directly derived from McIntosh's approach to organization development:

1. Environmental protection and enhancement
2. A healthy lifestyle
3. A sense of place
4. A sense of community
5. Economic and racial diversity
6. Convenient and efficient transportation
7. Energy conservation
8. Lifelong learning and education
9. Aesthetic design and high-quality construction
10. Economic viability[70]

The Ranneys selected "environmental protection and enhancement" as their first guiding principle because "[i]t was the core concept motivating" both the Donnelleys and the Ranneys.[71] Enhancement is the more interesting and innovative of the two elements. Many policies seek to protect nature where it exists, and such principles are simple and intuitive. The United States has an extensive network of natural preserves at every level of government, and the concept of government preservation precedes the founding of the country.[72] Using real-estate market forces to improve and enhance degraded land, however, is something new and more rare. The North American grassland ecosystem, which originally occupied 22 million acres across the state of Illinois alone, is now more endangered than rainforest habitat, a fact that is not appreciated by many Americans or even Midwesterners. Only 0.01 percent of the biome still exists, much of it carved up into small, isolated plots.[73] Gaylord Donnelley, however, recognized the loss, and he in fact owned one of those small undisturbed parcels, the Liberty Prairie.[74] The Prairie Crossing development, therefore, was an opportunity not only to protect what was left but to restore and regenerate what was lost, at least to the extent possible. Enhancement, Vicky said, also "drew on the work of the great naturalist Aldo Leopold, Frederick Law Olmsted, and others."[75]

The second principle, "a healthy lifestyle," was based in part on the opportunities that the specific site location offered the new community: farming and open space. George grew up near Prairie Crossing, and he understood the important role that agriculture plays in a community. Much of the farmland in the area had been degraded in his lifetime through the use of herbicides, pesticides, fertilizers, and hydrologic alteration. A developmental emphasis on organic farming, which was relatively new at that time, would provide fresh local produce while still treading "lightly on the land," a guiding philosophy the Ranneys had observed at the Sea Ranch. A network of trails connecting the open space had the potential to get residents out of the house and into nature. The outdoor exercise would also help fuel healthy lifestyles.

Guiding principles three and four, "a sense of place" and "a sense of community," are related and were inspired by Vicky's work on Olmsted. The Ranneys sought to ground Prairie Crossing in its historic past by bringing in local nineteenth-century structures such as the Byron Colby Barn and the Wright Schoolhouse, and by naming the streets after Native tribes and early white settlers. Rooting the community in its past, in the words of Vicky Ranney, "would remind us that others have lived on this land before, and others, to whom we have responsibility, will live here after us."[76]

"Economic and racial diversity," combined in the fifth principle, recalled the Ranneys' work in civil rights. As a member of John F. Kennedy's program Teachers for East Africa, Vicky taught at Nyakasura School at the foot of the Rwenzori Mountains in Uganda for two years in the early 1960s, shortly after the country achieved independence. And in 1964 she taught again, this time with George, at

Tougaloo College, an all-black institution near Jackson, Mississippi. The tenor of the difficult times made a strong impression on Vicky: "it was more scary than anything I experienced in Africa." As a result, social justice became an important principle for both Ranneys. "After Africa and Mississippi," Vicky explained, "the idea of living in a place that was an all-white or almost-all-white monoculture wasn't interesting."[77] Of all the guiding principles, however, economic and racial diversity would be the most difficult to achieve.

"Convenient and efficient transportation" and "energy conservation," the sixth and seventh principles, "were drawn from the realities and needs of suburban life."[78] George Ranney has an "extensive background" in transportation planning and is still an influential actor in regional mass transit. He helped bring rail service to Prairie Crossing in the mid-1990s. The availability of mass transit lessens the environmental impact of development. And in spite of the substantial conservation amenities the community offers, Michael Sands, the long-time environmental team leader, went so far as to say that he would not have supported Prairie Crossing without mass-transit service because of the negative externalities associated with automobile use.[79] The emphasis on energy conservation reflects the development's "environmental purpose" and was also influenced by George's work experience.[80] As an Inland Steel executive in charge of energy use, he understood the value of energy conservation. Energy efficiency was a requirement for all architects working in the planning and design process.

The eighth principle, "lifelong learning and education," is similarly rooted in George and Vicky's past. As both teachers and students, they understood the value of not only formal education but also the "conviction that learning is important throughout one's life."[81] Inspired by Robert Davis's Seaside Institute in Florida, the Ranneys created a not-for-profit foundation to promote conservation and sustainable agriculture in the region. Believing that education and learning can bind a community together, they helped bring the charter school to the development. The Byron Colby Barn furthers the mission by offering lectures and cultural events to the adult community.

The last two principles, "aesthetic design and high-quality construction" and "economic viability," speak to industry profitability. Gaylord Donnelley and George Ranney both knew that land costs money and that they would never have enough to protect the natural and historic character of the area by direct purchase. But they gambled that they could save the land through development if they engaged in conservation-friendly practices while adhering to important profit-making incentives. The development must be grounded in economic reality and pay its own way, they reasoned, for the conservation community to be both replicable and a viable alternative to conventional urban sprawl.

The guiding principles had influence beyond the boardroom. They were posted in the sales office, and even today, twenty years after initial occupation, the residents are polled annually regarding their importance and implementation. Throughout every stage of the developmental process, the principles provided a baseline for guidance. "They were real," said Linda Wiens, a long-time assistant to the Ranneys. She argued that the principles had "the commitment [of] all the members," and that whenever a conflict or question arose, the planning team "always referred back to the strategic plans." The planning and design team benefited from a diversity of opinions. Wiens stated that "each one had their pet preferences," which prevented any single principle, especially profits, from overwhelming the others.[82]

The Ranneys and the Prairie Crossing residents themselves believe that the principles have held up well over the years, and the Ranneys have stated that they would not change them. Second-generation conservation developments have widely copied the concept of a vision statement or set of guiding principles, in addition to adopting many of the individual principles themselves. Prairie Crossing's impact on other conservation communities is covered in chapter seven.

## The Liberty Prairie Foundation

The Liberty Prairie Foundation is a 501(c)(3) private foundation that portrays itself as a "nationally recognized . . . leader in developing and supporting enterprises that build and strengthen our local food system while enhancing the natural landscape."[83] It was created by the Ranneys to finance future conservation projects, develop public policy, and educate people about the importance of keeping the land healthy. Both George and Vicky Ranney are foundation board members and help guide its mission. The organization is funded in part by a tax on Prairie Crossing home sales and a legal agreement with a nearby landfill. Home sellers pay a tax of 0.5 percent of the sale price, and the proceeds help fund the Liberty Prairie Foundation. The Countryside Landfill (now owned by Waste Management, Inc.) also donates $.30 per cubic yard of waste to the foundation, which generates a sizeable income of $400,000 per year, nearly 40 percent of the organization's annual budget. The home sales tax was innovative for its time and has been copied at other conservation communities for similar public-interest organizations.

The Liberty Prairie Foundation is headquartered in the original Prairie Crossing farmhouse. George Ranney set up the initial sources of funding for it. The organization has an annual budget of $1.2 million and seven full-time staff members. Its stated mission is to provide "leadership and financial support for sustainable local food system development, social entrepreneurship, conservation, and environmental education."[84] The Liberty Prairie Foundation owns the hundred-acre Prairie Crossing Farm and helps fledging organic farmers get started in the business by allowing them to develop the trade on five-acre plots. With thirty acres designated for that purpose, farmers have up to five years to practice with organic farming techniques before starting out on their own. To date, the foundation's Farm Business Development Center has helped launch sixteen organic farm businesses. Beginning farmers can lease all of the equipment they need from the Farm Business Development Center. That allows them to get started in the business of farming as they learn the craft while avoiding large capital expenses. The foundation provides additional assistance by conducting annual reviews of the farmers' financials to help them understand "the business of business."[85]

Foundation staffers frequently travel throughout the country to speak, educate, and trade information with the relevant farming and conservation policy communities. The Liberty Prairie Foundation and the Gaylord and Dorothy Donnelley Foundation are founding members of Fresh Taste, a Chicago-based sustainable food collaborative geared toward promoting local food within a 200-mile radius of the city.[86] The Liberty Prairie Foundation is also a member of the Sustainable Agriculture and Food Systems Funders, which further supports local sustainable food production.[87] The organic and sustainable food industries are still in their relative infancy, and the Liberty Prairie Foundation spends most of its budget attempting to expand, nurture, and export sustainable agricultural practices.

## Prairie Crossing Farm

Having grown up on a farm, George Ranney is mindful of the harm that unsustainable agricultural practices can cause to the environment. The Ranneys disassembled the Byron Colby Barn and moved it to Prairie Crossing for reassembly. Today the nineteenth-century structure generates income for the Liberty Prairie Foundation by hosting a hundred weddings a year in addition to concerts, lectures, and other educational events. The foundation retained the original farmhouse on the property, along with the windmill and several other ancillary buildings. Horse stables permit owners to house and ride horses on the property, and the 100-acre farmland is worked by USDA-certified organic farmers.

Sandhill Family Farms has been the leading company farming the acreage for nine years. Sandhill grows "every vegetable imaginable" and sells the produce at farmers' markets outside the development and through a community-supported agriculture program that serves 550 families, 150 of which pick up directly from the farm.[88] All of its organic practices are documented, a requirement for maintaining its organic certification. Both residents and nonresidents can purchase produce on-site. Eggs, honey, and jam are usually available. Sandhill keeps free-range chickens for egg production only (no meat), with the flock consisting of approximately 350 laying hens. Some of the organic farmers who mentor through the Farm Business Development Center occasionally produce turkeys and pork for meat consumption.

The farm operation at Prairie Crossing was initially a challenge for the development.[89] It took some time to develop the business model, but during construction of the community, the farm proved successful in terms of marketing and home sales, community education, and environmentally friendly food production. Numerous second-generation developments have followed the Prairie Crossing lead, and some have expanded farming to much larger operations.

The Learning Farm at Prairie Crossing is situated on a three-acre-plot and includes "a children's garden, mobile henhouse for egg-laying chickens, fruit orchard, greenhouse and hoop house." Funded by the Liberty Prairie Foundation, the project was "founded with the purpose of educating and inspiring people to value healthy food, land and community through hands-on experiences on a working organic farm," says Vicky Ranney.[90] This farm-based education initiative is designed to promote sustainable agricultural practices, especially among young people. The Learning Farm is often used as an outdoor classroom for the students of the charter school.

The Prairie Farm Corps is an educational program that seeks to "lay the groundwork for a more resilient local food system by immersing youth in sustainable agriculture, providing mentoring, and reflecting on the collaboration between land and living systems." Based on the successful and nationally recognized Boston Food Project, the Prairie Farm Corps provides "an experiential paid work experience" to youngsters interested in learning about sustainable agriculture.[91] The program is highly competitive—several hundred people apply for only fourteen positions. It attracts a diverse demographic of students.

Sustainable agriculture is an integral part of the mission of the Liberty Prairie Foundation, and the organization has had a national impact developing policy in this area. Preservation of the environment and sustainable agriculture are the twin pillars supporting the conservation agenda of the Prairie Crossing development.

## Developing the Concept

The path to the Prairie Crossing development was not linear and involves numerous players beyond George and Vicky Ranney. Gaylord Donnelley's passion for conservation, commitment, and financial resources were instrumental in the incipient stages. After his death in 1992, Dorothy and her son and daughter, Strachan and Laura Donnelley, continued to support the project.[92] Strong community backing, including from fellow private landowners and public officials, generated sufficient resistance to keep urban sprawl from taking over the site and the reserve.

George and Vicky not only had a deep emotional connection to the land, they also believed in what they were trying to accomplish. Given the unproven nature of the development, which involved extensive and costly ecological restoration, there was a measure of risk in forging ahead with the $100 million project. Their commitment in the face of industry skepticism was important in the eventual success of Prairie Crossing.

The Heartland Development litigation in the 1970s provided the catalyst for preservation, and the settlement of the lawsuit led to an intriguing opportunity. Gaylord Donnelley's gradual realization that land preservation needed to pay its own way—that there would never be enough money to buy the land and set it aside—laid the foundation for the conservation community model. The answer to saving the land was to develop it, albeit in a profitable, conservation-friendly way that preserved nature and open space. Gaylord's advanced age and his close personal bond with his nephew led him to reach out to George Ranney to realize his vision, knowing he was not likely to see either the final product or the verdict on its success or failure. The family's strong tradition of public service was the driving force.

The Ranneys did not have a prior background in housing development; however, many of their past experiences were useful and helped organize and catalyze their thoughts. Teamwork between Vicky and George made the development possible. Both are Harvard-educated; true intellectual partners, they work well together, and their talents complement each other: what one lacks, the other has. George is a trained lawyer and has experience negotiating the corridors of power in Springfield as a former Illinois state deputy budget director, which proved invaluable when it came to urban planning and budgetary issues. Vicky contributed her knowledge of Olmsted's landscape architecture work and his profound influence on America. The Ranneys traveled widely, observing both successes and failures in urban development. In northern England, Vicky appreciated how effective local zoning ordinances were in preserving the ancient hedgerows of medieval times and how they enhanced community aesthetics. At the Sea Ranch, she observed the maintenance and protection of nature within the confines of the built environment. This gradual learning process, which over the course of twenty years integrated their green beliefs with their commitment to business development, predisposed the Ranneys to take advantage of Gaylord Donnelley's offer when it unexpectedly appeared.

Vicky's exposure to Olmsted convinced her that there was a better way to build communities. Backed by the real-estate value of the property, the Ranneys would incorporate natural aesthetics into the housing environment and integrate the citizen back into nature. By making nature part of the home, the built landscape had the potential to alter the social and political dynamics of the community, positively impact civic participation, and promote the public good.

# CHAPTER THREE

# SEA OF SUBURBIA

Suburbia will come to be regarded
as the greatest misallocation of
resources in the history of the world.

—James Kunstler

On a date lost to memory sometime in the mid-1980s, a catchy slogan and circular green symbol caught his eye. "Save Our Planet," the 4-by-4 inch card declared from the desk of a South Pacific hotel. Jay Westerveld, the ponytailed former pro snowboarder-cum-environmental activist, read on with a nagging skepticism: "Every day, millions of gallons of water are used to wash towels that have only been used once. You make the choice: A towel on the rack means, 'I will use again.' A towel on the floor means, 'Please replace.' Thank you for helping us conserve the Earth's vital resources," the card said. Westerveld was not fooled. Washing fewer towels saves money. The corporation, pursuing nothing more than the bottom line, was tugging on patrons' heartstrings solely in an effort to increase profits. In a momentary flash of insight, a new word was born: "greenwashing."[1]

Greenwashing—"disinformation disseminated by an organization so as to present an environmentally responsible public image"—has become common in the United States.[2] Marketing spin is specifically designed to mislead the public and consumers into believing that a company is green-friendly, thereby boosting profits and increasing market share. It can take many forms, from mild exaggeration to deliberate falsification. Giving the appearance of being green can positively affect corporate profits, and environmental claims can be difficult to prove or disprove, particularly for busy consumers. Is it possible that Prairie Crossing is merely a greenwashing community rather than a green community, a cynical advertising gimmick designed to cash in on the latest green marketing trends? This chapter will evaluate the development's primary land conservation practices: wetland and prairie restoration, open-space preservation, and plant and animal biodiversity. The impact on the environment of residents' behavior and the Homeowners Association's practices will be analyzed in chapter four.

## Contrasting Models of Environmental Protection

There are two contrasting models of environmental protection in the United States: land advocacy and land trusts. Though both models can trace their political pedigree back to the late nineteenth century, the land trust movement has only recently begun to challenge the dominance of the advocacy approach in the policy arena. Land advocacy groups, such as the Sierra Club and the National Wildlife Federation, are private-interest groups that seek to protect land by advocating government purchase or regulation. Land trusts are also private-sector organizations; they differ from advocacy groups in that they acquire land directly by private purchase or voluntary contractual agreement (e.g., conservation easement) without government sanction or involvement, the Nature Conservancy being the best-known example.

Private landowners, particularly in the West, often vigorously oppose and sometimes even despise the work of advocacy groups. These tensions have given rise to pro-development, anti-environmental groups such as the Wise Use movement.[3] Such groups are fiercely anti-regulation, though not necessarily anti-government; they are often willing to accept government subsidies, and are generally backed by the Republican Party. For an example of the intense opposition that government preservation can generate, we can look to the Tallgrass Prairie National Preserve in Kansas, a federal preserve designed to protect the same grassland ecosystem as that re-created at Prairie Crossing. Traditionally a red state, Kansas is among the states with the smallest portion of land under federal control, less than 1 percent. In spite of the dearth of federal regulation and federally owned land in the state and the relatively small size of the preserve, just 10,894 acres, Kansans have waged a "political war" over whether the Tallgrass Preserve should exist at all. Roadside signs at the entrance to the preserve headquarters read: "Private Lands in Private Hands." Kansans who oppose government regulation have gone so far as to kill endangered species on their private land for fear their discovery will lead to land-use restrictions.[4]

Ever since the Reagan presidency, environmental protection has been a highly charged, partisan issue, one that divides Congress, the statehouses, and occasionally the public, though polls generally show broad public support for protection on most issues.[5] The division between the parties is so strong that it has come to be called "the Great Green Divide." According to a 2012 report from the Pew Research Center, "No issue divides more along partisan lines than the importance of environmental protection."[6] Thoroughly wedded to Reagan's philosophy of less government, local control, deregulation, and a strong faith in the market, the GOP has forced land advocacy groups to play defense for most of the past three decades.

Land trusts, in contrast, have had more success. Their recent expansion, combined with the inherent efficacy of removing land from development, has prompted biological scientist Richard Brewer to call trusts the "most successful and exciting force in U.S. land conservation today and perhaps the most effective component of the whole environmental movement."[7] Thirteen hundred local land trusts, representing 1 million members, protect a total of 6.5 million acres of land in the United States. More than 80 percent of that acreage has been preserved since 1990, decades in which very little land was set aside at the state and federal levels.[8] Their voluntary nature and lack of government involvement has drawn considerably less objection from free-market conservatives.

Environmental public policy is highly dependent on issue framing. Frames, according to cognitive linguist George Lakoff, are unconscious cognitive structures that are "physically realized in neural circuits in the brain." These circuits are connected to the emotional centers of the brain, and political ideologies are also heavily influenced by systems of frames. Frames structure the way people think about the world. Lakoff writes: "All of our knowledge makes use of frames, and every word is defined through the frames it neurally activates. All thinking and talking involves 'framing.' And since frames come in systems, a single word typically activates not only its defining frame, but also much of the system its defining frame is in."[9]

Conservatives and liberals think differently about the environment because they employ very different frames when they do so. Conservatives' conceptual worldview centers on the "strict father" moral system.[10] Children need to be punished when they do wrong to develop the discipline required to live a prosperous and moral life. Government undermines this by helping people, which, Lakoff says, "takes away their discipline, and hence makes them both unable to prosper on their own and function morally."[11] For this reason, conservatives tend to support free-market forces and oppose welfare, entitlements, and other forms of government assistance. This is easily illustrated in the well-known biblical paraphrase "Give a man a fish, and he'll eat for a day; teach a man to fish, and he'll eat for a lifetime." For conservatives, the market exerts a discipline that is both natural and moral, for it helps people to help themselves. Consequently, they have vigorously opposed land advocacy and government intervention for the purpose of environmental protection.

Liberals, in contrast, tend to use the "nurturant parent" metaphor.[12] In this frame, it is entirely appropriate for government to intervene on behalf of people who may not be able to adequately protect themselves. For liberals, environmental regulation, such as the Clean Air and Water Acts, the Endangered Species Act, and the American Antiquities Act, which authorizes the president to protect federal land as national monuments, are all necessary and responsible uses of government authority. The nurturing parent frame is far more congruent with using government power to make the world a better place. Not only is it permitted under the frame, it is a moral imperative. Protecting the air, water, land, and fellow species is our collective responsibility. Until recently, liberals' preferred mode of protection has been the land advocacy approach through direct government action.

Given the policy complexity of many environmental problems, especially those involving a threat to the commons, the proper political response in most cases is government regulation. Not only are market forces inadequate to prevent a tragedy of the commons—the destruction of a common-pool resource through overuse—but it is the pursuit of economic self-interest that brings about the collapse. The global ocean fisheries are the classic example. Individuals, motivated by self-interest, maximize their profits by pulling as many fish from the sea as possible, eventually destroying the industry in the process as fish stocks collapse. Markets, however, can sometimes be harnessed for the public good, if they are properly incentivized.[13]

It may be possible to bridge the green partisan gap if environmental protection can be achieved through mechanisms acceptable to political conservatives, which often means reliance on the free market. Success has been achieved in the past using market-based frames to solve environmental problems. Perhaps the biggest environmental initiative to pass Congress since 1980, the 1991 Amendment to the Clean Air Act, succeeded under divided government, a Republican president and a Democratic Congress. The legislation, originally conceived in conservative think tanks, employed free-market mechanisms (i.e., cap and trade) and helped clean up acid rain with significant bipartisan support. Market forces have expanded into other green policy areas as well, including water markets, wetland mitigation banking, and "species banks" (investment trade in endangered species to offset the impact of development).

With the Great Green Divide a fixture in Washington and many statehouses for the foreseeable future, voluntary conservation initiatives that preserve green resources in an increasingly anthropocentric world, especially those that rely on market forces, stand a better chance of passage and implementation.[14] Prairie Crossing is one such initiative.

## Prairie Crossing's Principal Conservation Goals and Objectives

George and Vicky Ranney consciously sought to accomplish two primary conservation goals in developing the Prairie Crossing property. One of those goals, "environmental protection and enhancement," is also the first of the development's ten "guiding principles." What is unique about the Ranneys' approach to conservation is the attempt to improve the environment by developing the land. Traditionally, development has been considered the enemy of conservation and open-space preservation, and nature has been viewed as something separate from the urban landscape, as Robert Gottlieb observes: "In all the standard environmental histories, the roots of environmentalism are presented as differing perspectives on how best to manage or preserve 'Nature,' meaning Nature outside cities and the experience of people's everyday lives."[15] Prairie Crossing was meant to alter this preconception, place nature firmly within the context of urban development, and make the natural experience a part of the residents' everyday life. But the Ranneys did not merely seek to restore a local parcel of secondary grassland; they sought to create an urban development policy model that could be "replicated elsewhere," and they made that objective known in the last guiding principle, "economic viability."

Private land management is an essential link in the conservation management policy chain, one that the land advocacy approach, in particular, frequently ignores. Private landowners are "the primary planners of land use," and often the land that they own and manage is environmentally sensitive.[16] Private land use is critical in preserving ecosystem function. More than 90 percent of threatened and endangered species depend to some degree on private lands for their habitat. As the human population grows, and more and more land comes under development, conservation will become crucially dependent on urban policy decisions.[17]

The second conservation goal is perhaps even more ambitious than environmental enhancement. In creating Prairie Crossing, the Ranneys were seeking, in George's words, to "change the culture."[18] By changing the culture, he means to demonstrate not only that urban development can be compatible and complementary with the environment, but that whole communities would come to view themselves as part of the natural environment, with roles and responsibilities to act responsibly as stewards of the world in which they live. Though no one guiding principle encapsulates the change-the-culture objective, it is ubiquitous throughout the set of principles. For example, the guiding principle "a sense of community" directly evokes "volunteer stewardship" regarding "environmental programs." "Energy conservation" is guiding principle seven. The homes were designed to reduce energy consumption by 50 percent relative to conventional home construction. Principle seven also emphasizes communitywide recycling and composting programs. A wind turbine, the first in the area, powers the organic farm, helping to produce sustainable, quality foods for residents. A second turbine generates renewable energy for the on-site charter school. Principle six provides for "convenient and efficient transportation" to and from downtown Chicago via rail transport, on two separate lines within walking distance of the development.

The most challenging effort in terms of changing the culture is guiding principle eight, "lifelong learning and education," a cross-generational attempt to foster the conservation community concept. Prairie Crossing's charter elementary school serves two school districts, educating students not only from within the development but also from outside. Charter school status permits experimentation, and the school's curriculum is unique in that it "emphasizes citizenship and the natural environment." Several organizations affiliated with Prairie Crossing offer educational opportunities for adults as well as children, with on-site lectures and seminars at the community center. The teenagers who work for the Farm Corps on the Learning Farm come away from the experience not just with the "capacity to grow and cook fresh vegetables, and a hands-on introduction to sustainable agriculture," but with "job skills applicable to any career."[19] The farm emphasizes organic vegetable production, not the typical corn, wheat, or soybean monoculture. Gardening opportunities are also available. Adult community residents can rent plots for a full season for between $40 and $70, depending on size. The foundation provides gardening tips and information, and works in partnership with the College of Lake County, which offers personal enrichment courses on gardening and landscaping.

The ambience of the property and the development reinforces the strong emphasis on citizenship and the natural environment. Vicky Ranney sought to create "a sense of place" through the physical surroundings. In a bright contrast to the standard use of neutral exterior home colors, she based her color scheme on indigenous prairie forbs and flowers. She also named the streets after the early settlers of the land and native plants. The original nineteenth-century structures that were relocated to the development from the Lake County area and put to new uses provide a historical connection to the wider community.[20]

Prairie Crossing's guiding principles were no marketing gimmick or green-washing advertising ploy. The Ranneys maintain that the principles have "held up well" over the years. Support for their view comes from two other policy actors who have played prominent roles in the conservation management of the development, Steve Apfelbaum and Michael Sands. Apfelbaum is the chief ecological restorationist of the property and president of the company that performed the restoration work, Applied Ecological Services. Sands served as the environmental team leader for the development from 1995 to 2010, a position he created from scratch and one that carries important responsibilities, such as the prairie and wetland burns. Sands started as a contract worker for the development and decided to buy a home and become a resident. He is currently a senior associate for the Liberty Prairie Foundation. In interviews, Apfelbaum and Sands stated that the commitment of the developers was crucial in the planning, designing, and realization of the stages of the development. "Committed owners," Apfelbaum said, were "the biggest missing link" in the success of Prairie Crossing, meaning they were the most important puzzle piece in the conservation community policy model. Both Apfelbaum and Sands stressed the importance of the ten guiding principles, especially when conflicts arose between competing objectives, such as profits and conservation. Sands advised that in situations of conflict, striking a balance between competing goals is always the preferred outcome.[21]

It seems clear that the conservation community concept is contingent upon the strong commitment and support of various founders, both developers and members of the Homeowners Association, who invest considerable time and effort. When asked whether the Ranneys' unusual commitment to the conservation mission would be an impediment to the replication of the concept elsewhere, Apfelbaum disagreed. In his opinion, the concept was spreading for a reason he found to be quite "perfunctory": national water quality issues. The United States is experiencing problems with the quality and supply of water, particularly in the

West. Apfelbaum considers water quality issues to be the "driving force" behind the conservation community model, which he feels has been expanding on a "national" basis and is used "widely but [on a] localized" scale.[22]

## Prairie Crossing Environmental Protection and Enhancement

According to the Greenpeace project StopGreenwash.org, "green is the new black."[23] Businesses as diverse as Google, Walmart, and BP have embraced green marketing strategies to sell their products, and green marketing is on the rise, with 73 percent more green products offered in 2010 than in 2009. A recent study found that "more than 95 percent of consumer products claiming to be green" engaged in some form of greenwashing.[24] Prairie Crossing's developers marketed the development prominently as "a conservation community," one of the nation's first. The first of the community's ten guiding principles is "environmental protection and enhancement," and in many ways it is the most innovative aspect of the development. How successful was Prairie Crossing in protecting, enhancing, and improving natural habitats, water, and green space resources?

Prairie Crossing set aside 69 percent of the original property acreage, restoring 350 acres of prairie and wetlands on a 677-acre parcel. This open space is held as common property, a community public good that is legally protected in perpetuity from economic development, and in that sense it qualifies as a unique form of private land trust. In his book *Conservancy: The Land Trust Movement in America*, the first comprehensive treatment of the land trust concept, Richard Brewer defines land trusts as "private nonprofit organizations that protect land directly, by owning it."[25] Prairie Crossing is private; the Homeowners Association qualifies as an organization, though perhaps not in the classic sense; and the Homeowners Association owns the nonfarm common land, the 350 acres of restored prairie and open space. Regarding the nonprofit element of the definition, the development's situation is not as clear-cut. The Liberty Prairie Foundation, a nonprofit organization, owns the 100-acre farm. The Conservation Fund held conservation easements on the farm and the 350-acre prairie restoration until 2013, when both easements were transferred to Openlands, a Chicago-based conservation nonprofit. The Prairie Crossing Homeowners Association does not actively pursue profits in the way that a commercial business operation would. However, property values are a salient issue for most homeowners associations, and few governing decisions are made beyond the calculus of resale value. The profit-making motive of the developers in selling the original property further weakens any claim that the association qualifies as a nonprofit.

Prairie Crossing is in fact something new, a hybridized land trust, splicing a few genes from for-profit DNA and inserting them into the corpus of the established land trust policy model. Implicit in Brewer's definition is that a land trust substantively conserves the land under protection, as he further elaborates: "The best conservation is stewardship of the biosphere and its component interacting systems: the air and water, the woods and fields, the mountains, dunes, and swales."[26] John Randall, an ecologist for the Nature Conservancy, agrees that stewardship of the land is of crucial importance. In the 1950s, the Nature Conservancy operated under the premise that its mission of preserving the land could be accomplished by "buying land, fencing it, and letting it be."[27] Today, the organization actively manages its land trusts to guard against exotic invaders and other ecological threats.

Prairie Crossing clusters 359 homes on a parcel of land that conventional developers anticipated could hold 3,000 homes.[28] From the standpoint of open-space preservation, the development has been successful. Open-space preservation, however, is a necessary but insufficient condition to meet the stated conservation policy goal of protection, improvement, and enhancement of the natural environment. Conservation of the Prairie Crossing land—which before settlement was ecologically valuable primary grassland, a rapidly disappearing ecosystem in the contiguous United States—requires significant conservation management and ecological restoration expenditures. Was Prairie Crossing successful in this restoration when evaluated from an ecological perspective? The evidence suggests that the development did indeed create, maintain, and conserve the land from an ecological standpoint.

The remainder of this chapter, and all of chapter four, will analyze Prairie Crossing's record of conservation management in eight different areas. The first three, which directly concern environmental conservation, are discussed in this chapter: (1) wetlands restoration, preservation, and water quality, (2) biodiversity, and (3) prairie restoration and open-space preservation. The remaining five, which concern human culture as it affects conservation, are addressed in chapter four: (4) the Homeowners Association's conservation management practices, (5) the residents' conservation practices, (6) educational opportunities, (7) energy conservation, and (8) economic viability. Because open-space preservation also contributes to shifts in human culture, that subject receives some discussion in the opening of the next chapter as well.

## Wetlands Restoration, Preservation, and Water Quality

As described in chapter two, the land at Prairie Crossing was subjected to heavy glaciation, which produced the lakes of Lake County. The resulting soils are deep silt and clay loam derived from the glacial till parent materials. Formerly a land of great biological abundance, the property changed significantly after settlement. Here is how Steve Apfelbaum, the development's eco-restorationist, described the property: "The land has been modified by drainage improvements including an extensive tile system, agricultural tillage for perhaps 150 years, herbicide and pesticide use since the 1950s, and the elimination of native biological communities."[29] The extensive agricultural development of the original property site required equally extensive conservation restoration efforts by the developers to meet their goal of environmentally enhancing and improving the land. The Ranneys selected Applied Ecological Services to perform this work. Without outside funding or governmental assistance, Applied Ecological Services devised a stormwater treatment "train" system to improve stormwater runoff rates and stormwater quality (see fig. 1).[30] The Urban Land Institute calls the natural water treatment system "the first of its kind in the country."[31]

The "train" begins with swales, which are designed to capture storm runoff flowing into the system—which often carries copious amounts of non–point source pollution from streets and yards, such as motor oil, antifreeze, and herbicides—and channel it into extensive prairies, where the water begins to percolate into the soil and the solids begin to settle out. The prairies then allow the stormwater still on the surface to move slowly overland via gravity flow to the wetlands complex. The deep root systems of the native prairie grasses facilitate the further settling of solids and the removal of pollutants. The wetlands then serve as a temporary detention system, providing biological treatment by helping to filter toxins and sediment out of the water before sending it on to Lake Leopold, the final component in the system. The man-made lake receives 65 percent of the drainage from the development and continues the process of solids settling and biological treatment.[32]

The 22-acre lake is among Prairie Crossing's most prominent features. Man-made ponds and lakes are common marketing strategies of developers. Homes that have "beachfront property" or offer a pleasant view of water generally have higher original purchase prices and resale values. Many artificially created urban lakes and ponds, however, are so-called "wet deserts," biologically impoverished

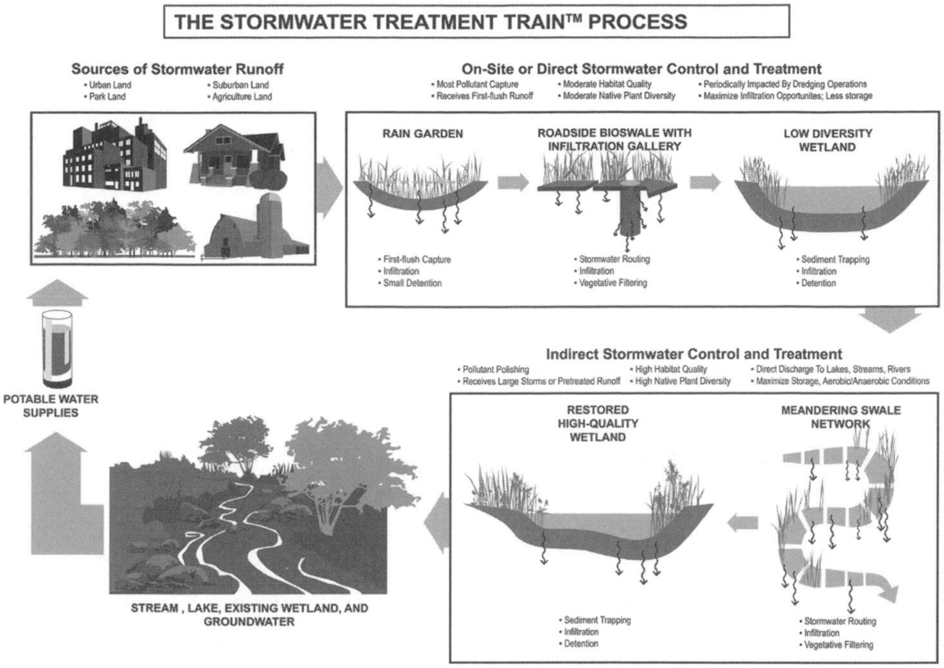

# THE STORMWATER TREATMENT TRAIN™ PROCESS

**Sources of Stormwater Runoff**
- Urban Land
- Park Land
- Suburban Land
- Agriculture Land

**On-Site or Direct Stormwater Control and Treatment**
- Most Pollutant Capture
- Receives First-flush Runoff
- Moderate Habitat Quality
- Moderate Native Plant Diversity
- Periodically Impacted By Dredging Operations
- Maximize Infiltration Opportunities; Less storage

**RAIN GARDEN**
- First-flush Capture
- Infiltration
- Small Detention

**ROADSIDE BIOSWALE WITH INFILTRATION GALLERY**
- Stormwater Routing
- Infiltration
- Vegetative Filtering

**LOW DIVERSITY WETLAND**
- Sediment Trapping
- Infiltration
- Detention

**POTABLE WATER SUPPLIES**

**Indirect Stormwater Control and Treatment**
- Pollutant Polishing
- Receives Large Storms or Pretreated Runoff
- High Habitat Quality
- High Native Plant Diversity
- Direct Discharge To Lakes, Streams, Rivers
- Maximize Storage, Aerobic/Anaerobic Conditions

**RESTORED HIGH-QUALITY WETLAND**
- Sediment Trapping
- Infiltration
- Detention

**MEANDERING SWALE NETWORK**
- Stormwater Routing
- Infiltration
- Vegetative Filtering

**STREAM , LAKE, EXISTING WETLAND, AND GROUNDWATER**

FIGURE I. Stormwater treatment train system created for Prairie Crossing by Applied Ecological Services. Courtesy of Applied Ecological Services. Reprinted with permission from Steve Apfelbaum.

greenwashing amenities that often suffer from poor water quality. They frequently contain waterfalls or water fountains and are sometimes drained and cleaned. Their banks may be lined with riprap or decorative stone, destroying any potential for the establishment of ecologically valuable invertebrate communities—the best biological indicator of wetland health.[33]

In contrast, Lake Leopold is home to an array of indigenous prairie wetland flora and fauna. Designed to be a self-sustaining ecosystem on a micro-scale, the lake and wetlands complex contains breeding populations of native Lake County flora that attract valued native macrovertebrates—large-bodied mammals, fish, and birds. The wetlands also provide habitat for reptiles and amphibians; however, these organisms tend to recolonize the area at much slower rates due to their limited mobility and have yet to invade the development in large numbers. They are, however, observable on and around the property. The water quality in the lake and the wetlands is excellent, according to Apfelbaum and Sands, exceeding the standards set by the Illinois Environmental Protection Agency in every category except chloride. Chloride levels spiked when the Village of Grayslake took over winter roadway maintenance, then decreased when the municipality stopped using road salt, falling below 230 mg/l level, the EPA-recommended maximum for aquatic life, in 2009. Lake Leopold also has exceptional water clarity. Secchi depth (maximum depth at which a black-and-white disk can be observed) averages exceed the Lake County average of 4.48 feet, with 2008 and 2009 values reaching or exceeding 7.0 feet.

One mistake the development did make in the wetlands restoration, Sands said, was in the orientation of Lake Leopold. The artificial lake is oriented primarily in a latitudinal, north-south direction. The developers did not take into account the prevailing southwest winds that buffet the region. The winds create chronic erosion problems that negatively affect some of the shorefront housing and the stability of the lakeshore in general. Simply rotating the lake by 90 degrees, said Sands, would have eliminated or greatly mitigated the problem. In retrospect, he also would have recommended that the lakefront houses be moved back from the lake because it would have facilitated maintenance of the wetlands (i.e., stabilization of sediment). The original rationale for the shorefront home sites was that they would garner a higher premium for the lake view. In practice, all the homes that have lake views receive the premium, and a buffer zone would have provided for easier maintenance.[34]

A second issue involving Lake Leopold and the stormwater treatment train is the size of the lake. Due to "early stormwater management permitting standards," the lake is twice as large as it needed to be to manage the flow of water. It remains full because of the relatively high annual rainfall that Lake County receives. Consequently, the water does not turn over as quickly as preferred. It takes twice as long to flush excess nutrients out of the hydrologic system.[35]

Applied Ecological Services created the lake and wetlands from scratch. Ecologically, the "very depleted" state of the original farmland property was the "single biggest disadvantage" that Prairie Crossing faced going into the project. Being heavily farmed for a century and a half and subjected to chemical applications for some fifty years, the land had "virtually no natural resources whatsoever." Drainage tiles had disrupted the natural flow of water, and pollution from the adjacent highway further exacerbated problems with the ecology and hydrology of the property.[36] Restoring the property to something approximating the original native ecology was an expensive undertaking. Not all conservation communities will require such extensive restoration. Utilizing existing native vegetation and natural drainage patterns, rather than filling in wetlands and creating artificial drainage through sewers and retention ponds, saves money, retains existing native habitat, and increases water quality and flood control. In the case of Prairie Crossing, every preserved acre of prairie grassland provides significant flood-control benefits. The prairie plants in a single acre can hold 12,000 gallons of water in their leaves to be returned to the atmosphere through evaporation.

Invertebrate biodiversity is the single best indicator of a wetland's condition, better than floral diversity or the fish, amphibian, and avian assemblages, though avian measures are also valuable. Unfortunately, hard data on invertebrate biodiversity and population rigor is not currently available. However, Prairie Crossing has conducted assessments of water quality and of floral and fisheries biodiversity. While Steve Apfelbaum has not done an empirical sampling of invertebrate biodiversity, he did offer a professional opinion based upon a "visual assessment." He found a "diverse and seasonally abundant macroinvertebrate fauna." Together with the healthy fish, avian, and plant community assemblages, which will be explored below, it is fair to conclude, based upon the data available, that the restored Prairie Crossing wetlands is an environmentally valuable ecosystem that is continuing to thrive and diversify.[37]

In 2006, Chicago Wilderness, a local environmental alliance dedicated to preserving the region's ecology, released *The State of Our Chicago Wilderness: A Report Card on the Health of the Region's Ecosystems*, a comprehensive assessment of the area's conservation fitness. In their summary of the longer technical report, the organization gave the region's wetlands a grade of D+, concluding, "The majority of the region's wetland communities remain in fair to poor condition." Given that the region has lost more than 90 percent of its pre-Columbian native wetlands to development, Prairie Crossing's modest efforts are important to the region's wetlands complex.[38]

## Biodiversity and Biotic Corridors

Prairie Crossing is biologically self-sustaining; its plant and animal communities survive and thrive on their own, managed but not supported by the Homeowners Association or its agents.[39] In other words, it is treated much like a national park: the grass is cut, prairie plants are burned, and pest species are monitored and occasionally extirpated, but the biological communities seek nourishment and breed, live, and die, on their own. Prairie Crossing is not a glorified garden or urban Eden. The local "ecosystem" of the property has real conservation and ecological value, serving as home to or urban refuge for flora and fauna that is frequently consumed, displaced, or altered by conventional economic development.

The original Prairie Crossing property was biologically impoverished. The substantial alterations that farmers made to the land for agricultural purposes were highly detrimental to the organisms that had previously occupied the space. Most of the pre-settlement flora and fauna died out or migrated to more suitable habitat. Sands and Apfelbaum both estimate the pre-development bird population at approximately 10 species, and no more than 15. Within a decade of occupation, "reliable birders" on the Prairie Crossing property were recording as many as 130 avian species a year, a tenfold increase over pre-development distributions.[40] Among the recorded species is the bald eagle, which has recently returned to the area. The Applied Ecological Services restoration has so successfully attracted bird life that the Evanston North Shore Bird Club now includes Prairie Crossing on its Lake County birdwatching circuit.[41] The 130 species total is 14 more than recorded at the Reed-Turner Woodland, a state nature preserve in nearby Long Grove. The Homeowners Association established a property-wide network of bluebird boxes to foster a population of this uncommon bird, formerly extirpated from the area due to habitat loss. With spectacular blue plumage on the wings and back and contrasting chestnut coloration on the chest and throat, this visually striking songbird may have helped boost residents' interest in the outdoors. The Homeowners Association considers the bluebird worth the effort. The resident survey revealed that 51 percent birdwatch in the complex and 61 percent maintain bird boxes and/or bird feeders. The development is also helping to boost the declining bobolink population. This increasingly rare grassland bird began nesting at Prairie Crossing less than a decade after occupation, though the relatively small size of the prairie habitat probably precludes viable long-term populations. A 2003 Lake Forest College undergraduate survey did not record the species.[42]

Some of the development's bird species are exotic invasives or can be considered pests, organisms that harm or crowd out valued natives. Prairie Crossing does take measures to eliminate invasives and pests and promote native species. With a fifth of the world's bird species on the "extinction path," habitat preservation is critical to the survival of 2,000 species worldwide.[43] Habitat loss is the number one cause of species extinction and endangerment. And sprawl's contribution to ecological problems is significant, as Richard Brewer observes: "Sprawl destroys forests, prairie remnants, and wetlands. What it doesn't destroy, it fragments. Between destruction and fragmentation, many animals and plants are lost and, as they go, biodiversity drops at every level from landscape to genes."[44]

The property's flora has undergone a substantive change. Formerly a monoculture of corn and soybean agriculture, with at best a small isolated fringe of native grasses that managed to survive the plow along fence posts and property lines, it is now home to 130 or more prairie plant species that are self-sustaining and indigenous to the Lake County region. Though natural ecological complexity is difficult to achieve through artificial means, the development's restoration efforts moved the previously depleted land toward natural system functionality within the first decade. A 2005 Applied Ecological Services assessment of botanical biodiversity found that two of three surveyed prairie planting transects had already achieved "remnant natural quality" status, with the third being "close." Seventy percent of the 94 species observed during the survey were native, though that value may understate the actual distribution of plant cover because it does not take species abundance into consideration.[45] Apfelbaum estimates the true native cover to be between 70 and 90 percent.[46] Given that the original farmland consisted of nearly 100 percent exotic species (i.e., corn and soybean monoculture), the ecological transformation of the Prairie Crossing restoration is significant.

Prairie Crossing's floral population provides the opportunity for natural dispersal of these species to nearby uncolonized areas and also contributes valuable genetic diversity for intraspecies breeding with flora on the adjacent Liberty Prairie Reserve, located to the east across a roadway. Higher species diversity has the added effect of increasing the biological community's "resistance to [exotic] invasions" because greater diversity is more likely to fill all available habitat niches, reducing opportunities for invaders. Ecologically, prairie restoration is very important due to the ecosystem's widespread extirpation over the last two centuries. More than 99 percent of the tallgrass prairie biome has been replaced by agriculture or urban expansion. In neighboring Iowa, less than one-tenth of 1 percent of the tallgrass is left from an assemblage that originally covered more than 85 percent of the state.[47]

Native plantings are not limited to community property. Residents can choose between two landscaping options for their personal property, a 70/30 percent ratio of native meadow/turf grass (i.e., a mix of prairie and traditional bluegrass lawn) and a 70/30 percent ratio of turf/native meadow. To "approximate a wild ecosystem," Homeowners Association management burns the common areas every two to four years, varying the time of year to mimic natural disturbances. Residents who would like to burn their private landscaping can enroll in educational seminars on the subject. Some of the residents contract out their prairie burning, but Sands stated that "everyone does some burning." Approximately

150 residents engage in burning in the course of managing their properties.[48] The burning events are impressive technical enterprises. Prairie Crossing burns eight to ten acres at a time, producing a twenty-foot wall of flame that often generates considerable interest among the residents.[49]

The burns are ecologically important. Not only do they eliminate dead vegetation, regenerate growth, and return nutrients to the soil, they help control and eradicate invasive species. Prairie plants are well adapted to fire ecology. Nearly 80 percent of the biomass of a tallgrass prairie can be found below ground (fig. 2). The roots of a compass plant, for example, may extend fifteen feet or more below the surface, which allows the plant not only to tap deep reservoirs of water but also to survive the high temperatures of prairie burns. Exotics, such as purple loosestrife, a common and problematic invasive in the Midwest, often have shallow root systems, which burning easily destroys. The extensive root systems of the tallgrass prairie benefit urban environments in two additional ways. They capture carbon underground when they die and decompose, unlike trees, which release the bulk of their carbon directly to the atmosphere, albeit slowly; and they assist in flood mitigation by absorbing and storing relatively large quantities of water. In contrast, note the shallow root system of the traditional Kentucky bluegrass lawn at the far left of figure 2. Planting natives can bring multiple benefits.

The wetlands habitat, with its good water quality, provides a suitable nursery for a healthy native fish population. Applied Ecological Services imported four species of endangered local minnows: blackchin and blacknose shiners, the Iowa darter, and the banded killifish. (A fifth endangered species, the pugnose shiner, was also introduced, though accidentally.) Formal evaluation of the fish introduction at Prairie Crossing resulted in a technical science article in the February 2012 issue of *Fisheries*, the journal of the American Fisheries Society. The authors, led by U.S. Geological Survey scientist Jeffrey Schaeffer, concluded that the fish introduction experiment was successful: "Success was likely due to a combination of unique design features and prior habitat preparation that resulted in clear water conditions that supported dense vegetation. . . . We suggest that well-designed storm water systems such as Prairie Crossing can play a role in biodiversity conservation, especially in urban landscapes that would support no aquatic diversity otherwise."[50] The five species are reproducing on their own, sustaining their populations into the seventh generation. This experiment in faunal reintroduction is a substantial public good. These are endangered (blacknose and pugnose shiner) and threatened (blackchin shiner, banded killifish, and Iowa darter) fish that have no value as game fish—exactly the kinds of species that have disappeared

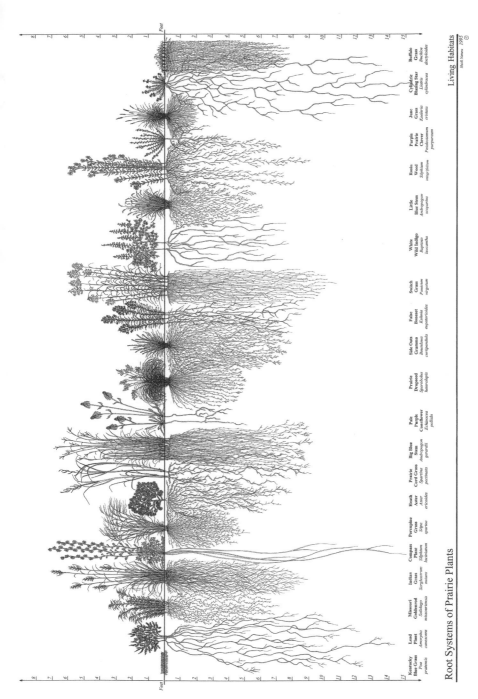

Root Systems of Prairie Plants

FIGURE 2. Root systems of prairie plants. For comparison, note shallow root system of Kentucky bluegrass at far left. Courtesy of Living Habitats. Illustrator: Heidi Natura, copyright 1995. Reprinted with permission from Heidi Natura.

from habitats the world over because they are of no commercial value. Prairie Crossing's populations of these fish have been used as "source populations that led to subsequent downstream emigration and recolonization of sites within their historic range within the Des Plaines River watershed."[51] The conservation impact of Prairie Crossing has extended beyond the community's borders.

Human development of the land in North America since the arrival of Europeans has put immense pressure on native biological communities. Over time, development—commercial, residential, and the industrial activities that support the American suburban lifestyle—carves up the land into smaller and smaller parcels or "islands" of ecologically pristine or relatively pristine land.[52] "Island" is in fact a very good descriptive metaphor for the phenomenon, for native biological communities literally become small pockets of "land" surrounded by a "sea" of sprawling economic development.

In 1967, Robert MacArthur and Edward O. Wilson co-authored the book *The Theory of Island Biogeography*, which revolutionized the science of ecology. Though they originally studied ants on oceanic islands to explain the biogeographic distribution of species, MacArthur and Wilson actually crafted an extraordinarily rich theoretic model applicable to a wide range of ecological contexts, including suburban sprawl. Most people think of an island as a small mass of land surrounded by a large body of water. In an ecological context, however, it can be much more. An island can be a cool microclimate on a 3,000-meter-high mountain surrounded (i.e., isolated) by a "sea" of sweltering low-altitude sagebrush desert. An island can be a lake surrounded by a "sea" of land, for a lake is in effect the "reverse image" of an island.[53] Or an island can be a plot of native woodland or a patch of farmland surrounded by a "sea" of suburban sprawl, as environmental author Scott Weidensaul notes: "MacArthur and Wilson originally applied their principles only to true islands, but ecologists have long since realized that the same rules hold for figurative islands as well, isolated fragments of habitat like forest patches surrounded by suburban sprawl or pieces of grassland in a sea of crops."[54] The key variable involved is insularity, precisely the ecological scenario that sprawling development creates.

The equilibrium theory of island biogeography is a highly mathematical, quantitative paradigm that laid the foundation for modern theoretical ecology. Conceptually, however, in studying sprawl it is not the complicated mathematics that concerns us. MacArthur and Wilson argued that in any ecological context that fits the biogeographical analogue of an isolated island, species equilibrium would eventually be achieved through the influx of immigrating species balanced by the loss of species already present through extinction. Whether the equilibrium level would settle on a relatively large or small number of species would depend on two crucial theoretical constructs, the species-area effect and the distance effect.

The species-area effect determines how many species (not individuals) can thrive in a given area of land.[55] The effect of area on the number of species is "one of ecology's oldest and most profound generalizations."[56] Data gathered from diverse organisms and ecosystems has consistently shown a strong relationship between the two. The carrying capacity of different ecosystems may vary; for example, the Arctic can support fewer species than the tropical rainforest.[57] However, each tenfold decrease in area brings about a roughly twofold decrease in species diversity. Smaller patches of land harbor smaller numbers of species; they do not retain the full complement of species at lower population densities. Biodiversity, in other words, decreases with loss of habitat. Suburban sprawl and other human activities tend to fragment ecosystems into small, isolated habitats or islands of native landscape. This fragmentation significantly reduces the capacity of the land to support native organisms. The presence of invasive species and climate change further exacerbate the problem. And artificial structures that create isolation between parcels of land, such as a multi-lane urban highway or a large border fence between countries, can also reduce overall diversity, even though the separation between habitats appears minimal, by preventing the migration of certain types of organisms.

The distance effect refers to the distance an island lies from sources of possible species replenishment, such as a small patch of virgin prairie surrounded by urban development. The greater the distance from sources of species immigration, the lower the predicted level of species equilibrium. All things being equal, the equilibrium theory predicts that a 100-square-mile island preserve would reach equilibrium at a higher level of species diversity than ten dispersed and isolated 10-square-mile island preserves totaling the same area.

The equilibrium theory has tremendous relevance for conservation in general and suburban sprawl specifically. As sprawl eliminates native green space and farmland, these lands become increasingly isolated from each other in a sea of artificial urbanity. As the islands of green space are developed, species diversity will inevitably decline, not only because the tracts of green become smaller and less numerous, but also because sources of species replenishment become more distant.[58] Floods, drought, disease, and harsh weather may extirpate extant species on island isolates, and distance then precludes their replenishment. As MacArthur and Wilson presciently wrote in 1967, "The same principles apply, and will apply to an accelerating extent in the future, to formerly continuous natural habitats now being broken up by the encroachment of civilization."[59] In fact, equilibrium theory has raised concerns about whether even large national parks can faithfully preserve biodiversity over the long term. As Frank Preston, an ecologist who laid some of the mathematical groundwork in population biology that led to MacArthur and Wilson's paradigmatic breakthrough, explained it, "If what we have said is correct, it is not possible to preserve in a State or National Park, a complete replica on a small scale of the fauna and flora of a much larger area."[60] Apex predators are often the first organisms to disappear, and they sometimes play important ecological roles as keystone species, those that have disproportionately large impacts on local ecosystems.

Placed in this ecological context, the consequences of suburban sprawl, developed in an uncoordinated and unplanned manner and played out nationally but on a local scale, can be serious. Combined with the possible effects of greenhouse gas–induced global warming, the long-term prospects of North American biodiversity could be uncertain. Before the rise of civilization, plants and animals could simply migrate latitudinally in response to climate change. Now highways, cities, and other human development block their path. If Preston is indeed correct, maintenance of biodiversity in urban environments will be absolutely essential to preserving functioning natural ecosystems and the economic services they provide to mankind—annual global services estimated to be worth between $125 and $145 trillion a year in 2011 dollars.[61]

Figure 3, reproduced here from *The Theory of Island Biogeography*, very simply and graphically illustrates habitat fragmentation for Cadiz Township in Green County, Wisconsin, not far from the Prairie Crossing development. The initial map from 1831 reveals pristine pre-settlement woodland and oak savanna untouched by nonnative human activity. By 1882, more than 50 percent of the township has been subjected to development and significant fragmentation. Just twenty years later, islands of woodland of various sizes are emerging from the surrounding developed land. In 1950, the final map in the series, the formerly contiguous woodland of Cadiz Township has been reduced to fifty-six small fragmented islands of forest in a sea of human development. Since 1950, throughout the entire country, the creation of the interstate highway system, the reliance on strip malls and big-box retailing, and the spread of suburban sprawl have accelerated the process of habitat alteration, fragmentation, and homogenization.

The answer to the problem of island biogeography as it applies to urban sprawl is the creation of biotic corridors, ecological linkages between source habitats.

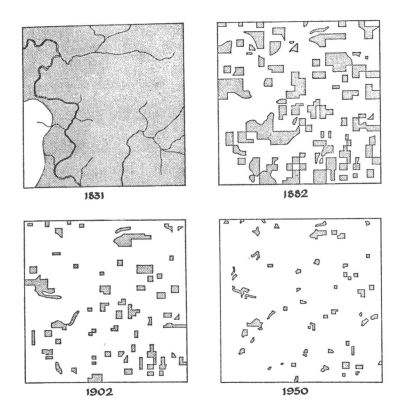

FIGURE 3. Habitat fragmentation in Green County,
Wisconsin, 1831–1950. Shaded areas represent woodland
habitat. Courtesy of John Curtis. Reprinted with permission
from University of Chicago, copyright 1956.

Because economic growth and development are the lifeblood of our capitalistic system, eventually most of our natural habitat will be eliminated or degraded unless developers can either improve existing land that has already been altered (e.g., farmland) or maintain the environmental viability of natural land that is being developed (e.g., maintain existing wetlands and natural habitats in new developments). Ecological improvement through development is the primary goal of Prairie Crossing's developers. A central question in my environmental analysis of Prairie Crossing was whether it could actively create, promote, and maintain biotic corridors with surrounding areas of biological value. I found that the development has engaged in all three activities.

Michael Sands, Prairie Crossing's first environmental team leader, stated that the developers intentionally created "connections and corridors" for regional organisms and endeavored to "avoid actual sinks," habitats that exclude or extirpate particular species. It was a complicated process, according to Sands, because a habitat source for one species may by its very nature be a sink for another.[62] Apfelbaum confirmed Sands's opinion on the establishment of biotic corridors. Applied Ecological Services employed GIS mapping to connect the lake and wetlands complex with the Des Plaines River. Wetlands connectivity is crucial; Bruce Babbitt characterizes it as "the first step in restoring [a] land's ecological functions."[63] Applied Ecological Services had hoped to expand westward to create a greater corridor link with the Fox River thirteen miles to the west, but it was not possible because there were several miles of land that was unsuitable for the linkage. The wetlands complex with its attendant fish population extends the range and habitat for the great blue heron rookery at the nearby Almond Marsh Forest Preserve, which is located a little more than a mile to the northeast. The herons can frequently be found fishing in Prairie Crossing's wetland banks and waters. Conserve Lake County, a local land trust that was started in 1995 by Michael Sands's wife, Betsy Dietel, and is loosely affiliated with the development, has purchased one property adjacent to Prairie Crossing to the west. The Liberty Prairie Reserve and Oak Openings, owned by the Lake County Forest Preserve District, abut the property to the east. The developers paid half the cost of a roadway underpass leading to the Liberty Prairie Reserve, and Prairie Crossing staff assisted in the expansion of the reserve itself. It was important to the Ranneys to open Prairie Crossing up to the public in an effort to establish contact and create dialogue with the larger community.

The Liberty Prairie Reserve is a public-private partnership that provides a relatively large-scale vision for permanent environmental protection and sustainable agriculture in central Lake County. A master plan updated in 2013 governs the reserve, which spans nine separate government entities (e.g., county, city, village, and township). The Liberty Prairie Reserve boundary is not a political jurisdiction and was not created by an act of government; it was formed through a collaborative process involving public and private stakeholders.[64] Twenty-three different landowners own agricultural acreage within the 5,770-acre reserve, which includes a wide variety of land uses. Nearly 3,400 acres are natural areas and farmland, including three substantial county forest preserve holdings: Almond Marsh, Independence Grove, and Oak Openings. These holdings preserve a contiguous array of important habitats, which are necessary to accommodate animals that require land diversity in their lifecycles. Wetlands, oak savanna, graminoid fen, sedge meadow, and a heron rookery can be found within the reserve's conservation lands. At least eighteen state and federal threatened or endangered plant and animal species find sustenance there, including slender bog arrow-grass, a rare remnant survivor from the last glacial retreat approximately twelve thousand years ago.[65] Eighteen notable conservation holdings exist in the reserve, held by eight different government entities or private organizations, including Prairie Crossing, the Nature Conservancy, Conserve Lake County, the Illinois Nature Preserves Commission, and Openlands. They range in type from conservation easement to fee simple ownership to Prairie Crossing's Homeowners Association covenant.[66]

Prairie Crossing's contributions to regional biodiversity are important. Chicago Wilderness graded the region's birds, reptiles, amphibians, and insects all C–. The region's fish communities scored a D+. The "highest conservation concern" regarding the region's avifauna is grassland species, and though the acreage at Prairie Crossing is relatively small for area-sensitive birds, both bobolink and dickcissel have been observed in the development's grassland habitat.[67] Amphibians have been slow to return due to their limited dispersal abilities. Their presence is currently limited to several species of frogs. Prairie Crossing is providing much-needed habitat for many at-risk species and is doing so through development of the land, which is generally viewed by Chicago Wilderness as the number one cause of habitat destruction.

## Prairie Restoration and Open-Space Preservation

The Prairie Crossing Homeowners Association has not conducted a follow-up botanical assessment since the initial 2005 survey, citing the high cost as the reason. Project restorationist Steve Apfelbaum, a trained ecologist, provided his professional opinion on the continued ecological evolution of the property since the last assessment.

Noting that the prairie grassland ecosystem took between 2,000 and 7,000 years to naturally establish itself after the glacial bulldozers wiped the environment clean, Apfelbaum stated that Prairie Crossing is "on track" to becoming a natural ecosystem, though it is not yet there. The wetland areas have progressed more quickly than the drier grasslands, but both are moving in the right direction, he says. The objective of the restoration effort, according to Apfelbaum, is to "jump-start the ecological process of recovery." While acknowledging that it is uncertain when or whether Prairie Crossing will achieve the status of a truly natural system, he nevertheless called the development a "tremendous asset" and "a very valuable ecosystem from an availability perspective," meaning that it is high-quality habitat of "real value" for a host of vanishing grassland species across all taxonomic boundaries.[68] Birds, insects, amphibians, and reptiles that depend on the once-dominant grassland ecosystem can find a niche, survive, reproduce, and be a possible source population for other suitable areas that may be established later.

Nearly 70 percent of the 677-acre development is preserved as open space, 350 acres of it in the form of restored wetlands and prairie. In striking the balance between environmental preservation and profits, both Apfelbaum and Sands stated that the developers repeatedly turned to their guiding principles for direction, deliberately seeking "never to maximize" any one of those principles. The most cost-effective way to preserve open space, Sands argued, was to cluster all the homes in one corner of the property. The developers rejected that design because they felt that the homeowners would then have less "investment" in the well-being of the land. By being closer to the conserved open space, living among the wetlands, the prairies, and the organic farm, the residents would presumably have a greater "connection to the land" and perhaps feel an obligation to act as stewards of conservation. Apfelbaum was also quick to point out that economic viability was one of the ten guiding principles, and that it was imperative to maintain competitiveness vis-à-vis conventional development or risk becoming an "oddity" or a failed housing experiment.[69]

Prairie Crossing has its critics, and one of the most vocal has been Chicago-area real-estate analyst Steve Hovany. In terms of open-space preservation, Hovany questioned the developers' business acumen in creating and maintaining the organic farm on the property. He felt that it was a financial drain on the development and argued that importing a farmers' market would provide the community with all the benefits of convenient organic produce without any of the drawbacks of managing a farm. He argued that farming does not make money, and that residents do not want a farm so close by: "Living next to a farm field doesn't turn people on," he said.[70]

Michael Sands strongly disagreed with Hovany. He viewed the farm as a great marketing tool, a lure that appealed to many prospective buyers. He felt that it positively affected the pace of sales and also increased the value of the homes. The resident survey provides some evidence to back up that assertion: 12 percent of those selecting a write-in response for the "most important" factor in their decision to move to Prairie Crossing chose the farm, the second-largest write-in category. A second reason Sands supported the inclusion of the farm in the final design for the development is that it is "very profitable."[71] The developers farmed the land for the first eight years. During the last decade, Prairie Crossing has leased the farmland to Sandhill Family Farms, an organic farming partnership that is turning a profit while avoiding many of the negative externalities associated with conventional agriculture, the principal one being water pollution.

Prairie Crossing's prairie restoration is perhaps the development's most important conservation element. It has both symbolic and ecological significance. Illinois has been known as the "Prairie State" for more than a century, a verbal testament to the vast open grasslands that once carpeted the state. Of the original 22-million-acre ocean of tallgrass and forbs, only a few scattered virgin remnants survived the systematic agricultural transformation.[72] Lost in the effort to tame the prairie was our nation's biological heritage. Capitalism has achieved many great accomplishments for mankind, including longer and healthier lifespans and more comfortable lives, freedom from the harsh daily realities of sustenance, and shelter procurement. A major drawback of capitalism, however, is that it is very difficult to put a "price" on public goods, such as ecosystem services, clean water and air, biological diversity, and aesthetic vistas.[73] Questions such as "How much is clean air worth?" and "How much is prairie worth?" are difficult to answer. Capitalism struggles with these concepts, and consequently profit-seeking activities often result in negative externalities, the loss of valuable economic services and public goods by society at large in favor of the parochial profits of a few. Such has been the case for the prairie ecosystem in the United States.

Ecologically speaking, the prairie ecosystem provides many services of economic value for society. The prairie functions as both water filter and purifier, and that is the central premise behind the Applied Ecological Services stormwater treatment train system employed at Prairie Crossing. It also provides natural stormwater detention, delaying the flow of water to surface hydrologic systems. Conventional developments often employ the retention pond, little more than a large grassy depression that fills with water during periods of heavy precipitation. These depressions are not "ponds" or wetlands in any biological sense. They are a monoculture of exotic invasives that do not settle solids, process biological toxins, or provide sustenance or shelter to native organisms. They require weekly maintenance during the growing season and, to maintain an appearance acceptable to homeowners, often require large doses of fertilizers and other chemical applications that may adversely affect animals many thousands of miles from the source of their original usage. Prairie grasslands are highly diverse ecosystems that provide a variety of rich ecological niches for wildlife.

In contrast, urban sprawl is often home to an impoverished assemblage of species due to habitat destruction and fragmentation, which disrupts symbiotic relationships and predator-prey ratios. For example, deer overpopulation, a direct consequence of predator elimination, has resulted in the overgrazing of native plants, human fatalities through automobile accidents, and death and disease for the deer themselves. The monoculture of urban-sprawl neighborhoods eliminates ecological niches and reduces the species carrying capacity of the land. Many summertime bird species winter thousands of miles away in the tropics. Their short stay in the United States, however, is a crucial part of their lifecycle, for they come here to breed. Without the varied niches provided by prairie and wetland habitats, neighborhood bird diversity in Illinois dwindles to a dozen very common species, the most common, such as the English sparrow or European starling, often being exotic invasives.

Though it has not yet achieved the full status of a natural system, the prairie grassland restoration at Prairie Crossing nevertheless has real ecological value. The Environmental Protection Agency cites the development as a leading example of native landscaping in the Midwest.[74] A "tremendous asset" is how ecologist Steve Apfelbaum described the restoration effort in 2013.[75] It returns to the region many species that have been extirpated and provides habitat for many species that are endangered, threatened, or uncommon. In 2006, the most recent year for which a summary report of the state of Chicago's ecology is available, Chicago Wilderness graded the region's prairies a D.[76] Fragmentation is blamed as one of the chief causes for their "poor" condition. In re-creating valuable wetlands and prairie grassland habitat and linking them to the Des Plaines River watershed and other nearby natural areas, Prairie Crossing has proven that it is possible to improve the environment through development.

Humans also impact the environment through their behavior, and suburban sprawl has been widely criticized for intensifying that impact, particularly regarding transportation and water consumption. The next chapter analyzes Prairie Crossing's influence on community culture and residents' green behavior, the second of the development's conservation goals.

# CHAPTER FOUR

# CHANGING THE CULTURE

These buyers want to keep up
with the Joneses. We are trying to
change what the Joneses are doing.

—Michael Sands

Prairie restoration and preservation at Prairie Crossing plays a secondary role, mainly cultural in nature—and equally as important as the development's primary ecological purpose. The prairie acts as the symbol of Prairie Crossing, giving the development not only a name but also a character, the first impression a prospective buyer assimilates. The prairie and open space provide a positive feedback loop for the conservation agenda, offering for adult residents a sense of connection to the land, and for children a playground to stimulate the natural experience. This is an essential element of the development if the conservation community concept is to provide a model of best practices for regional and national export.

The prairie may also act as a source of spiritual renewal, leading to changes in how residents view their place in nature. In *Reinventing Eden: The Fate of Nature in Western Culture*, environmental historian Carole Merchant argues that environmentalists such as the Ranneys are seeking to "recover the original garden [Eden] by restoring nature and creating sustainability." Rather than acting as "dominators" of the earth, as Americans have for centuries—reversing the flow of streams, paving the land in asphalt, and building skyward in steel and concrete, for example—people may seek an alternative to domination and "cooperate with nature and each other in healthier, more just, and more environmentally sustainable ways." What is needed is what Prairie Crossing provides: an economically viable market-based alternative to environmentally degrading conventional development. Merchant's "Recovery Narrative" seems to fairly describe the approach the Ranneys have pursued in creating Prairie Crossing.[1]

Vicky Ranney, in particular, seems to have a highly emotional, if not spiritual, attachment to the Prairie Crossing project and the conservation community concept. That emotional connection to the land has rubbed off on some residents. For example, a resident who moved to Illinois from the East Coast for employment stated that he no longer viewed the Kentucky bluegrass lawn as something to aspire to. He simply had always taken the front lawn for granted and had never thought about the ecological consequences of having one. The ambience of Prairie Crossing's prairie landscape changed his perspective on natural beauty. He now views the deep green "corporate lawn as a sterile monoculture."[2] Michael Sands, who originally came to the development with only a financial stake as a contracted employee, became a resident and is very emotionally invested in the property.

## Homeowners Association Conservation Management Practices

For the conservation community concept to become a successful model of "best practices," available for export to other markets, the commitment to the model must extend beyond the original developers. The Homeowners Association, which has been governing Prairie Crossing for more than a decade, must embrace the conservation ethic and propagate it over time, as new homeowners come and go. Conflicts between conservation and the bottom line (i.e., property values) must be satisfactorily resolved without undermining the conservation mission, and economic viability must be maintained. Prairie Crossing appears to have managed the potential for conflict, preserving the conservation agenda and also remaining financially sustainable.

The Homeowners Association board is responsible for managing the common property, which includes the 350-acre prairie and wetlands complex. The Homeowners Association contracts out environmental maintenance to various companies, including Integrated Lakes Management, Applied Ecological Services, and Landscape Concepts, with an annual budget totaling $82,000. Integrated Lakes Management performs lake monitoring, water quality monitoring, fish conservation, and selected weed management of Lake Leopold and the ponds. Applied Ecological Services is under contract to perform weed control, associated burns, and selected mowing of restored prairie and wetland areas.

Landscape Concepts performs fertilization, weed control, turf mowing in the common area, and maintenance of trees and plantings. These environmental expenditures amount to approximately 36 percent of the annual operating budget, which is funded through a monthly assessment fee.

In managing the development, the Homeowners Association has consistently employed an eco-centric approach, with perhaps one exception. Residents are permitted to use herbicides and fertilizers on their private property, though they are encouraged to adopt eco-friendly practices through a voluntary weed-management program that contracts with a private company for turf aeration and three yearly applications of a stable low-dose fertilizer. This practice helps mitigate harm to the environment but does not eliminate it. The effects of chemicals, even for such pedestrian applications as lawn care, can have a deleterious impact on ecosystems as far away as the Arctic. The development could have adopted a blanket ban on chemical use, and the Homeowners Association's failure to do so is a valid criticism of its conservation management policies.

Despite this exception, the conservation management program is solid and progressive. The common agricultural property is organically farmed, which somewhat offsets the chemical usage on private property. As the environmental manager, Michael Sands was hired by the Homeowners Association to draft and maintain management plans for the common areas. Sands is part of a conservation policy network and met frequently with conservation professionals, land trust conservators, developers, municipal politicians, and environment volunteers. He developed written plans, created maps and visual aids, and maintained a database for managing and conserving the common areas. Sands's role as a founder of the development was critical to the success of the conservation program. In his opinion, one that the Ranneys share, Prairie Crossing would not have been possible without someone with his commitment and expertise. Sands's educational background suited him well for the position. He has a Ph.D. in animal science/international agriculture from Cornell University. It may not be possible to establish a conservation community in circumstances of extensive restoration without someone with the ability and perspective to manage a natural-resource base and to strike a balance between cost management and profit and ecology. In Sands's words, "A developer simply cannot build and walk away."[3] Other than the initial conservation commitment of the developers, the expertise and commitment of the Homeowners Association's conservation manager is the most important link in the policy chain. If Sands were to leave Prairie Crossing (and his home is currently for sale), he is of the opinion that someone else would have to fill the void. At this relatively mature stage of the development, it would be possible for others to follow Sands because he has created a substantial framework for future management. Having an environmental founder available at the incipient stages of development is important. The developers must provide one if someone does not emerge naturally.

Prairie Crossing opened for initial occupation in 1994, and the last single-family home sold in 2004.[4] Sands and the Ranneys agree that the first year was the most crucial phase for the development. For the Ranneys it was necessary to show prospective buyers that the developers were "serious" about the conservation amenities by investing in those elements first. Sands felt that the education of the homeowners, which started with a sales pitch that emphasized the development's guiding principles, was essential. The developers also encouraged the nonvoting participation of homeowners in board decisions, which made a difference in addressing homeowners' concerns and making them feel invested in the community and the conservation mission. The developers created six committees to produce written recommendations pertaining to the guiding principles and the design of the development. The committees, consisting of ten to fifteen residents who rotated in and out, encouraged others to get involved and immersed residents in the culture and ethic of the conservation community concept. This relatively high level of participation is in stark contrast to conventional homeowners association developments, which are often dominated by just a few individuals.[5]

To change the culture—that is, to increase environmental awareness and shift resident behavior toward sustainability, the stated ultimate goal of the developers—Prairie Crossing and its management practices must attract the uninitiated, those unfamiliar with or not already practicing green-friendly behaviors. Otherwise, the development will suffer from the "preaching to the choir" phenomenon, and the community will effectively become little more than an enclave of previously established conservationists. Sands acknowledges that "to a certain extent," Prairie Crossing's initial homebuyers may have decided to come to the development via "self-selection." By self-selection he does not mean that the development intentionally sought conservation-minded buyers, but rather that the nature of the product inevitably attracted those types of individuals. The developers did initially "select" for community-oriented buyers, however. Sands called these first-phase (i.e., pre-construction) buyers "risk-takers."[6]

During the pre-construction first phase, Prairie Crossing spent "a lot of time" stressing the importance of community, from the moment the prospective buyers walked into the sales office. This emphasis was very important, perhaps critical, in getting the community agenda to take root. Sands believes that in the second phase of the development, when the houses began to materialize, many buyers purchased their homes irrespective of the conservation agenda, buying only because they thought they were getting a "good deal," making a good financial investment. The resident survey provides some evidence for that assertion. The single most important motivating factor for purchasing a home in Prairie Crossing, chosen by nearly 38 percent of the respondents, was the design and quality of the homes.

It was those second- and third-phase buyers, mainstream homeowners who bought for economic and not conservation reasons, who represented the "greatest challenge" for the developers. But it was a challenge that Sands was determined to tackle: "These buyers want to keep up with the Joneses," he said. "We are trying to change what the Joneses are doing." Rather than seeking change through coercive compliance, in which people alter their behavior in hopes of being rewarded or in fear of being punished, the developers strove to implement change through conformity, which instills new behavior as people watch, listen, and follow new cultural norms.

Of all the environmental threats to native North American organisms, only habitat destruction poses a greater danger than exotic invasive species, and it is likely that invasives will eventually top the list of the nation's "engines of ecological disintegration."[7] A 1998 study found that 49 percent of endangered species in the United States were threatened by exotic invaders. The consequences are more than ecological. By 1999, according to ecologist David Pimentel, the United States was already spending $137 billion a year fighting invasives.[8] The problem is global in scope, involving everything from rabbits in Australia to gray squirrels in Europe to Eurasian honeysuckle and emerald ash borers in North America.

The Prairie Crossing Homeowners Association takes various steps to combat invasives. For house sparrows, the association employs sparrow traps. The house sparrow is an aggressive European invasive that "rapidly [took] much of the New World by storm," breeding continuously year-round and crowding out native species. Deliberately introduced by humans more than a century ago, house sparrows still enjoy a competitive advantage over native birds because they left their natural enemies—the parasites, pathogens, predators, and competitors— behind in their home range. House sparrows in North America are afflicted with only half as many parasites as their European counterparts, making it easier for them to seize niches formerly occupied by native birds that are still fighting a full complement of natural enemies and competitors.[9] By employing traps and removing these invasive birds from the development, Prairie Crossing gives a boost to native birds, such as the eastern bluebird and the bobolink, that were previously extirpated or diminished. The development also spends $4,000 per year addling Canada goose eggs and harassing these pest birds to mitigate reproduction and motivate the species to avoid the property.[10] Though native to North America, the Canada goose was formerly a migratory species that now stays year-round and has greatly expanded its range and population numbers to the detriment of other species. In an effort to avoid using herbicides, Prairie Crossing has also utilized biocontrol methods to fight the invasive plant Eurasian water milfoil, which established itself as the dominant plant in Sanctuary Pond. Weevils, a predatory insect that preferentially consumes the milfoil, were employed, with minimal success, from 2002 to 2009.[11]

Many homeowners associations limit public access to their properties, often using fences, gates, and even private security services to keep out nonresidents. Prairie Crossing departs significantly from that model. The Ranneys decided early on that if they wanted to change the culture, the common areas of the development would have to be open to the public to allow nonresidents to experience firsthand the conservation community concept. To enhance public access, the developers paid half of the construction costs for an underpass linking Prairie Crossing to Oak Openings and Almond Marsh, two Lake County Forest Preserve District properties. Prairie Crossing has been public since its inception, though the Homeowners Association retains the legal right to make the development private should any unforeseen consequences develop. This was done as a necessary protection to ensure the economic viability of the development should problems with public access arise.[12]

In line with its stated goal of creating community, the Prairie Crossing development has facilitated the organization of various groups of volunteers that not only provide an opportunity for resident interaction but also advance common goals. The residents who are recruited for "Prairie Patrols" adopt an area within the development that they work four times per year, pulling weeds, picking up trash, and performing any other needed conservation tasks. Taking responsibility for a specific area, which generally includes their home and the surrounding common areas but also the homes of others, creates a sense of obligation and connection both to the land and to their fellow residents. The Prairie Patrols are popular, which probably creates a positive feedback loop encouraging even greater participation through a sense of community obligation. Sands is of the opinion that Prairie Crossing's conservation agenda creates community and "brings

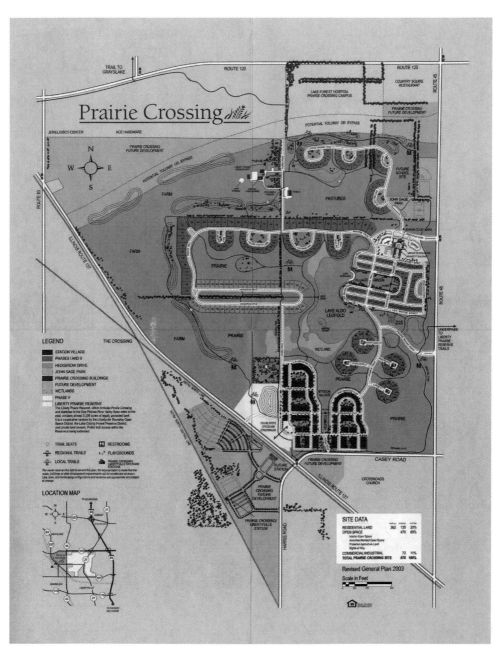

MAP 1. Prairie Crossing site plan. The diagram does not include the Station Square and Station Village condominiums. Courtesy of Prairie Holdings Corporation. Reprinted with permission from Vicky Ranney.

PLATE 1. Frank Lloyd Wright design with yellow coneflower and prairie plantings in the foreground. Photographer: Maryanne Natarajan.

PLATE 2. Three young residents catching frogs and interacting with nature in the re-created wetlands. Photographer: Maryanne Natarajan.

PLATE 3. Prairie Crossing organic farm and windmill.
Photographer: Maryanne Natarajan.

PLATE 4. Reflection of homes off Lake Leopold.
Photographer: Maryanne Natarajan.

PLATE 5. Village green and gazebo as viewed from the prairie west of Lake Leopold. Photographer: Maryanne Natarajan.

PLATE 6. American Foursquare (red) and Midwestern farmhouse designs. Photographer: Maryanne Natarajan.

PLATE 7. Lake Leopold shoreline with prairie restoration
in foreground. Photographer: Maryanne Natarajan.

PLATE 8. American Foursquare (white with red roof) and farmhouse designs on Lake Leopold. View is from photographer's front porch. Photographer: Maryanne Natarajan.

PLATE 9. Field of native compass plants (*Silphium laciniatum*). The plant is named for its tendency to orient its basal leaves in a north-south direction. Compass plants sometimes exceed ten feet in height. Photographer: Maryanne Natarajan.

PLATE 10. Prairie wetlands restoration.
Photographer: Maryanne Natarajan.

PLATE II. Fall prairie burn. Photographer: Maryanne Natarajan.

PLATE 12. Prairie Crossing hiking path, with Sanctuary Pond and horse stables in background. Photographer: Maryanne Natarajan.

PLATE 13. Open-space prairie restoration. Photographer: Maryanne Natarajan.

PLATE 14. Hiking path near Station Village and Square. Note the variety of housing colors, a departure from industry standards of the time. Photographer: Maryanne Natarajan.

PLATE 15. Prairie Crossing's developers tried to re-create the yesteryear small-town charm absent from many suburban-sprawl communities. Photographer: Maryanne Natarajan.

PLATE 16. Great blue heron fishing in Prairie Crossing's re-created wetlands. The community anchors the northwest corner of the Liberty Prairie Reserve, a 5,770-acre public-private partnership designed to preserve and protect prairie grassland habitat and agricultural land. Photographer: Maryanne Natarajan.

PLATE 17. Farmhouse homes with views of wetlands and prairie. Reprinted with permission from Vicky Ranney.

PLATE 18. Prairie Crossing Charter School with wind turbine and Byron Colby Barn and silo. Photographer: John Watson.

PLATE 19. Prairie Crossing Charter School with student bicycles. Photographer: John Watson.

PLATE 20. Native prairie plant diversity near Lake Leopold.
Note towering prairie dock forb (*Silphium terebinthinaceum*) and eastern
bluebird nesting box in middle foreground. Photographer: John Watson.

people together."[13] The Homeowners Association also organizes volunteers for activities outside the development, such as roadway cleanup. The survey found that a third of residents had volunteered to take part in development-sponsored activities.

## Resident Conservation Practices and Behaviors

Many sprawl-related environmental problems are the cumulative result of private choices that individual citizens make. Such citizens are presumably acting as what are known in rational choice theory as self-interested utility maximizers.[14] Those behavioral choices may be highly beneficial for the individual but are possibly harmful to society's collective interests. Alfred Kahn coined the term "the tyranny of small decisions" to describe this type of market failure.[15]

If Prairie Crossing is to serve as a policy model devoted to mitigating or reversing the negative effects of urban sprawl, the resident population of the development should exhibit an interest in conservation and act on it. Increasing environmental awareness is a necessary but insufficient condition, for it is cumulative behavior—the tyranny of small decisions—that ultimately creates negative externalities. Understanding one's own contributions to environmental degradation is of little value if it does not reverse or mitigate the behavior. Awareness without mitigation is very common in American society. Today, virtually no one is ignorant of the negative effects of smoking, yet one out of five adults continues to smoke. The connection between enjoying a steak or burger and environmental degradation is far less obvious to the average citizen, and perhaps less pressing, than the link between cancer and smoking. Increased environmental awareness alone cannot change the culture. Changes in behavior must accompany any changes in awareness.

To study residents' behavioral changes, I employed a resident survey. All surveys are a snapshot in time, and the Prairie Crossing survey dates to an important time frame in the development: shortly after the community reached full occupation in 2006. The survey was able to capture the motivations and mindset of the community's founding residents shortly after they had purchased their homes and moved in. The data shows that the first residents were not all "tree-huggers" and firmly established green activists; most were buyers whose first priority was home quality, not the conservation agenda. And because of the housing bubble of 2008, which slowed home turnover, many of the residents from the survey still live in the Prairie Crossing development. Additional surveys on the support for and implementation of the guiding principles, conducted annually by the Prairie Crossing Institute, indicate that support for the conservation agenda has not diminished over time.

In exploring behavioral changes, I surveyed residents on a variety of green-friendly activities and also tested for pre-development conservation propensities. I sent the survey via U.S. mail to all 354 occupied single-family households (the condominium complex was not yet built), receiving responses from 210 households, for a return of 59 percent—a sufficiently high rate from which to draw firm conclusions. To measure the impact of Prairie Crossing's policy on the environmental awareness of its residents, I asked two questions regarding whether moving into the development had increased their awareness of local and national environmental issues. The results showed that the residents themselves believed that living in Prairie Crossing had raised their awareness of environmental issues, particularly at the local level, with 84 percent reporting an increase. In regard to national environmental issues, the increase was substantial but not as dramatic, at 58 percent. The greater concern about the local environment is significant, in that residents' impact at the national level is likely to be limited to contacting their congressional representatives, voting in elections, and making financial donations to public interest groups. While these activities are important, involvement in local issues regarding development of land, volunteerism, and educational activities may have an equal or greater impact on conservation, if the individual can translate that awareness into action.

To measure the impact of Prairie Crossing's guiding principles, policies, and procedures on residents' environmental behavior, I employed a five-point survey rubric designed to quantify their before-and-after environmental activism.[16] Lower values indicate greater levels of activism. The results revealed that the residents themselves perceived that Prairie Crossing had positively affected their environmental behavior. The pre–Prairie Crossing measure produced a mean of 3.26, a value falling between "occasional" and "inactive" environmental activism. The "occasional" category had the highest modal value, twice the value of the next-highest category, which was "inactive." The post–Prairie Crossing measure produced a mean of 2.73, a value falling between "occasional" and "active," a movement of more than half a category level (0.531) toward greater environmental activism. In the post–Prairie Crossing group, "occasional" again was the highest modal category; however, it exceeded the "active" category by only four households, with percentages of 32.5 for "occasional" and 31.6 for "active." Furthermore, the "very active" category nearly tripled between pre- and post-survey measures, with the "inactive" and "non-participant" categories dropping 42 and 41 percent, respectively. After-the-fact self-reflective survey instruments certainly have a measure of error, but given the high rate of survey completion and the clear movement toward greater activism in each category, it appears that exposure to the conservation agenda of Prairie Crossing was in part responsible for the reported increase in residents' environmental activism.

Additional survey data supports the conclusion that residents enjoyed some limited success in translating increased awareness into conservation behavior. When asked to "describe the community's degree of participation in conservation activities," 74 percent selected "high" or "very high," with 24 percent choosing "moderate" and only 2.5 percent selecting "low." No one selected the "very low" response. Nearly all residents, more than 96 percent, recycle their household waste, which is higher than the Midwest regional average of 70 percent and the national average of 77 percent. Significantly, 65 percent reported that they conserve water usage, and 47 percent had made attempts to lower their material consumption. These behaviors have considerable conservation value. Water is an indispensable developmental resource that is becoming more scarce in many areas of the United States, particularly the West. Material consumption is also a salient issue. Landfill space is increasingly in demand, and many consumer products are made of plastic, a petroleum-dependent substance. More than 50 percent of residents reported burning native plants on their private property, erecting bird boxes or bird feeders, and contributing money to green-friendly candidates or interest groups. Nearly 50 percent engaged in composting, and 44 percent walk or ride a bicycle for daily errands when possible rather than drive.

Resident behavior also impacted the ecology of the Prairie Crossing land itself. Eighty-two percent of the respondents planted native species on their private property. An additional 57 percent participated in prairie burns on their property, a practice that imitates prehistoric ecology and fosters native flora regrowth.

Where the development's conservation agenda failed to take significant root is in changing popular social behaviors with a significant conservation impact. Only 23 percent of respondents reported driving fuel-conserving vehicles, a point of contention for many development residents, according to current Homeowners Association board member and former president John Breen.[17] Several residents on the development's internal email list have lamented the fact that some residents drive Hummers and other SUVs while living in a conservation community. In spite of the easy walking distance to two Metra rail lines, only 35 percent utilized mass transit or a carpool to get to their jobs. And given the relatively small number of residents driving fuel-efficient cars, it appears that Prairie Crossing is still contributing to regional traffic problems, greenhouse gas emissions, and foreign oil dependency.

Another area where residents could improve is in reducing the number of households that plant nonnative flora, which was reported at more than 43 percent. Only 39 percent selected the 70/30 ratio of native meadow to conventional turf landscaping. It is possible that the development could reduce the impact of exotic invasive plant species in the future through increased educational efforts. As Yvonne Baskin argues, many Americans simply do not fully understand the threat that invasive plants pose to the environment. People often mistakenly believe that planting *anything* green is conservation friendly: "The concept that not everything green is benign and interchangeable, or that anything green could cause ecological degradation, is still a hard sell in many quarters. Being 'green' in the sense of being environmentally aware does not yet seem to require an understanding of the threat of plant invasions."[18] Convincing homeowners that plants can have a dark side is an uphill battle, one that requires increased educational efforts.

The role that individuals and communities play in exotic plant invasions is substantial and significant. Oftentimes it is homeowners themselves who create the problem, as exotic plants escape from gardens and home landscaping to invade the ecosystem at large. In the United States, 82 percent of woody plant invaders started out as landscape or garden plants. As ecologist Forrest Starr points out, "The real diversity of sleepers [incipient exotic weeds] is down here in people's yards. This is where things are going to start, and this is where the winnable battles are, so that's where we've been focusing." What residents plant in their yards has real ecological consequences.[19] Prairie Crossing residents, while probably more aware than the typical suburban resident, still plant too many exotics on their property. The Homeowners Association's Environmental Stewardship Committee has recently taken steps to educate residents about the dangers of invasive plants. *Meadow Mix*, the community newsletter through which the association disseminates news and information on the community, has a column each month called "Econotes" in which the committee offers timely conservation advice. The July 2013 column informed readers how to eradicate two lesser-known invasives, crown vetch and birdsfoot trefoil. The committee also publishes a handbook providing descriptions and control information for the twelve most harmful invasives.

Homeowners Association board member John Breen, noting among other things the considerable number of SUVs within the development and the very low number of hybrids, believes that Prairie Crossing has changed some behaviors of residents, but not many. "Most people," he said, "brought their behaviors with them."[20] Breen's opinion, although anecdotal, does underscore the failure of the policy model to impact conservation behaviors in select areas, in this case fuel conservation, the most obvious and well-known behavior in the public consciousness. It appears that the residents did bring this behavior with them, because it is firmly ingrained within their lifestyles and very difficult to change, a point that Ann Forsyth also noted in her analysis of the new town communities.[21] Planting nonnative plants is a behavior not commonly understood to be ecologically deleterious. For this reason, future targeted educational efforts by the Homeowners Association may prove fruitful in limiting exotic plants on private lots. Prairie Crossing has had both successes and failures in this policy area, and there is room for improvement.

## Educational Opportunities

Robert Thompson, professor of marine affairs at the University of Rhode Island, performed several case study analyses on green developments, including Prairie Crossing, in an attempt to discern the cognitive barriers to ecologically sensitive land management. He identified three categories of barriers: internal, external, and problem recognition. Thompson employed sixty randomly selected telephone interviews with Prairie Crossing residents as his database, sampling less than a third as many households as my survey. He found that for eco-problem recognition, a lack of local ecological knowledge, difficulties in recognizing environmental problems, and the absence of an emotional investment can create barriers to good land management.[22]

My own research shows that Prairie Crossing has cultural programs and practices designed to break down all three of these potential barriers. The development's successful land stewardship appears to correlate with increased awareness of local environmental issues—nearly 85 percent of residents reported such an increase and attributed it to moving to Prairie Crossing. This increase in awareness also appears to be a contributing factor in the reported increase in environmental activism. Prairie Crossing combats knowledge deficits with both formal and informal educational settings.

Because Prairie Crossing integrates housing with the prairie ecosystem, the development provides opportunities for residents to perceive direct connections between environmental policy actions and problems, particularly regarding water management and prairie ecosystem management. Residents can see the water-retention capabilities of the land because the stormwater treatment system is in plain sight. The movement of water is readily apparent. Similarly, prairie burning by the Homeowners Association dramatically demonstrates the ability of fire to regenerate biological growth. The very high level of conservation participation reported by residents illustrates the emotional connection they have to the land. Residents walk the property, erect bird boxes, plant native species, burn the grasses on their private property, and conserve water. The Homeowners Association encourages and fosters all of these activities through in-house classes, Conserve Lake County seminars, and conservation information disseminated through *Meadow Mix*.

Prairie Crossing has largely been successful in breaking down external barriers and influencing social norms. Wildflowers and native prairie landscaping are noticeable on private properties. Frequent social events, such as community events at the Byron Colby Barn and the prairie burnings, create opportunities for the transmission of social norms and implicit rules. In the survey, 83 percent of residents reported engaging in conservation-related activities with neighbors, and 74 percent rated community participation in conservation-related activities as "high" or "very high." Some residents I interviewed, however, had long-term concerns about maintaining the relatively high level of involvement. One resident expressed apprehension that over time, as homes change hands, commitment to the green agenda may taper off. While the prairie landscape can be visually spectacular during some seasons, it can appear "weedy" at other times, and on occasion some new owners have removed their private prairie plantings and replaced them with conventional suburban exotics. Nonnative landscape replacement is not common, but as one resident said of the practice, "it's been done." Continued education of new residents is the key to maintaining the community conservation commitment.

Prairie Crossing has had less success in overcoming certain internal barriers to taking pro-environmental actions. Residents have not taken maximum advantage of mass transit and have continued to drive low-mileage vehicles. Sands stated that the topic was very contentious and frequently was discussed on the community email list. Presumably, residents prefer their freedom, convenience, and status to the satisfaction of engaging in behavior that mitigates global warming, air pollution, and energy consumption. Global issues such as energy and climate change are probably beyond the capability of the conservation community policy model to address, even though they are the result of cumulative tyranny-of-small-decisions behaviors. Even with the powerful green visual stimulus of the wetlands and prairie, the tendency to free-ride prevails over the individual's perceived contribution to abstract global environmental problems. My research here supports Hal Rothman's assertion that inconvenience and expense will override environmental quality if the perceived personal cost is too high.[23]

Education and community building are among Prairie Crossing's guiding principles. The development offers many educational opportunities for both residents and nonresidents. Conserve Lake County, a conservation organization with ties to the community, is headquartered at nearby Almond Marsh and holds environmental education events and seminars there that are open to the public.

In-house seminars, or "burn schools," are given annually to educate residents and assist them in prairie burning on their private property. Informal learning occurs during Prairie Patrol activities and volunteer roadside cleanup, and for nearly twenty years it occurred during socializing at the recently closed farmers' market. The market, which was also open to the public, fulfilled a significant function in educating nonresidents about the conservation community concept. In fact, it was where some of the residents first learned about the development. The decision to close the farmers' market was a difficult one. It was prompted by a variety of factors. When the market opened in 1996, it was a a novel way for residents to purchase organic produce on-site. The success of the community-supported agriculture program, an increase in the number of on-site farm businesses, and competition for nonresident customers from markets in Grayslake, Libertyville, and Mundelein eventually made Prairie Crossing's farmers' market unsustainable.[24] But in the early years of the development, it played an important role in creating community and disseminating conservation information.

Education is not limited to the resident community or the local community at large. Sands estimates that 15 percent of his paid time was spent educating visitors, many of whom were mayors, developers, and journalists who had come from across the country to see Prairie Crossing and the conservation community concept for themselves.[25] Sands is also a prominent member of a formal policy community that discusses and tackles conservation issues. Applied Ecological Services, Steve Apfelbaum's company, also features Prairie Crossing on its website, offering the development as a conservation policy example of best practices for future developers.

## Energy Conservation

Energy conservation is Prairie Crossing's seventh guiding principle, and the development is successful in several related areas. Prairie Crossing was "the nation's first community-scale demonstration project of the U.S. Department of Energy's Building America program."[26] Energy-saving construction techniques, designed to Leadership in Energy and Environmental Design (LEED) standards, helped reduce energy consumption by approximately 50 percent relative to comparable local construction. Prairie Crossing's architects used an integrated design approach to "make maximum use of the interaction between the building envelope and its heating and cooling system." Some of the energy-saving techniques included double-glazed argon gas–filled windows with low-e glass, efficient framing that allows for the inclusion of extra insulation, and interior placement of ductwork to prevent air leakage.[27] The energy efficiency of the homes makes a significant contribution to energy conservation. Buildings are responsible for almost a third of the nation's energy usage and generate 30 percent of the nation's greenhouse gas emissions.[28] Christine Ervin, who served as the U.S. assistant secretary of energy during the Clinton administration, praised Prairie Crossing as a model development for energy efficiency: "I think you'll serve as a beacon to many communities across the country," she said.[29]

The Prairie Crossing development as a whole has not remained static; it has continued to grow and seek improvement. A 120-foot-high, 20-kilowatt wind turbine powers the organic farm and serves as a symbol and a constant visual reminder of the principle of energy conservation. It was built in 2002 at a cost of $45,000. A second, 2.4-kilowatt turbine, erected in 2011, provides renewable energy and green symbolism for the charter school. Two students originally developed the idea for the newer turbine as a school project.

Though the design of the community has been innovative and successful, the efforts of individual residents to conserve petroleum resources have been largely unsuccessful. The automobile is the dominant mode of transportation for most residents. The suburban culture of transportation convenience still has a strong hold on the community. The energy footprint of Prairie Crossing is smaller than that of conventional sprawling developments, but there is still room for improvement in the lifestyle of the residents.

## Economic Viability

Landscape restoration takes resources, and considerable effort was required to return the land at Prairie Crossing to an ecological condition reminiscent of its pre-European state. Not all conservation communities will require similar expenditures. Conservation construction is very site specific, though it can be adapted to almost any suitable circumstance. Contrary to conventional wisdom, conservation construction actually saves money. An Applied Ecological Services study of ten conservation communities found that green construction cost, on average, 22 percent less than traditional housing construction. Landscaping costs are higher; however, the real savings come from infrastructure costs. The clustering of homes, the narrower roadways, the use of permeable surfaces for walking paths, and the employment of natural water drainage produced significant savings. Conservation stormwater management and roadway costs produced savings on average of 39 and 18 percent, respectively. A 2005 study by the Conservation Research Institute estimated cost savings for green construction at $2,500 to $3,700 per lot. The infrastructure savings at Prairie Crossing totaled $1.375 million—$2,000 per acre—through the construction of narrower streets, the elimination of sidewalks, curbs, and gutters, and a decreased reliance on storm sewers. Similar savings have been recouped in ecosystems as diverse as the scrubland of Texas and woodlands in Tennessee.[30]

Market research has shown that potential homebuyers are willing to pay for green amenities. A 2008 National Association of Realtors study found that "more than 90 percent of first-time home buyers said that environmentally-friendly features were an important criterion in selecting a home."[31] Regarding Prairie Crossing specifically, the development was successful in achieving economic viability. A market analysis generated for the Ranneys by Robert Charles Lesser and Company revealed that houses at Prairie Crossing sold at $139 per square foot, a premium of 33 percent relative to comparable construction in the Lake County market. Studies of other conservation communities across the country have produced similar economic projections.[32]

The Ranneys are not permitted to reveal the profits earned by the Prairie Holdings Corporation because of a nondisclosure agreement. Additionally, the collapse of the housing bubble in 2008 complicates the evaluation of current prices. However, an examination of sale prices from 1994 to 2014 provides some insight into the success of the development beyond Lesser and Company's market analysis. In November 1994, the first Prairie Crossing homes began to sell, with prices ranging from nearly $180,000 to $250,000. In comparison, the average home price in Lake County at that time was considerably lower—$120,000. Several years later, in 2000, the larger homes, those between 2,500 and 3,500 square feet, were priced between $365,000 and $427,000. And in 2007, the most expensive homes in the development sold for up to $650,000.[33] The collapse of the housing bubble in 2008 had a negative effect on housing prices nationwide, and Prairie

Crossing was no exception. However, prices have since improved. Home resale prices in 2013 ranged from $243,000 to $395,000, with a mean of $324,000 and a median of $315,000, and in the fall of 2014, listed home prices were ranging from $274,000 (three bedrooms, 1,767 square feet) to $565,000 (four bedrooms, 2,986 square feet). The Carton Team, a realty group with experience selling Prairie Crossing homes, reported that properties in the development averaged $134 per square foot through the first nine months of 2014.[34]

The economic downturn had a greater negative effect on the Station Village condominiums. Half of the units were unsold when the market went into decline. Units that were initially selling for between $329,000 and $499,000 in 2005 and 2006 sold for considerably less in 2011, when the last unit sold.[35]

Additional outside factors beyond the control of the developers have also had a negative impact. A proposed tollway and power plant initially slowed sales. Local organizations allied with the Liberty Prairie Reserve, including the Liberty Prairie Foundation, negotiated a settlement permitting a scaled-down, environmentally friendly expansion of Illinois Route 53/120, which borders the reserve's northern boundary. The power plant proposal was defeated, in part by resident activism, and is no longer a threat to the reserve. A negotiated agreement with Waste Management, Inc., which owns a landfill that can be seen from parts of Prairie Crossing, helped to "insulate [the] developers and residents against potential negative impacts" from its operation. Waste Management agreed to buy any listed Prairie Crossing homes that did not sell after 180 days. In the wake of the downturn, the company purchased dozens of homes, many of which it still owns. To avoid saturating the market, the company sells a few homes at a time while renting the rest.[36]

Recently published research lends support to my hypothesis that conservation communities such as Prairie Crossing can positively affect the behavior of residents. A study by Thomas Macias and Kristin Williams of the University of Vermont in Burlington employed data from the General Social Survey to explore the effect social capital has on environmental values. Drawing off of Putnam's thesis in *Bowling Alone*, Macias and Williams reason, "people who have stronger social ties may care more about the environment" because "those social ties can be mind-broadening." Interacting with neighbors, as opposed to family, appears to open people's minds to greater possibilities regarding environmental issues. The "shared assumptions in tight-knit family circles," in contrast, appear to diminish these concerns.[37]

Social interaction with neighbors translated directly into more conservation behavior, including driving less, using less water and household energy, and buying more chemical-free produce. People who spent more time interacting socially with relatives were more likely to drive more, and "also less willing to sacrifice for the environment by paying higher taxes or higher prices for various consumer objects." The findings of Macias and Williams suggest that conservation communities have the potential to increase green activism and behavior in greater society: "Policies that foster social interactions at the community level through online forums, neighborhood organizations or local opportunities to volunteer may prove in the long run to be at least as important to addressing environmental crisis as social marketing aimed at promoting efficiency improvements." Given that so many environmental problems involve the tyranny of small, incremental decisions made by ordinary citizens—water and energy use, consumption of material goods, production of household waste and greenhouse gases—any policy that can promote and reinforce eco-friendly behavior can provide a solid foundation for tackling some of the serious environmental problems we face in the latter half of the twenty-first century.[38]

# CHAPTER FIVE

# A GEOGRAPHY OF SOMEWHERE

You can't know who you are
until you know where you are.
—Wendell Berry

Nature is not a place to visit.
It is home.
—Gary Snyder

Prairie Crossing has made an innovative contribution to urban public policy: a conservation agenda and practices. The developers, however, aspired to do more. They actively sought to avoid the "cookie-cutter" ambience, plasticity, and sameness of suburbia that journalist James Kunstler notably called "the geography of nowhere." The goal of Prairie Crossing was to create a geography of somewhere, a place where residents would feel invested enough to volunteer their time to create genuine community.

The Ranneys specifically formulated the development's guiding principles three, four, and five to address some of the problems that trouble contemporary American communities. Their intention with the third principle, "a sense of place," is to create an atmosphere of uniqueness and home, a location where the residents feel a sense of investment in the land and physical structures. This principle draws off of and expands many of the concepts the New Urbanism movement espoused.

With the fourth principle, "a sense of community," the Ranneys moved beyond the built and physical environments to encourage social interaction among residents and also between Prairie Crossing and the larger communities of Grays-lake and Lake County. The creation of community serves a dual purpose for the development. It creates and enhances social capital, and as the descriptive text that expands on the principle explains, it also provides "places where people can meet to enjoy and care for the land," which serves to reinforce the conservation ethic. Guiding principle five, "economic and racial diversity," seeks to remedy the tendency toward exclusivity and homogeneity in community housing, frequent problems for various types of development.[1] "Common-interest housing was first used to create exclusivity," Evan McKenzie writes, "and later it became an instrument of exclusion."[2] Prairie Crossing's developers reject exclusivity, believing that "a mix of incomes and races is essential to the future of our society."[3]

Together, these three guiding principles strive to lay the groundwork for a new kind of housing community, one that does not passively wait and hope that a positive and engaging community life will spontaneously emerge from the physical design and built environment. This chapter details the efforts the developers have made to foster positive community living and a sense of place through landscaping, architecture, education, community events, Homeowners Association participation and governing, and land conservation. The development's goals are ambitious: creating economically and racially diverse housing with a sense of place and community that conserves the land while turning a competitive profit. It is a significant departure from the standard land economics model of common-interest development, which in the past has focused on the calculus of profit by housing "more people on less land."[4]

## Satisfaction with the Homeowners Association

In "Trouble in Privatopia," McKenzie details the many problems that occasionally beset everyday life in common-interest developments. Internal disputes, conflicts, lawsuits, and even violence have sometimes characterized living in this relatively new alternative to the traditional neighborhood development. McKenzie's research has shown that these problems are "not just isolated neighborhood conflicts." He writes, "For some, CID [common-interest development] living means having to fight to defend a semblance of privacy and personal freedom, while the few residents who enforce the rules enjoy a degree of personal power over their neighbors that the Constitution denies to public officials."[5] Residents may be denied the right to engage in behaviors and practices considered commonplace in many traditional neighborhoods—having pets, displaying the American flag, parking a vehicle in a driveway or on the street, erecting backyard fences or swing sets, even using the back door as an entrance or exit.[6] This "business as usual" atmosphere generates hostility and diminishes the quality of life for millions of Americans, many of whom, because of geographic and financial restraints, have few alternatives to the common-interest development when it comes to home-ownership. No state supreme court has yet held common-interest development communities accountable to state constitutional provisions. In 2007, the New Jersey State Supreme Court ruled in favor of the Twin Rivers Homeowners Association in a lawsuit filed by some residents claiming violations of the free speech and right of assembly clauses of the state constitution. In the words of McKenzie, "the case was a significant victory for those who seek to shield associations from any form of constitutional scrutiny." And though there has been "a sharp turn in the direction of more intense state regulation" of common-interest developments, these communities still experience a fair amount of conflict.[7]

Prairie Crossing's residents, however, do have alternatives to common-interest development living. With mean and median family incomes of $135,000 and $128,000, respectively, they have options available to them that are closed to the typical prospective homebuyer and could readily avoid homeowners associations, if they so desired.[8] How does Prairie Crossing compare to conventional common-interest developments? Has the community avoided many of the common homeowners association pitfalls, or has it also experienced trouble building its unique version of ecotopia?[9]

To test residents' level of satisfaction with the Homeowners Association's governance, I utilized an ordinal survey question. Overwhelmingly, the respondents appeared to be at a minimum satisfied with the association's handling of private government affairs. Nearly 92 percent selected the "satisfied" or "very satisfied" category, with slightly more than one in five reporting very high satisfaction. The residents' high level of satisfaction with Homeowners Association affairs may be related in part to their relatively high level of involvement in association government. Nearly 28 percent reported their level of involvement as "very active," with 58 percent reporting "somewhat active" and less than 14 percent as "not very active." Given the reported high levels of satisfaction with living within the community after a decade under Homeowners Association rule, it appears that governance is less of a problem at Prairie Crossing than it is in conventional common-interest developments.

In spite of the inherent problems of common-interest development living, "people who live in condominiums and homeowners associations are overwhelmingly pleased with their communities," according to Tom Skiba of the Community Associations Institute.[10] Polling by IBOPE Zogby International indicates that 70 percent reported their overall experience as being "positive," with roughly 10 percent reporting a "negative" experience. The results were somewhat mitigated by the fact that only 37 percent stated that they would live under a homeowners association again, with 26 percent stating that they would not consider living in a homeowners association–governed development in the future. The three most important positive facets of common-interest development living, as reported by Zogby, were property maintenance, safety and security, and enhancement of property values. The three most important reasons for rejecting common-interest development living were rules and restrictions, fees and costs, and the desire for more privacy.[11]

The polling seems to suggest nationwide satisfaction among common-interest development residents. Though more than a quarter of the respondents reported that they would not move into another common-interest development home, only 8 to 12 percent, depending on the polling year, reported dissatisfaction with their present common-interest development. With 63 million Americans living in common-interest developments, however, even that low rate of dissatisfaction rate translates into more than 6 million unhappy households, many of them perhaps experiencing the serious difficulties detailed in *Privatopia*.

The residents of Prairie Crossing are comparatively wealthy and have abundant housing alternatives available to them, including the option to avoid common-interest development living entirely. How do they compare to national trends regarding future home purchases? When asked in the survey, "Would you consider moving into a conservation-oriented community again?" 83.3 percent answered "yes," 14.8 percent "maybe," and only 1.9 percent "no." These results differ markedly from those obtained in the Zogby poll and seem to indicate a strong preference for a form of living that emphasizes community and an altruistic agenda.[12]

## New Urbanism and the Creation of Place

New Urbanism is a revival and reinterpretation of traditional urban planning. It seeks to replicate in modern town design the great sense of place found in many old American towns, such as Scarsdale, New York, Alexandria, Virginia, and the Georgetown section of Washington, D.C. New Urbanist architects strive to re-create the pedestrian-friendly design, graceful architecture, and old-town atmosphere captured so well by those late nineteenth-century and early twentieth-century American towns that avoided modern demolition and urban redesign. In stark contrast, some critics of sprawl argue that postwar suburban development designs reflected America's strong reliance on the automobile, and sometimes resulted in repetitive neighborhoods and monotonous designs, best epitomized by Levittown, New York, and Palm City, Florida. Urban neighborhoods were not immune, as downtown areas became "a no-man's-land brutalized by traffic," where nobody walks, and the mixed-use street was replaced by "an 'analogous city' of pedestrian bridges and tunnels," similar to the suburban mall.[13] What contemporary town planning needed, New Urbanists reasoned, was a rebirth of old ideas.

In the early 1980s, Seaside, a small resort community in the panhandle of western Florida, helped spark interest in and media attention to New Urbanism. Designed by the husband-and-wife architectural team of Andres Duany and Elizabeth Plater-Zyberk, Seaside employs a variety of old architectural designs, from pitched roofs and wooden shutters to pedestrian-friendly mixed-use buildings that connect "seamlessly" to nearby preexisting neighborhoods. Front porches face the street, encouraging people to get outside and interact, while garages are relegated to the rear of the houses, where they are accessed from an alley. Village greens and squares, gazebos, parks, and open spaces provide meeting places and sources of social engagement. Seaside's financial success and innovation made the development an icon for the incipient neotraditional movement.[14]

Capitalizing on the interest and appeal surrounding New Urbanism and inspired by the work of Frederick Law Olmsted, Prairie Crossing's developers sought to enhance community relations and participation through the deliberate design of the landscape and built environments. Olmsted favored village space that mixed rural and urban, with curved streets that slowed traffic, public squares and parks, and houses set back from tree-lined streets. His goal was to create an urban environment set in "natural beauty and quiet."[15] Vicky Ranney sought to incorporate many of his ideas into the conservation community model for Prairie Crossing, hybridizing Olmsted's rural elements with New Urbanism architecture.[16] In addition to Vicky's background in social justice issues, she has worked with numerous cultural and conservationist groups, such as the Illinois Humanities Council, Friends of Parks, and the Chicago History Project. Her life experience made her uniquely qualified to refine the concept of community and place.

A "sense of place" can mean different things to different people. No one definition is necessarily definitive. For this case study I define having a sense of place as living in an environment where people have an emotional connection to and investment in the built and physical environments. A "place" *belongs* to the individual and is greater than the sum of its parts. A place is something that people experience and value, something more than a mere location where they eat, sleep, and perform perfunctory life-sustaining functions. A sense of place is a state of being in which the place becomes a part of the person experiencing it, and in turn the place reflects the values of the person who finds meaning in it.

Vicky Ranney began constructing a sense of place by grounding the development's ambience in the property's past. She named streets after the area's indigenous wild plants (Bluestem Lane, Turks Cap Road) and the land's original settlers and native inhabitants (Amos Bennett Street, Potawatomi Road). Departing from the industry standard of using only neutral colors for the homes, she selected a "spectrum of colors" based on prairie plants to offset the "cold, dreary winter weather" of northern Illinois.[17] The Ranneys were inspired by old homes and homesteads they found in Lake County; they toured the area with their architect, selecting elegant designs they wanted to emulate. The result was a mix of Midwestern, Victorian, farmhouse, bungalow, and Frank Lloyd Wright homes that incorporated energy efficiency into the design. Homebuyers were able to semi-customize the final product, providing that the changes were approved by an architectural committee. In retrospect, George Ranney says he would have limited the designs and customizing because the process was "too confusing, too time-consuming, and too expensive."[18] The resulting architecture and landscaping is distinctive and reflects the rural milieu of a simpler time and place. The existing farmhouse from the original farmland now serves as the conservation headquarters for the Liberty Prairie Foundation and property maintenance. The charter schoolhouse is a local Lake County structure and dates to 1857. It is topped by a small belfry and functions as an environmental resource library for the school. The Byron Colby Barn is also an original local structure, built in 1885, which was disassembled, transported, and reassembled timber by timber. It serves as a community center and also generates rental income for banquets, concerts, and weddings. These historic buildings add a yesteryear quality to the development.

Prairie Crossing also creates a sense of place through various resident activities. The working farm, rather than a negative as some critics suggested, became a hub for resident recreation. Both livestock and organic crops are raised on the farm, providing opportunities for adults and children. More than one-quarter of the residents reported having volunteered on the farm at least once, and 11 percent of residents participate in horseback riding. The Byron Colby Barn community center and the farm amenities proved to be a draw in attracting residents to Prairie Crossing. More than one in five selected the barn as the first, second, or third most important factor in their decision to move to the development, and when allowed to write in a factor, nine of forty-three households mentioned the farm or its animals as having played a role in their decision to purchase their property.

Outdoor activities have also helped shape residents' perception of place. Half of the residents take advantage of the property's abundant wildlife by birdwatching. There are several visually impressive resident bird species that likely drew people into the hobby on at least a novice basis. The nest boxes distributed by the Homeowners Association have been successful in boosting eastern bluebird populations. Red-winged blackbirds are abundant and can be heard and seen every day from most locations within the development. And bobolinks, while not common, are acoustically unique and offer spectacular in-flight flashes of color. The lake and pond have also motivated residents to take to the outdoors. Nearly a third of residents ice-skate on the frozen bodies of water, and more than a third have boated on them. More than 40 percent have engaged in organic gardening. This activity has numerous positive feedback loops. In addition to fostering a personal connection to the land, it provides local produce, which diminishes residents' ecological footprint, and it facilitates greater environmental awareness as residents seek out information to increase their yields.

The results of the 2006 survey suggest that the development was successful in drawing residents out of their homes and establishing a place with ambience that people want to experience. The results of annual surveys conducted by the Prairie Crossing Institute, which are discussed at length in chapter seven, also suggest that participation in community life has remained strong and perhaps even increased in the ensuing years. Prairie Crossing opened for initial occupation in 1994, several years before the publication of Robert Putnam's *Bowling Alone*, which detailed the nation's long-term trend toward civic and social withdrawal. Prairie Crossing's residents have proved to be an exception. The developers stressed community from the outset, starting with the sales pitch, and through integration of the built and ecological environments they have created a positive sense of place that their residents seek out for interaction.

## Creation of Community

Like "sense of place," "community" is a somewhat ambiguous term. Clearly, community is usually related to a sense of place. A place that people do not value or meaningfully experience is less likely to generate community. Yet a sense of community is greater than the sum of the built and physical environments and is more than a vague "feeling" on the part of the residents of a place. Putnam argues that the decline in civic engagement in America during the last several decades is due to "the replacement of an unusually civic generation by several generations . . . that are less embedded in community life." As far back as the early 1960s, Melvin Webber understood the challenges that technology would create for community life and called for a new definition of community, one severed from proximity and based on personal bonds unconstrained by the limits of territory. Other scholars have quantified these bonds, framing "modern community as complex and varied networks of primary social ties."[19] The rise of the Internet and its many social networks has proven Webber prescient. And though cyber social networks have facilitated social activism and engagement in many ways, that engagement also has its limits. Social network activism is both less personal and less committed. As Malcolm Gladwell argues, "the revolution will not be tweeted. . . . Facebook activism succeeds not by motivating people to make a real sacrifice but by motivating them to do the things that people do when they are not motivated enough to make a real sacrifice. We are a long way from the lunch counters of Greensboro."[20]

Community entails "participation in the social life of a place" and involves the communal sharing of social experiences, territory, traditions, institutions, common goals, and political or economic structures.[21] A place with community, therefore, should offer abundant occasions for social engagement and interaction, exhibit a high level of civic participation, and provide opportunities for residents to work collaboratively toward shared goals that will help to bind them together. Does Prairie Crossing exhibit any of these qualities?

The residents of Prairie Crossing officially share a common purpose in connection to the conservation agenda, the first guiding principle in the community's charter. This is a legitimate altruistic goal that moves beyond the customary goals of many conventional developments such as maintaining and enhancing property values, the status goals of wealthy prestige communities, the retirement goals of lifestyle communities, or the security goals of gated and walled communities. This is not to say that Prairie Crossing's residents are not concerned about maintaining and enhancing property values or acquiring status. The development has garnered its fair share of media attention and has assuredly conferred a measure of status on its homeowners. It has also maintained property values (when considered in the context of the housing bubble). Although the most important factor that residents reported in their decision to move into the development was the design and quality of the homes, they seem to have embraced its conservation goal as their own. More than eight in ten stated that they would consider living in a conservation community again, with less than 2 percent ruling it out. Reported conservation-related activity within the development is high, at 74 percent. And although certain specific behaviors (e.g., use of mass transit and high-mileage vehicles) were practiced at lower than desirable rates, many others (e.g., conserving water and lowering material consumption) were practiced at relatively high rates. The conservation agenda does not appear to have been divisive. There have been no complaints at the charter school regarding its environmental curriculum, and only 1.6 percent of residents who responded to the survey reported being "dissatisfied" or "very dissatisfied" with its "emphasis on the environment and citizenship."[22] Further evidence of the residents' collective support of the conservation agenda is their movement toward greater environmental activism and awareness. Clearly, not all of the residents have embraced conservation. Several derisively referred to Prairie Crossing as the home of "fruits and nuts"; however, the resident survey shows a dominant trend toward collective involvement.

The residents also showed signs of significant political and civic engagement. Political participation is evaluated in the following chapter. Regarding civic participation, more than one-quarter of residents indicated that they had volunteered within the community on the development's farm, and one-third reported participating in roadside cleanup or environmental reclamation. When asked to describe the community's degree of participation in conservation activities, 74 percent of residents rated the level of participation as "high" or "very high." Survey write-in activities involving an altruistic component included volunteering with Conserve Lake County, Prairie Patrols, and prairie burning. More than half of those surveyed reported contributing money to green-friendly interest groups.

The primary communal institutions within the community are the Homeowners Association and the Prairie Crossing Charter School. Residents appear to be directly involved in their private governance; more than 27 percent reported that their fellow residents are "very active" in their association government, with 58.1 percent describing the same involvement as "active." Moreover, 92 percent of residents reported being "satisfied" or "very satisfied" with the results of that governance. In contrast, when Edward J. Blakely and Mary Gail Snyder asked the same question to gated community residents, only 6 percent of residents reported being "very active." Also in the Blakely and Snyder survey, 55 percent of gated community respondents reported being "not active" in the private government, compared to only 13 percent at Prairie Crossing.[23] Prairie Crossing's residents compare favorably to both gated communities and all communities employing a homeowners association regarding communal maintenance of their governing institutions.

In 1995, Betsy Dietel, a resident of Prairie Crossing and the wife of Michael Sands, founded the Liberty Prairie Conservancy, with a mission "to protect and restore the Liberty Prairie Reserve's natural ecosystems, to preserve the area's agricultural, historic and archeological heritage, and to improve public access to the reserve." The Liberty Prairie Reserve contains 3,383 acres of permanently protected natural land that is home to several hundred native plants and animals, and preserves a variety of habitats, including prairie, woodland, oak savanna, wetland, graminoid fen, sedge meadow, and stream corridor. It supports twenty-eight endangered or threatened species. In 2004 the Liberty Prairie Conservancy expanded into a regional land conservation organization, and in 2012 its name was changed to Conserve Lake County to better reflect the enhanced scope and vision. Conserve Lake County has embraced an ambitious goal: to "realize a Lake County landscape where, by 2030, at least 20 percent of the County is preserved forever as natural areas, parks, trails, farmland, and scenic views."[24] The organization is loosely affiliated with Prairie Crossing and is headquartered nearby in the Liberty Prairie Reserve at Almond Marsh. It sponsors a significant outreach and education program that gives presentations to groups and offers one-on-one property visits. It also holds workshops and classes and organizes volunteer workday projects. In 2011, Conserve Lake County launched one of its most successful programs, Conservation@Home. The program was originally created by the Conservation Foundation, a nonprofit organization that focuses on land and watershed conservation in the remaining four regional collar counties of DuPage, Kane, Kendall, and Will. Conservation@Home assists homeowners in transitioning their conventional Eurasian landscaping to a more eco-friendly landscape that incorporates native plantings and provides habitat for songbirds, butterflies, and other sensitive indigenous organisms. Conserve Lake County offers consultations to property owners and certifies those properties that meet its eco-standards. Certified owners receive a sign that states: "Conservation@Home: This property supports clean water, rich soil and resilient ecosystems." It is an aspirational program designed to change the accepted social standard of home landscaping, one property at a time. Three years into the program, six hundred properties are enrolled, and approximately half of those have achieved certification.[25]

Using "participation in the social life of a place" as a working definition of community, I tested for its presence in Prairie Crossing by employing questions adapted from a survey used by Blakely and Snyder.[26] I asked residents to describe the "community feeling" in the development on an ordinal scale of "neighborly and tight-knit," "friendly," "indifferent," and "distant or private." More than nine in ten residents described the community as at least "friendly," with 38 percent selecting "neighborly and tight knit." Only 3 percent perceived the development as "distant or private." In contrast, Blakely and Snyder's data revealed that only 8 percent of the surveyed residents of gated communities described their developments as "neighborly and tight-knit"; 28 percent characterized their community as "distant or private," more than nine times as many as chose that option in the Prairie Crossing survey.[27] The results from all communities with homeowners associations do not differ appreciably from those for gated communities: 8 percent characterized their community as "neighborly and tight-knit," 58 percent as "friendly," and 30 percent as "distant or private." When asked to compare Prairie Crossing to "most communities [they] have previously lived in," more than three out of four residents rated the development as "more neighborly," with 17 percent rating it as the same, and 5 percent finding the community "less neighborly." The general feeling among the residents supports a finding for the creation of community and positive social interaction in the development, but more evidence is needed.

To make the case for creation of community, the residents of Prairie Crossing need to actively engage and participate in its social life. To measure this, I again utilized a question from Blakely and Snyder and developed several new questions designed to further explore the social engagement process.[28] The Blakely and Snyder comparison asks residents to "describe the level of involvement of residents in association-sponsored activities other than governance (i.e., social or charitable events)." In gated communities, Blakely and Snyder found relatively low levels of resident participation in non–governance association activities: 13 percent reported that they were "very active," 41 percent "somewhat active," and 46 "not active." Prairie Crossing's residents were remarkably active in comparison: 53 percent characterized themselves as "very active," 43 percent as "somewhat active," and 4 percent as "not active."

To further explore social interaction, I asked residents to estimate how frequently they socialized with their neighbors. The results revealed a relatively active social life within the community. Slightly more than half reported social activity with neighbors one or more times per week, and nearly a quarter reported once per month. Only 5 percent reported socializing only once a year or never. When the residents were asked to list various social activities they had engaged in, their responses ranged from a high of 97 percent for walking the development's system of trails to a low of 11 percent for horseback riding. More important in terms of community relations is that nearly 83 percent reported having taken part in at least one of these social activities with a fellow Prairie Crossing resident. Fifty-seven residents listed twenty-four write-in social activities they had engaged in at Prairie Crossing, including bonfires, concerts, lectures, potluck dinners, and the farmers' market. On the strength of the survey responses, which sharply contrast with the relatively inactive engagement of gated and non-gated homeowners association communities, it seems reasonable to conclude that Prairie Crossing, which stresses community involvement from sales pitch to post-occupation, has succeeded in generating and fostering a distinct sense of community.

## New Town Movement

In the late 1960s and early 1970s, a group of ambitious young planners and developers sought to shake up the suburban design paradigm that had ossified in the United States since the 1950s. The new town movement, as it came to be called, was a "grand experiment," unlike anything built before or since.[29] The target was sprawl and its many externalities—cookie-cutter repetitiveness, stale architecture, environmental degradation, long commutes, and social isolation. The aims were bold, entailing coordinated master-planned communities ranging in size from tens of thousands to hundreds of thousands of residents, with retail, recreational, and employment opportunities. The three biggest, best-known, and most influential communities of the movement are Irvine, California; Columbia, Maryland; and The Woodlands, Texas. Of the three, The Woodlands, as its name implies, had the greatest environmental impact and legacy. Where does Prairie Crossing, as an exemplar of the conservation community policy model, fit in relation to this movement?

The Prairie Crossing developers shared characteristics and motivations with many of the designers and developers of the new town communities. Like the Ranneys and Donnelleys, developers James Rouse (Columbia) and George P. Mitchell (The Woodlands) could rely on "elite social networks" and draw on considerable financial resources. All three developments were backed by patient money, considerable wealth derived from other business sectors. Mitchell was an oil and gas magnate, Rouse earned his fortune in mortgage banking and shopping center development, and the Irvine Company dealt in large-scale agriculture. The Irvine Company had owned the land (called the Irvine Ranch) for a century and was "essentially forced into developing" by government action that raised property taxes and by a proposal to use the land for a new campus for the state university system. The impetuses for Columbia and The Woodlands were different. Like Prairie Crossing, they were the "pet projects" of their founding developers. All three were profit-making ventures that sought to "solve at least some of the problems of incremental and uncoordinated suburban growth."[30] Mitchell, in particular, was driven by his enthusiasm for the environment and sustainability, and his life and interests in some ways paralleled those of Gaylord Donnelley, though Donnelley was by far the more committed and accomplished environmentalist.

Mitchell was not quite Donnelley's contemporary, having been born nine years later, in 1919. Both served in World War II, led Fortune 500 companies to prosperity, and created philanthropic foundations in their own and their wives' names. Mitchell shared Donnelley's unique ability to think creatively, and after pioneering the technologies that launched the present-day shale gas revolution, he became an "unlikely environmental warrior" by creating The Woodlands, campaigning for "tight governmental regulation of fracking" to protect the environment, and "champion[ing] sustainability."[31] Where Mitchell diverges from Donnelley is in the duality and tension between his "twin passions—fracking and sustainability." How did "the father of fracking," a polluting technology, come to turn over a green leaf?

Like Vicky Ranney, Mitchell had an environmental mentor, though his was a peer and collaborator rather than a reasoned voice from the distant past. Ian McHarg, a Scottish-born landscape architect, influenced Mitchell in much the same way that Olmsted influenced Vicky Ranney. Mitchell purchased several large tracts of land in the 1960s with the original intention of building conventional residential and light industry developments. The prospect of obtaining federal loan guarantees for a new town development through the Title IV and Title VII programs convinced him to reconsider.[32] Prompted by a colleague to read McHarg's newly published *Design with Nature*, Mitchell found his vision for the development that would eventually become The Woodlands. He hired McHarg to team up with William Pereira, a Chicago-born architect best known for having designed the Transamerica Pyramid in San Francisco, to build a green-friendly community.

The rapidly evolving science of ecology, a discipline that was increasingly relying on mathematics and quantification, heavily influenced McHarg's approach to landscape design. Just a few years before his involvement with The Woodlands, Robert McArthur and Edward O. Wilson published their paradigm-shifting work

*The Theory of Island Biogeography*, which suggested that the fragmentation of habitats by sprawl could trigger a decline in biodiversity. McHarg hired specialists in geology, hydrology, soil science, botany, wildlife management, and climatology so that the new development would track as lightly as possible upon the land.[33]

Like Olmsted a century earlier, McHarg was deeply moved by his childhood experiences with nature. The countryside provided a refuge from industrial Glasgow, which he called "a no-place, despondent, dreary beyond description, grimy, gritty, squalid." Here is how he described his design philosophy:

> We need nature as much in the city as in the countryside. In order to endure we must maintain the bounty of that great cornucopia which is our inheritance. . . . It is not a choice of either the city or the countryside: both are essential, but today it is nature, beleaguered in the country, too scarce in the city which has become precious. . . . Let us then abandon the self-mutilation which has been our way and give expression to the potential harmony of man-nature. The world is abundant, we require only a deference born of understanding to fulfill man's promise. Man is that uniquely conscious creature who can perceive and express. He must become the steward of the biosphere. To do this he must design with nature.[34]

Mitchell was hooked; he wholeheartedly embraced McHarg's environmental worldview.[35]

The result was a green-oriented community, though not the first comprehensive conservation community. In a 1998 book, McHarg and co-editor Frederick Steiner would claim that The Woodlands was "the best example of ecologically based new town planning in the United States during the 1970s."[36] McHarg's design emphasized hydrology—protecting water systems, limiting runoff, and permitting the recharge of aquifers. It also incorporated the native pine forest of the region into the urban landscape with limited alteration. Preserving the natural drainage system was essential to save the natural vegetation.[37] George Ranney stated that he was familiar with The Woodlands but did not specifically cite it as a model or inspiration for Prairie Crossing. Riverside, Seaside, and the Sea Ranch played greater roles in the Prairie Crossing design process than any of the new town communities.

The name of the community—The Woodlands—emphasized the most prominent and innovative element of the development, a strategy that Prairie Crossing would adopt years later. Unlike developments that bulldoze the trees and then name the subdivision after them, The Woodlands actually lives up to its name, and in such circumstances the name is laden with green symbolic value. It calls attention to the natural environment every time it is invoked.

It is not possible to make an in-depth comparison of the residents of The Woodlands and Prairie Crossing at the level of their behavior; however, there is some evidence regarding the behavior of The Woodlands' residents. In her comprehensive examination of the three new town communities in her well-received book *Reforming Suburbia*, Ann Forsyth states that homeowners in The Woodlands "have both promoted and undermined the ecological concept." Presumably seeking a more conventional suburban appearance, some residents trimmed the natural vegetation to increase their lawn size. Recycling came late to the development, and even then it was kick-started by a volunteer group. The community is completely automobile dependent, and residents have actually opposed the introduction of bus service.[38]

In some respects, it is difficult to compare The Woodlands and Prairie Crossing because of the advances in technology that separate the two eras. However, compared to the developments of its own time, The Woodlands was more progressive in many areas: open-space preservation (16 percent), use of native vegetation, attention to natural hydrology, and Mitchell's funding of sustainability awareness through various means. The biggest failure of not only The Woodlands but all three new town communities was that they neglected to promote a viable alternative to the automobile. The Woodlands' landscape design has also been criticized: "a number of environmental activists have complained that in some areas only a 'veneer of woods' or 'a forest façade' remains and that the focus on hydrology has detracted from the attention paid to maintaining corridors for wildlife." As an alternative to sprawl, Forsyth calls The Woodlands a "mixed success."[39]

The new town community of Columbia also had an energetic founder, James Rouse. Somewhat like George Mitchell, Rouse had internal contradictions. A vociferous critic of suburban sprawl, it was Rouse in the 1950s who actually "pioneered the speculative air-conditioned shopping mall," that oft-despised yet ubiquitous element of urban sprawl. Columbia, however, did an admirable job of protecting environmental values. It set aside 38 percent of the land as open space—mostly public parks and hiking paths—and it protected its riparian habitats. But social issues were most important to Rouse, and they provided Columbia with both a vision and a focus. Rouse viewed the development as an opportunity to help inner urban areas, and to "promote human growth and values such as lifelong learning, civic participation, and the mixing of diverse populations."[40]

Racial and socioeconomic diversity were crucial issues for Rouse, and he made social mixing a "centerpiece" of the Columbia development. To accomplish this, he utilized the village concept. Presently, Columbia has nine residential villages, consisting of roughly 3,500 households grouped into smaller neighborhoods, and one mixed-use town center. To obtain a social mix, Rouse built different housing sizes and types within each village. He set schools in the village centers so that children could walk to class. Columbia is a fully functioning town with employment opportunities. The center includes a college and hospital, theaters, restaurants, inns, and a community center and shopping mall.[41]

Columbia opened in 1967, the same year the landmark Supreme Court case *Loving v. Virginia* legalized interracial marriage. And by chance, the first new baby in the community was born into an interracial family. The open housing policy of Columbia proved to be successful. Since its inception, approximately one-fifth of the population has consistently been African American; the figure provided by the U.S. Census for 2010 was 25.3 percent. Forsyth's research showed that early on, the residents understood the racial uniqueness of the community. Some even referred to Columbia as a "reservation," in the sense that to leave it was to enter a different (i.e., primarily negative) kind of world regarding racial relations.[42]

Socioeconomic integration proved to be more difficult to achieve than racial integration. The developer's need for profits is the likely cause. Early African American residents were wealthy, and actually had higher average earnings than the white residents. Forsyth attributes the lack of success in attracting economically diverse residents to the difficulties in providing low-income housing in new construction.

The Irvine Ranch is the largest of the three new town communities. The original plan called for extensive development; however, the long-term developmental process allowed for changing environmental attitudes to influence the design, and today more than 50,000 acres, much of it coastal scrub, are preserved as open space. Politics played a role in the preservation. The 1993 listing of the California gnatcatcher as a threatened species, a bird that has suitable habitat on the Ranch, prompted negotiations and an eventual agreement to set aside land for a wildlife preserve, albeit one with a seventy-five-year sunset provision. The acquisition of the Irvine Company in 1983 by Donald Bren, one of the world's wealthiest men, also aided the preservation cause. Bren was interested in leaving behind a philanthropic legacy.

Of the three communities, the Ranch has received the most criticism. The architecture, in particular, has generated strong and mostly negative reactions. But Irvine is also the community that has evolved the most over the decades of development. As Forsyth notes, "The story of the Irvine Ranch is at least in part a transformation in perceptions of the land—from an economic view held by the agriculturalists at the Irvine Company, one based on long-term returns, to one more focused on protection of the land itself both for human enjoyment and because of its more intrinsic features. . . . Land that was later seen as habitat and an important legacy was at the time [i.e., the design and planning stages] regarded as scrubland and as hillsides amenable for development because of location and views."[43] Irvine, like Columbia and The Woodlands, is based on a village structure that incorporates shopping, recreation, and light industry into the design. The housing has often been described as "monotonous," with one *New York Times* critic describing the homes as "less architecture than . . . quick, efficient packaging of a comfortable level of middle class taste done as neatly with buildings as Sears or J.C. Penney has ever been able to do it with clothes."[44] The Irvine developers, however, successfully avoided commercial strip development, and broke new ground in creating attached upper-income housing. Most of the housing targeted the high end of the market, with the percentage of subsidized affordable housing measuring only in the single digits. The development is heavily reliant on the automobile, with all the associated negative externalities that come with it, although by the late 1990s the city had managed to generate significant employment opportunities close to home, an estimated three jobs per household.[45]

Regarding quality-of-life issues, Irvine has fared well. In 2000, the *Ladies' Home Journal* ranked Irvine as the best city in the nation for women. A telephone survey the same year found that 95 percent of residents rated the quality of life there as excellent or good, with 64 percent selecting "excellent." In fact, residents in independent surveys rated all three communities highly. The new town movement proved successful in creating a sense of place and community.[46]

Though the new town communities share many similarities with Prairie Crossing, there are also many distinct differences. The most noteworthy differences are related to the scale, time frame, and type of development. With respect to scale, Irvine, the largest of the three communities, is home to 211,906 people (2010 U.S. Census), consists of more than 51,000 households, and covers nearly 30,000 acres. The Woodlands is the smallest of the three communities, yet still relatively large: 93,847 people, more than 19,000 households, and nearly 28,000 acres.[47] Prairie Crossing is just a fraction of the size of The Woodlands, and consequently is a totally different kind of development—the modest subdivision. Since the vast majority of real-estate development in the United States is small-scale subdivision,

Prairie Crossing offers a policy model that has the potential to make an impact on local ecology if it becomes accepted as industry best practices.

Because of the immense scale of the new town projects, time frame represents another important distinction. All three communities are still in the process of development. Prairie Crossing took only seven years from conception to the initial occupation, and required an additional fifteen years to reach full occupation, including the Station Village condominiums. While the Irvine development has changed its focus considerably over the years, Prairie Crossing represents a mode of development that more closely resembles typical urban development, one that focuses on a relatively short time horizon.

New town developments also represent a different type of development. They were designed to be self-contained towns or cities—large-scale developments that offered a significant range of employment opportunities, something far beyond the scope of Prairie Crossing and the standard subdivision.

Ann Forsyth's comprehensive analysis of the new town movement found it to be a viable alternative to sprawl in many respects, but one with definite limitations: "The case study developments certainly didn't change the whole culture, but they shifted preferences a little."[48] In areas of housing affordability, energy use, and influencing market trends, substantive change proved exceedingly difficult.

## The Prairie Crossing Charter School

The Prairie Crossing Charter School opened in 1999, initially teaching kindergarten through second grade. It has since expanded through eighth grade, and attendance is capped at 432 students. A nonexclusive, nondiscriminatory institution, the school serves the wider community; children from the Prairie Crossing development are not given priority.[49] Admittance is based on a lottery system in accordance with state law, though siblings of current students get priority if space permits.[50] It is not funded by property taxes, as are traditional Illinois public schools. State funding follows the student, irrespective of school district, with additional charter school funding provided by private donors and an annual auction and plant sale. The school's sponsor donors are a mix of local and environmentally friendly businesses.[51]

A Prairie Crossing resident originally conceived the idea for the charter school, and the Ranneys helped bring the project to fruition. The building is located next to the Byron Colby Barn near the entrance to the community. Charter schools in Illinois have greater freedom to experiment with innovative curriculum than do traditional public schools. The Prairie Crossing Charter School uses a curriculum based on environmental learning, which is not bound by the four walls of the classroom. The school has a library devoted to the environmental curriculum, located in a mid-nineteenth-century one-room schoolhouse that was moved to the community in 1996 from nearby Libertyville. Weather permitting, the students can be found out on the community's trails, sitting on mats, drawing, writing, or observing nature. The school has five guiding principles: (1) partnership with parents, (2) environmental stewardship, (3) ecological understanding, (4) academic rigor and innovation, and (5) promoting personal responsibility.[52]

The school endeavors to accommodate lower-income students. The $100 books, materials, and activities fee may be waived if a child is eligible for the federal school lunch program. A payment plan for the fee is also available. Because the school has a small student body that is dispersed over a relatively large geographic area—two school districts—it does not offer bus service. To accommodate families with transportation issues, there is a carpool program, as well as a parent volunteer program to transport students to and from home. Dozens of students, however, ride their bikes to school when the weather permits.

The school's curricular emphasis on the environment has the potential to sow discord in a congressional district that has elected representatives with diverse voting records.[53] The unique curriculum, however, does not appear to have stirred any controversy over time. Former principal Maria Sanborn did not report any concern or complaint about liberal bias in 2005.[54]

The launching of the Prairie Crossing Charter School was a success, unlike that of the charter school at Celebration, Disney's New Urbanism community that was built a stone's throw from the Magic Kingdom in Florida. A public relations disaster from the very beginning, Celebration School experienced student withdrawals, negative newspaper publicity, attempts to "stifle debate" about perceived inadequacies, and confrontational public meetings.[55] In contrast, Prairie Crossing's school has won multiple awards and currently has more requests for admittance than seats. It is considered one of the top elementary schools in the state; in 2014 it ranked 29th out of 866 Illinois public schools.[56] Recently, however, the school has been embroiled in controversy.

The Prairie Crossing Charter School serves two separate districts, Woodland 50 and Fremont 79. In May 2014, Woodland 50 filed a lawsuit against the Illinois State Charter School Commission, the Illinois State Board of Education, and the Prairie Crossing Charter School alleging that millions of dollars in state aid intended for Woodland was being "siphoned away" to the charter school and impairing Woodland's ability to serve its at-risk students. Nearly a third of Woodland's student body is considered at-risk, up from 18 percent just five years ago. Less than 2 percent of Prairie Crossing students fall into that category. Woodland received only $450,000 of an eligible $3.5 million in state aid; per state law, the remainder followed the students to the charter school. The lawsuit is an attempt to overturn the Illinois State Charter School Commission's 2014 five-year reauthorization of Prairie Crossing's certificate. "We believe Prairie Crossing Charter School is not fulfilling its state-mandated special purpose to educate at-risk students," said former Woodland board president Mark Vondracek.[57]

Geoff Deigan, executive director of the Prairie Crossing Charter School, argued that the real problem derives from the way Illinois funds education:

> The reality remains that PCCS, as a public school, is entitled to public dollars to educate its students. Woodland's claim that money is being "*siphoned*" to PCCS is not revealing the entire story. In Illinois, funding for public education actually follows the student. Unlike Woodland, who can issue tax referendums and receives property taxes through all residents within their district (whether they attend their school or not), PCCS's only revenue stream from the State is in the form of Per Capita Tuition Charge (PCTC) for students that attend our School. The PCTC is derived by the current funding formula (using General State Aid) that the State created to ensure that schools receive fair and equitable funding for each student they educate.[58]

Taking into consideration local property taxes and state aid, Woodland receives more money per student than Prairie Crossing.[59] The charter school engages in an outreach program for "educationally disadvantaged and at-risk students." The school has "developed flyers, PSAs, newspaper ads, press releases, and cover letters for flyers" toward that end. To further increase its exposure, Prairie Crossing has placed ads in *Reflejos*, a local Spanish-language newspaper.[60] The charter school argues that these efforts to increase minority student enrollment have been hindered by the state mandate of blind lottery admissions. The State Charter School Commission acknowledged the problem and granted renewal for five years at 100 percent funding, with a mandate of a "robust outreach" program for recruiting at-risk students. The Woodland District 50 lawsuit counters by arguing that Prairie Crossing's policies "construct barriers that deter increased at-risk student enrollment" through two principal means: the school lacks a Limited English Proficiency Program, and it does not meet the transportation needs of those students.[61] Executive Director Geoff Deigan publicly stated that Woodland's allegations are "unfounded."[62] Deigan, however, did not respond to repeated requests for an interview.

Diane Ravitch is a historian of education and a research professor at New York University. She is harshly critical of charter schools in general. In her education blog, she wrote: "Charter schools were created to help the neediest students. Now, however, many charters skim off the most advantaged students and avoid those who are needy. This harms the public schools, removing their best students and overloading them with the students who require the most services." Calling Prairie Crossing a "textbook case of charter skimming," she argued that "[t]he charter's avoidance of high-needs students is blatantly unfair."[63]

In an email exchange in which I questioned Dr. Ravitch about how the Prairie Crossing Charter School skims, she acknowledged that she had "not conducted research at the school."[64] She asserted that the lottery system used at Prairie Crossing is a "sorting mechanism" and that "the least functional families do not apply."[65] She did not specify any discriminatory policies or practices at the school or any related to "skimming." Instead, her objections seemed to be based on a strong philosophical opposition to charter school systems in general: "Charter schools are a form of privatization of a public service. They have less accountability or transparency than public schools. As the charter industry grows, it is being overtaken by rapacious chains that operate for profit. Even in states where for-profit charters are not legally allowed, the board may hire a for-profit to run the school."[66] The critique, however, is not a good fit for the Prairie Crossing Charter School.

Prairie Crossing is a nonprofit public school. The parallel public school district receives $200 more per student per year than does Prairie Crossing, which receives its funding directly from the state. The school's lottery system for admittance is mandated by state law and transparent; the annual draw is open to the public. All students who apply have an equal chance of selection; the school cannot cherry-pick its applicants. The school does not discriminate on the basis of academic performance. Students cannot be dismissed for poor grades. The remedy for failing to meet standards is repeating the grade. The school has, however, been criticized by the Illinois Board of Education "for its failure to educate students matching or even approaching the demographics of [the] Woodland [School District]."[67] As a result, it has launched an outreach program to advertise its availability to Spanish-speaking families. The application forms are available in Spanish, both online and in-person. Prairie Crossing's school is also subject to state accountability. The school charter has to be renewed every five years by a commission created by statute for that purpose. The most recent renewal vote, in April 2014, passed 5–4, a fairly narrow margin and not indicative of a bureaucratic rubber stamp. As this book goes to press, the lawsuit is still pending. In hearings, the presiding judge appeared to be critical of the charter school's reliance on carpooling for school transportation.[68]

The value of the charter school system in Illinois is that charters are essentially policy laboratories; they are permitted to experiment with curriculum, and Prairie Crossing has taken maximum advantage of this freedom.[69] The school employs an innovative environmentally based curriculum, which is congruent with the community's conservation agenda. The curriculum is premised on breaking down traditional barriers between subjects and using interdisciplinary units based on environmental themes. The school practices constructivist teaching and learning methods. Constructivism is premised on the idea that learning occurs when students are actively engaged in the learning process, constructing meaning by building on, adding to, or discarding previous knowledge and meaning. Learners do not passively receive knowledge but help construct their own through active engagement.[70] The approach has proven effective; the school's performance ranks in the top 5 percent in the state.

The charter renewal lawsuit has marred the school's otherwise highly successful academic performance. The lawsuit raises some legitimate issues; however, based upon the legal record, there is no evidence of bad faith on the school's part. The at-risk student population of the Woodland District has increased significantly in the last five years, from 18 to 30 percent. And the blind lottery requirement mandated by state statute presents problems for recruitment. The outreach program, which emphasizes foreign language advertising, may make a difference. In the school's fifteenth year of existence, its charter has been extended through 2019 pending appeal.

## Economic and Racial Diversity

"Economic and racial diversity" is the development's fifth guiding principle. The developers sought to extend the benefits generated by the conservation community model to all races and a mix of incomes because they view diversity as "essential to the future of our society." A wide variety of scholarship has stressed the importance of socioeconomic and racial diversity. Former secretary of labor Robert Reich has warned of the self-perpetuating tendency for the wealthy to seek out segregation of various forms, a phenomenon he calls "the secession of the successful." New Urbanist architect Andres Duany has argued for an end to the spatial inequities between the rich and poor that have led to what he refers to as "the balkanization created by sprawl." Urban scholars Blakely and Snyder have studied the movement toward "forting up"—the inclinations of the wealthy not only to sequester themselves behind gates and walls but also to hire their own private security forces to patrol their streets.[71]

In gated communities, the employment of physical barriers is a common method for achieving exclusivity. Wealth can serve the same purpose, and often produces racial homogeneity as an unfortunate byproduct. The ability to move into a particular type of housing is based on a requisite level of income, below which purchase is not possible. The preservation of open space in conservation communities comes at a price, as does green restoration, such as the resurrection of the extirpated grassland ecosystem at Prairie Crossing. And as Peter Huber, senior fellow at the Manhattan Institute, argues in his "Conservative Environmental Manifesto," "wealth is green": "The rich man secures his genetic posterity through quality, not quantity. . . . He puts some of his wealth into charity, some into art, some into his bird feeder, and some into the prairies beyond. . . . [T]he only form of poverty that is green is the poverty chosen freely by the man so rich—so rich in capital, so rich in spirit—that he freely chooses to spend his treasure preserving and advancing more life than his own."[72] Steve Hovany, a real-estate analyst from the Chicago area, estimates the Prairie Crossing preservation "premium" at 20 percent. Developer George Ranney placed the cost at a somewhat lower but still significant 14 percent.[73] Is the preservation premium an unavoidable consequence of conservation policy? And what effect did it have on economic and racial diversity at Prairie Crossing?

To evaluate whether Prairie Crossing succeeded in achieving the diversity goals set forth in the guiding principles, I again relied on resident surveys. The Ranneys acknowledge that they have had difficulty meeting their goal of racial diversity.[74] The results of the survey reflected that difficulty. Thirty households neglected to answer the race question. Of the 178 (out of 354 households) that did respond, 90 percent identified themselves as white, 5 percent as Asian, 3 percent as Hispanic, and less than 3 percent as African American. Although several African American residents cited the goal of racial diversity as a reason for moving into the development, Prairie Crossing has not even come close to achieving it. The most likely reason is the relatively high price of the homes, which were selling for between $299,900 and $439,900 in January 2004.

The relatively high cost of the homes has also negatively affected the goal of economic diversity. The survey found a mean household income of $134,671 for the 149 households that responded to that question. The median income was a similar $127,500. The residents are not wealthy retirees; the mean age for 181 reporting households was 46.5 years, with a median of 44 years. Clearly, Prairie Crossing residents are wealthy by any standard—national, regional, or local. The median household income for the development was three times the national average of $44,473 in 2004 dollars. It was also roughly three times the state average of $45,787. The 36-unit condominium complex was not included in the original survey because it was still under construction at that time. The two-to-three-bedroom units range from 1,700 to 2,700 square feet and are selling for $160,000 to $180,000 in 2014 dollars. The condominiums have full access to trails, footpaths, and all conservation amenities, though the complex is segregated from the homes in the southwest corner of the property. The inclusion of the condominium complex has undoubtedly lowered resident incomes for the development and may have slightly increased the racial diversity; however, the survey data shows that the development has not been able to meet the goals expressed in the guiding principles.

Prairie Crossing's residents are also highly educated. The mean and median levels of education for the 179 responding households were 18.1 and 19 years, respectively, which roughly corresponds to earning a master's degree. Though Prairie Crossing retains the right to restrict outsiders, to its credit it welcomes nonresidents on its trails and to its farm. A trail system links the property to the Liberty Prairie Reserve. It is possible to interact within the development with nonresidents of different backgrounds; however, it is likely that such interactions are relatively infrequent. From an educational, economic, and racial perspective, the development is probably best characterized as a fairly homogeneous, if not segregated, enclave.

## Creating a Geography of Somewhere

A confluence of several factors gave rise to suburbanization in America. Middle-class expectations about residential space began changing in the latter half of the nineteenth century, as public space became more crowded and congested and the urban environment became increasingly more polluted.[75] The middle class responded by seeking "separation and willful blindness" by commuting to and from the workplace without having to confront "the true nature of the urban society in which they lived."[76] Changes in technology made the separation of home and work possible, but they did not drive it. Economic elites seeking to increase the value of their landholdings on the urban periphery propelled the initial expansion of electrified trolleys and mass transportation.[77]

The federal government encouraged sprawl with carefully crafted policies designed to make use of surplus industrial capital. Housing construction boomed in the 1920s. In the 1930s, the newly created Federal Housing Authority underwrote home mortgages that helped further fuel suburban expansion. An increase in homeownership coincided with a dramatic increase in consumer durable goods—more residential space requires more stuff to fill it.[78] Though other forms of urban development, such as community-based social housing, were economically viable, and perhaps even socially preferable, suburban sprawl in America was a deliberate economic strategy that both local business elites and national politicians consciously promoted.

Veterans returning home from World War II touched off a frenzy of development. Following the war, subsidized loans from the Federal Housing Authority and the Veterans Administration facilitated the purchase of middle-class homes, often with little or no down payment. "Developers quickly learned" to capitalize on these subsidies. The application of mass production technology to housing construction significantly lowered costs, and in the process "revolutionized home building."[79] In the late 1940s and early 1950s, whole new towns sprang up on agricultural land, including Levittown on Long Island, which became home to more than 80,000 new residents.

Postwar economic expansion and aggressive effective marketing helped produce a new social status paradigm, the American Dream, as Judd and Swanstrom explain, "In the two decades after World War II, the suburban home, complete with a patio, barbecue grill, and a tree in the yard, occupied center stage in the American Dream. The suburban house was more than a physical structure; it was also the promised path to success."[80] This rapid development, with little regional planning, in pursuit of a very narrow definition of status and socioeconomic success, could not be easily undone when future generations began to understand the costs in environmental, energy, and social capital resources.

Prairie Crossing achieved its goal of creating place and community, two of the developer's original guiding principles. The extensive restoration of native grasses, prairie forbs, and indigenous fauna fostered a greater connection to the land among residents and prompted most of them to engage in a variety of socially enriching outdoor activities and to value civic participation, the subject matter of the following chapter. Both the development and the conservation community compared quite favorably to other communities that the residents had previously lived in. The conservation agenda did not prove to be divisive, and the continued emphasis on community over time helped Prairie Crossing avoid some of the pitfalls of living in a common-interest development.

The achievement of racial and economic diversity, however, remains elusive. The cost of buying green at Prairie Crossing is the probable cause of a rate of minority ownership that measures in the single digits. The addition of adjacent "granny flats" and a larger condominium complex with mixed-use development could have expanded opportunities for those with lower incomes. Granny flats were part of the original vision for the development; however, they were dropped in the face of residents' opposition. Limiting the customization of housing designs would also have lowered the costs of the single-family residences, perhaps further expanding opportunities. The lack of diversity at Prairie Crossing, however, is not an inherent flaw in the conservation community policy model. Green housing is very site specific, and several second-generation green communities have managed to attract a diverse demographic, a topic covered in chapter seven.

Amazon, perhaps the ultimate purveyor of the consumer durable goods that fill suburban homes, sells a bumper sticker that resonates: "Suburbia: Where they cut down the trees and name the streets after them." That pithy phrase speaks to the many critics of suburban sprawl. It was the repetitive monotony of sprawl, that "geography of nowhere" quality so many twentieth-century subdivisions have, that motivated the Ranneys to take a risk and try to create a new form of housing with a sense of place and community—a geography of somewhere.

# CHAPTER SIX

# CIVIC PARTICIPATION

For the first two-thirds of the twentieth
century a powerful tide bore Americans
into ever deeper engagement in the life
of their communities, but a few decades
ago—silently, without warning—that tide
reversed and we were overtaken by a
treacherous rip current. Without at first
noticing, we have been pulled apart from
one another and from our communities
over the last third of the century.

—Robert Putnam, *Bowling Alone*

Numerous scholars have noted that Americans are no longer as socially and politically engaged as they used to be. Evan McKenzie has explored this "culture
of non-participation" in the context of private governance in common-interest
developments. Oftentimes, residents fail to contribute in a meaningful way to the
process of making decisions about the management of their community. Many
such developments are run by the same small, select group of people year after
year. Edward Blakely and Mary Snyder similarly found a "lack of participation"
in community affairs in gated communities, some of which they described as
"fortresses." Whereas in the 1960s and 1970s Americans exhibited a high level
of social involvement, active in bowling leagues, PTA, church events, and civic
and political affairs, Robert Putnam found that there is now a "central crisis" of
non-participation "at the heart of our society." Americans have withdrawn from
civic participation on many different levels and undermined the nation's pool
of social capital.[1]

Prairie Crossing is by form and necessity a private government. Without the collective interests of a homeowners association, the restoration of prairie and wetlands in a common-interest property would not be possible. For the conservation community concept to succeed and spread as a policy model, such developments have to generate and sustain enough participation to avoid the problems that hinder conventional common-interest developments and foster non-participation in the era of suburban sprawl.

George Ranney thought the development's strong emphasis on community and promotion of a public-interest conservation agenda might lead to higher rates of political participation. But greater political engagement is not the only logical outcome of this policy model. Another, equally plausible scenario suggests that adding an extra layer of responsibility could result in less resident participation in community affairs due to the additional drain on the limited time and resources available to each individual. The effort required to manage the conservation of common properties while also maintaining and managing the traditional common-interest development infrastructure could result in less participation.

In exploring the political participation of Prairie Crossing residents, I distinguished between local and national levels of participation. I defined local political participation as being involved in private government through the Homeowners Association and voting in county, township, and municipal elections. I defined national participation as voting in national elections and engaging in political activity such as working for a candidate, attending a political rally or meeting, and influencing others to vote. Employing questions taken from the American National Election Studies (ANES) database (a record of public voting practices, opinions, and attitudes during election years since 1948), I utilized the survey to compare the political participation of Prairie Crossing's residents to that of the national cohort.[2]

## Prairie Crossing Local Political Participation

Common-interest developments frequently suffer from the kind of civic disengagement that McKenzie describes.[3] In assessing the participation of Prairie Crossing's residents in their community's private government, I relied upon the resident survey and also interviews with principal actors within the Homeowners Association. The unusually high rate of return of the survey itself—59 percent for a mass mailing—suggests a willingness on the part of residents to become involved in community affairs. The survey and interview data were at odds. More than 85 percent of residents in the survey characterized residents' involvement in the Homeowners Association as at least "somewhat active," with 28 percent selecting "very active." Less than 14 percent selected "not very active." Former Homeowners Association president and current board member John Breen and former conservation manager Michael Sands, in contrast, characterized participation as generally poor, based on residents' level of attendance at the association's meetings, and considered it similar to participation in conventional homeowners associations. However, it is possible to participate in governance without attending meetings by reading newsletters, reading and posting comments on the development's email list, discussing issues with fellow residents, and passing on comments and suggestions to Homeowners Association board members outside of the board meeting setting.

There is some evidence to support this social-networking mode of participation. Breen stated that residents frequently post to the email list, often within minutes of receiving information by email, telephone, or newsletter. Responses to postings are also common, timely, and occasionally "heated," depending on the topic. The survey recorded a relatively high degree of social contact among residents. More than 54 percent reported socializing with neighbors one or more times per week. And given the opportunity to write in community activities they had engaged in, residents listed a dozen activities that provide an opportunity for political networking, including bonfires, lectures, potluck dinners, and the farmers' market. Residents' satisfaction with Homeowners Association governance is also very high. Given an ordinal choice on the survey ranging from very satisfied to very dissatisfied, nearly three-quarters reported being at least satisfied with the governance, with less than 2 percent claiming to be very dissatisfied.

Though attendance at Prairie Crossing Homeowners Association meetings is poor and does not significantly depart from the level of attendance for conventional common-interest developments, the residents' involvement in private government cannot be fairly characterized as a "culture of non-participation." Residents appear to be reasonably well informed about governance, and as the impassioned exchanges on the email list demonstrate, they participate using technology when community circumstances sufficiently motivate them.

Homeowners association boards are often controlled by the same few people, year after year. Some individuals enjoy the power and influence and regularly seek reelection. Other communities suffer from apathy and a general lack of participation, which makes it difficult to fill board positions. Prairie Crossing's board exhibits a willingness to share the workload. Five different residents took turns as board president from 2005 to 2014. The Prairie Crossing Homeowners Association also employs several permanent committees staffed by residents, such as the Environmental Stewardship Committee and the Architectural Review Committee, and occasionally ad hoc committees that make recommendations about specific problems or issues. The association appears to govern with a fair degree of transparency. The eight-page monthly newsletter *Meadow Mix* keeps residents updated on community proposals and rules changes and provides contact information for feedback. The Environmental Stewardship Committee and Architectural Review Committee have their own monthly columns located on the same pages every month, making it easy for residents to stay informed about important community issues. Conserve Lake County, the Prairie Crossing Farm, and the Liberty Prairie Foundation also have regular monthly columns. A "Quick Picks" section on the front page highlights the coming month's community activities. And once a year, as the following chapter details, the Homeowners Association publishes the results of its annual resident survey on the community's guiding principles.

## Prairie Crossing National Political Participation

The 2004 presidential election was dominated by the Iraq War, and in some red states also by specific social issues such as same-sex marriage. Congressional elections, however, while occasionally influenced by presidential coattails, still have a significant local component.[4] Such was the case in Prairie Crossing's Eighth Congressional District in 2004, and the outcome revealed the latent capacity of conservation communities to respond to salient environmental issues. This election pitted a relatively unknown Democratic challenger against a thirty-year incumbent branded as one of the "Dirty Dozen" legislators in Congress by the League of Conservation Voters. Prairie Crossing voters provided nearly 15 percent of the margin of victory for the greener candidate. Subsequent elections from 2006 through 2012 did not have the same environmental component.

To measure Prairie Crossing's involvement in national political activities in the 2004 general election, I employed fifteen questions taken from the ANES database. The questions fall under the category "Public Opinion and Electoral Behavior" and cover a wide variety of political participation activities, including voter turnout, voter registration, working for a party or candidate, wearing a campaign advertisement, attending a political meeting, influencing others to vote, interest in national political campaigns and general public affairs, and watching or reading about political campaigns. The value of using the ANES database is that it provides a control group, national in scope, with which the activities and opinions of Prairie Crossing's residents can be compared.

As measured against ANES data, Prairie Crossing's residents appeared to have significantly higher levels of participation in many areas of specific political activity. They exceeded the ANES control group by substantial margins in seven of the fifteen measured categories, even when that control group was adjusted to fit the development's demographics for median age, education, and income (see table 1).

For example, during the 2004 presidential campaign, nearly 36 percent of Prairie Crossing's residents reported attending a political meeting, a considerably higher rate of attendance than the 7 to 8 percent recorded for Americans of comparable median age and income demographics or the 12 percent recorded for comparably educated Americans in the ANES survey. According to the ANES survey, no year in the last several decades saw a level of participation on the national level comparable to that in Prairie Crossing. More than 98 percent of the development's residents reported reading at least one or two magazine articles about the campaign, more than double the figure for their education and income counterparts on the national level and more than triple that for their overall age group. Nearly half of residents reported reading "a good many articles," the same percentage of the control group for education and income that reported reading at least one article. Working for a party or candidate shows a high degree of commitment to a candidate or cause and generally requires a considerable time investment. Prairie Crossing's residents reported a very high level of participation in this area. Across all demographic groups, "working for a party or candidate" produced results in the low single digits, none higher than 6 percent. In the survey, nearly 23 percent of residents reported participating in a campaign, more than four times as many as in their overall income demographic.

Perhaps the nature of the 2004 congressional campaign in the development's district can partially explain the high level of participation. As I detail in the next section, the Eighth Congressional District election that year was a closely contested race. The two candidates, long-time Republican incumbent Phil Crane and Democratic challenger Melissa Bean, offered very different leadership visions for the district, particularly regarding environmental issues. Bean ran on a green-friendly platform, receiving an endorsement from the Sierra Club; she opposed many of President Bush's anti-environmental initiatives. In stark contrast, Crane had had a poor environmental voting record throughout his career. The clear

TABLE I. Comparison of Political Participation Activities
in the 2004 General Election

| Activities | Survey responses in the American National Election Studies (ANES) database* | | | | |
| --- | --- | --- | --- | --- | --- |
| | Age: born 1959–1974 | Education: college degree | Income: 96–100th percentile | All national respondents | Prairie Crossing residents |
| Attended a political meeting | 7% | 12% | 8% | 7% | **36**% |
| Care who wins congressional election | 62% | 76% | 73% | 66% | **89**% |
| Read about campaign in newspapers | 61% | 81% | 78% | 67% | **81**% |
| Care who wins presidential campaign | 85% | 94% | 86% | 85% | **97**% |
| Tried to influence how others vote | 47% | 55% | 58% | 48% | **60**% |
| Gave money to help a campaign | 8% | 22% | 31% | 13% | **45**% |
| Wore a button or put a sticker on a car | 22% | 21% | 24% | 21% | **38**% |
| Read magazine articles on the campaign | 29% | 46% | 46% | 28% | **99**% |
| Worked for a party or candidate | 2% | 4% | 5% | 3% | **23**% |

*ANES respondents selected to fit Prairie Crossing's demographics for median age, education, and income.

difference between the environmental policy platforms of the two candidates
may help to explain the high level of activism on the part of Prairie Crossing's
residents, especially given the residents' reporting that living in the development
had greatly increased their awareness of both local and national environmental
issues. In contrast, the development's interest in the presidential campaign was
not appreciably different from that of the control groups, even in light of the
contentious nature of the Iraq War at that time. Residents also reported much
higher rates of campaign contributions to candidates and parties, and higher rates
of using a campaign button or bumper sticker advertisement. Lastly, residents
reported a much higher interest in general public affairs when controlled for
demographics, with more than 60 percent reporting that they were interested

"most of the time," compared to 39 and 37 percent, respectively, for the education and income control groups.

Relative to their national peers (i.e., age, education, and income) Prairie Crossing's residents do not stand out in most of the basic areas of political participation, such as voter turnout, voter registration, or gathering information from the convenient news sources. When considered in the light of non-mainstream political activity, however, such as attending meetings, contributing money, displaying campaign messages, and seeking additional campaign information, they excel. They also appear to be far more interested in local political issues. Residents attributed their unusually strong interest in local environmental concerns to their residence at Prairie Crossing. Given the relatively high-profile role that the environment played in the 2004 congressional election, it is reasonable to conclude that this may have been a factor in the enhanced interest in that race.

## Prairie Crossing Voting Behavior

Unfortunately, Prairie Crossing's residents are not seated in a self-contained voting precinct, which would have made it easy to analyze their voting behavior. Since the development's initial occupation in 1994, its residents have been divided into two voting precincts. Redistricting following the 2010 census moved them from the Avon 45 and Fremont 123 precincts to Avon 50 and Fremont 110. The Fremont 123 precinct consisted wholly of Prairie Crossing residents.[5] Fremont 110 contains a relatively small number of nonresidents. Voter registration totals can vary daily as voters move in and out of the precincts. In June 2014, Fremont 110 had 334 registered Prairie Crossing voters out of a total of 386 (87 percent). Both Avon precincts, however, contained a majority of non–Prairie Crossing residents. In June 2014, Avon 50 had 350 Prairie Crossing voters out of a total of 896 (39 percent).[6]

It is, however, possible to draw reliable conclusions regarding residents' voting behavior. Between 2003 and 2012, Lake County conducted thirteen local, state, and national elections involving Prairie Crossing precinct candidates.[7] In each of those elections, the Fremont precincts exceeded the Lake County average for voter turnout. In several cases, the Fremont turnout surpassed the average turnout by a wide margin. For example, in the local election of April 17, 2007, Fremont 123 turnout was 43.42 percent, compared to a county average of 17.12 percent. In another local election, in 2003, Fremont 123 nearly tripled the county-wide average of 21.90 percent. Out of 481 precincts in Lake County, Fremont precincts had the highest voter turnout in three elections and placed in the top three in six of nine elections (precinct-level data is not available for the four elections predating November 7, 2006). The lowest turnout ranking relative to other county precincts occurred in the April 5, 2011, local election, a 34.8 percent turnout and forty-fifth ranking. But even this low turnout was more than double the county average of 15.04 percent.[8]

Avon 45 and Avon 50 (post-2010) precincts are combined voting districts that contain a majority of non–Prairie Crossing voters. Conclusions regarding voting behavior in those precincts are somewhat tentative; however, the data trends in the same direction as that for the self-contained Fremont 123 precinct and the Prairie Crossing–dominated Fremont 110 precinct. For example, though voter turnout was never higher in the Avon precincts than in the Fremont precincts, in all thirteen elections Avon voters outvoted the county average by at least 5.94 percent. The mean departure from the county-wide average was +7.85 percent.

For three elections between 2003 and 2005, I attempted to estimate the full Prairie Crossing voter turnout for the two precincts. Assuming that non–Prairie Crossing voters in the Avon 45 precinct turned out at the county average, I estimated the full Prairie Crossing community turnout for two local elections for village trustee in 2003 and 2005, and also the presidential general election in 2004.[9] The odd-year elections produced similar estimates of 47.5 and 48.3 percent voter turnout, both of which exceeded the county average by more than 20 percent. The 2004 general election produced a reconstructed estimate of 90 percent for Prairie Crossing voters, exceeding the rate for their Lake County counterparts (72 percent) and the national mean (77 percent). The resident survey provides an independent check for the reconstructed 2004 estimate; it reported a voter turnout of 92.3 percent. Compared to their specific demographics, Prairie Crossing voters voted at a rate slightly higher than their mean income level (89 percent) and less than a percentage point lower than their mean educational level (93 percent).[10]

In 2004 Prairie Crossing was approaching full occupancy, and the congressional election in the Eighth District that year provided an interesting test of the community's commitment to green activism. Republican congressman Phil Crane had been the district's representative for three decades, handily winning his previous election with 58 percent of the vote. His Democratic challenger for the district's House seat in 2004 was Melissa Bean. The two candidates offered clear-cut choices on environmental policy issues. Crane's League of Conservation Voters environmental scores were 6, 5, 13, and 10 percent, respectively, for the last four sessions of Congress prior to the 2004 election.[11] In 2004 he was named one of the "Dirty Dozen" by the League of Conservation Voters, the group's trademark list of the worst anti-environmental incumbents, for having demonstrated "a blatant bias toward corporate polluters and special interests over Illinois families."[12] Bean countered with a campaign endorsed by environmental organizations. The higher turnout for the presidential election produced an upset. Bean narrowly defeated the long-time incumbent by just 874 votes out of more than 146,000 ballots cast. Prairie Crossing's contribution to Bean's victory was 130 votes, or 14.9 percent, above Bean's district-wide winning margin of 50.2 percent. Bean's tenure in office rewarded environmental voters. The difference between Crane's and Bean's environmental legislative voting records in the 108th and 109th congressional sessions was 74 points. Her lifetime League of Conservation Voters scorecard totaled 85 when she left Congress in 2011.[13]

The resident survey data revealed a high level of attentiveness regarding the Crane-Bean congressional campaign. More than 78 percent responded that they were "very much interested" in the 2004 campaign, 25–30 points higher than the ANES education and income control groups. Caring about who won the congressional election generated differences of 12–16 percent relative to the education and income control groups. In contrast, the interest in the presidential campaign among residents was not appreciably different from that of the control group. Though the data cannot specifically link the Bean votes to green activism, it is likely to have played a role given the environment's relatively high profile in the election.

The survey results date to 2006. Has anything changed in the development in the intervening years? The Homeowners Association, with the help of the Prairie Crossing Institute, still conducts an annual survey on the guiding principles and makes it available to all residents in a report posted on the community's website and in summary form in *Meadow Mix*. The annual survey does not provide extensive data on resident behavior, as did the detailed original survey, but it does provide insight into residents' support for the conservation agenda and the sense of place and community, which remains strong. Analysis of voting data also confirms that civic participation has remained high. The organizations and institutions affiliated with Prairie Crossing have continued to extend their reach since 2006. In 2012 the Liberty Prairie Conservancy changed its name to Conserve Lake County to better reflect its expanded vision. The Homeowners Association is not dominated by the same few individuals, and participation on the board has been healthy. *Meadow Mix* continues to reflect resident interest and participation in conservation and community.

Every year in the survey, the Homeowners Association asks residents to rate two questions related to the guiding principles on a scale of 1 to 10 (10 being the highest): "How important is this principle to you?" and "How well has Prairie Crossing as a community implemented this principle over the last year?" Residents are also given an open-ended opportunity to write in comments regarding any of the guiding principles. Their feedback helps the association identify and address community problems. The surveys generally produce a response rate of between 15 and 25 percent. The results show that the residents themselves take the guiding principles seriously. During the years 2006–2010, no principle mean ranked lower than 7.6 in terms of importance, and only six times over that five-year period did a principle score lower than 8.0.[14] The median for importance surveyed between 8.0 and 10.0 for every principle during the time frame. Implementation in every survey lagged behind importance.

With respect to community implementation of the principles, the residents viewed economic and racial diversity as the only principle that was not being realized.[15] That principle had a mean ranging between 3.6 and 5.1, with a median of 4.0 every year except 2010, when it was 5.0. The annual surveys identified economic and racial diversity as "the most difficult principle to achieve." The survey mean for economic viability ranged between 6.7 and 7.3 and was the second-lowest-rated principle for implementation. The biggest concern regarding economic viability, according to write-in comments, was high county taxes. The remaining principles all scored high in survey mean implementation: environmental protection and enhancement, 7.4–8.8; a healthy lifestyle, 7.7–8.3; a sense of place, 7.7–8.9; a sense of community, 7.8–8.8; convenient and efficient transportation, 7.0–7.2; energy conservation, 6.7–7.3; lifelong learning and education, 7.2–8.1; and aesthetic design and high-quality construction, 7.2–7.7. Overall, the survey suggests that residents have embraced all of the guiding principles and rate the community's implementation of them as successful, with the exception of economic and racial diversity.

## Running for Office

The residents of Prairie Crossing have an extensive record of public service at the state and municipal levels of government. At least twelve residents have held elected positions in ten different offices. Several have noteworthy records of service. Sandy Cole has served as the 62nd District representative in the Illinois General Assembly since 2007. She is also a former Lake County board member and Forest Preserve commissioner. Michael Bond was elected to one term in the Illinois State Senate from the 31st District after serving on the local Woodland District 50 School Board. Jeff Werfel and Ron Jarvis served together as trustees for the Village of Grayslake from 2011 to 2015. It was Werfel's second stint as a trustee for Grayslake. He is also on the board of directors for the Central Lake County Joint Action Water Agency, a public utility that provides drinking water for more than 200,000 people in the county. Prairie Crossing residents have held positions on several other government boards, including the Grayslake Library Board, the Grayslake District 27 School Board (high school), the Grayslake Park District Board, and the Prairie Crossing Charter School Board. At least seven residents have been members of the Charter School Board since 1999. For a modest-sized subdivision, Prairie Crossing residents have amassed a significant record of public service involving the environment, education, water policy, and state, county, and municipal government in just twenty years of existence.[16]

## Has the Culture Changed?

Prairie Crossing is a common-interest development, managed by a private government by both design and necessity. It could not preserve open space and create, maintain, and conserve the land without at the same time owning common property held in trust for the public good. Several scholars have noted a trend of withdrawal from civic participation in American society over the last few decades. Common-interest developments, while offering many potential benefits, also frequently experience a "culture of non-participation." In a fast-paced society in which even small children have a full plate of social obligations, the need for citizens to participate in private governance adds another layer of responsibility for people already encumbered by multiple commitments. Prairie Crossing represents an experiment in urban policy that seeks to increase that governing burden further by adding yet another responsibility, stewardship of the land. An important question regarding conservation communities is whether the additional burden will cause further withdrawal from civic participation.

Prairie Crossing's developers sought to change the culture by emphasizing community, beginning with the sales pitch and continuing through occupation and daily community life. The data reveals that they have achieved a measure of success. Surveys suggest that residents are both active in community governance and satisfied with the results. Participation in local affairs does not end at the development's borders. Residents' participation in municipal elections has been much higher than that of their Lake County peers. Local voting in the self-contained Prairie Crossing precinct in the 2003 and 2005 consolidated elections equaled or exceeded the national turnout for congressional elections in 1974, 1986, 1990, and 1998, which traditionally have much higher levels of turnout. The 2003 turnout also equaled or exceeded the national turnout in 1958, 1970, 1978, and 1994. More than eight in ten residents reported that moving into the development had increased their awareness of local environmental issues, compared to 58 percent reporting the same for national environmental issues. And Prairie Crossing policies have had an impact locally. The Village of Grayslake changed its zoning ordinance to permit small lot construction, "as small as the developer cares to build," as long as at least half of the property is preserved as contiguous open space. Zoning was formerly limited to one-acre lots.[17] Numerous residents have also served as officeholders in a diverse array of government bodies.

On the national political stage, Prairie Crossing residents have remained active. The residents vote in national elections at much higher rates than the mean national voter turnout; however, their turnout has not differed appreciably from that of their peers when controlled for education and income levels. Where Prairie Crossing residents have excelled is in organized political activity. They attend meetings, display campaign messages, contribute money, work for a party or candidate, and seek additional campaign information at rates considerably higher than those of their income and educational demographics. There is sufficient evidence to suggest that Prairie Crossing's emphasis on involvement in community affairs has produced an increase in civic participation.

# CHAPTER SEVEN

# NATURE'S SUBURB

> Never doubt that a small group
> of thoughtful, committed citizens
> can change the world. Indeed, it
> is the only thing that ever has.
>
> —Margaret Mead

In *Changes in the Land,* environmental historian William Cronon persuasively argues that the New England colonists held a concept of property markedly different from the Native American belief—a contrast that caused ecological transformation beginning when the first colonists arrived in the region and continuing through the nineteenth century. The colonial emphasis on land as a private commodity traded in the marketplace (rather than Native usufruct rights of land held in common for its value in renewable natural products) changed the land dramatically in less than two centuries. Land speculation that tended to ignore ecological qualities generated good profits for speculators and "marked an important new way of perceiving the New England landscape, one that turned land itself into a commodity."[1] This decoupling of economics from ecology resulted in the extirpation and extinction of scores of species, the introduction of exotic invasives, and in many cases a total reordering of the natural landscape throughout much of North America.[2]

Prairie Crossing as an exemplar of the conservation community policy model is a concerted remedial attempt to bring economics and ecology back into balance after nearly four centuries of careless, if not reckless, land development. As a lone development, Prairie Crossing cannot impact the national or regional ecology. For that, the conservation community policy model must take root, spread throughout the real-estate industry, and achieve acceptance within diverse political jurisdictions.

## Prairie Crossing as Policy Model

Two categories of policy attributes contributed to Prairie Crossing's success: constitutional organization and physical construction. Constitutional organization refers to the internal policy approach, organization, and structure of the development corporation that plans and builds a given community. The critical element of the organization is the presence of a committed developer. Both Steve Apfelbaum, who headed the restoration work, and Michael Sands, who headed the environmental management team, emphasized this component. Apfelbaum referred to committed owners as "the biggest missing link"—the most important element—in the policy process.[3] Without a strong commitment from the developer, profit incentives and corner-cutting can overwhelm a project and mitigate or destroy the conservation value of the development. Secondly, while perhaps not absolutely necessary, the adoption of a set of guiding principles is important. The Ranneys repeatedly emphasized the value of the principles they drew up for Prairie Crossing, adding that they have "stood up well" over time. Sands stated that the principles were very useful as a foundation to which the developers returned whenever conflicts arose between profits and conservation. The developers never sought to maximize any single guiding principle. Sands spoke of "constant tradeoffs" between competing principles.[4] A set of guiding principles, therefore, can give structure to the planning and development process, which is ongoing and not merely relegated to the blueprint planning and conceptual stages. The implementation of Prairie Crossing's principles has largely been successful, and the residents themselves have embraced them.

Another crucial element of constitutional organization is the presence of an environmental policy founder. Michael Sands, a resident of Prairie Crossing, played this role there from the beginning. He created the position of "environmental team leader" from scratch, and he helped transition the community to new conservation management when he stepped down in 2010. George Ranney stressed the necessity for an environmental manager to work with the developers of a project such as Prairie Crossing, characterizing Sands's role as as critical and "necessary to keep things on track" and ensure the "integrity" of the planning and developmental process. Ranney believes that it is best for such a leader to emerge from within, as Sands did, and be someone who has an "investment" in the community. Sands is of the opinion that if a suitable candidate does not emerge naturally, the developer will need to find someone with natural resource experience to nurture the development through the critical early stages. Even a mature community needs experience and commitment.[5]

A committed emphasis on community that begins with the sales pitch is recommended to reinforce social expectations and to effect the change in cultural norms needed to achieve both conservation and community goals. Encouraging and even soliciting residents' early participation on various committees during the construction phase will help solidify a base of positive participation. At Prairie Crossing, rotating residents on and off committees that substantively impact policy before the Homeowners Association takes over has empowered the residents and fostered an emotional commitment to the community. When residents are given such opportunities to engage with the policy process, they feel as though their opinions matter.

The creation and maintenance of a permanent educational network can make residents more environmentally conscious and help strengthen their commitment to the conservation agenda. At Prairie Crossing, burn schools, Liberty Prairie Foundation programs, Conserve Lake County seminars, Prairie Patrols, Colby Barn lectures, and the *Meadow Mix* newsletter all contribute to the high level of local ecological awareness. Such enhanced awareness with reinforcement of acquired green-friendly behaviors is required to change the culture and reverse the pervasive trend of the tyranny of small decisions. When a conservation-based curriculum is offered at the local school, as it is at the Prairie Crossing Charter School, the importance of conservation is passed along to new generations. The charter school is open to students from outside the community, and those children take the ideas that they learn back to their homes in the larger community.

Similarly, the creation and maintenance of a community network that organizes cultural events can help bind residents together and also permits the integration and transmission of social norms that break down barriers for not only ecological land management but also the creation of distinct community. Prairie Crossing has always been open to the public, and the community's contributions to causes such as the underpass walkway enabling easier access to the Liberty Prairie Reserve help promote the development's conservation mission and open-space preservation to greater Grayslake.

Prairie Crossing's environmental team leader, the Liberty Prairie Foundation, and some of the community's residents have been active within the network of conservation policy organizations, and that involvement has been essential to the export of Prairie Crossing's conservation community concept to other regions of the country. As policy learning takes place through on-site visits and through the exchange of trade secrets, the development can serve as an example of best practices. Only through the substantial export and replication of the Prairie Crossing policy model can it help to mitigate regional and possibly national environmental degradation.

The second category of Prairie Crossing's policy structure is the physical construction of the community. Spreading the homes throughout the property helped foster within the residents a greater emotional commitment to the land. Clustering the homes within one corner of the complex would have preserved the same quantity of open space in a more cost-effective manner, and would have yielded the same conservation benefits, but it would have reinforced and symbolized the "man apart from nature" cognitive and psychological construct. Having wetlands and prairie in their own backyards has helped integrate the residents into nature. It also encourages hands-on stewardship as residents construct bluebird boxes, plant native species in their yards, and cyclically burn their private plantings. Particularly in the Midwest, where nearly all of the tallgrass prairie ecosystems have been destroyed or extensively modified, it is important to have place-based ecological restoration that provides biotic corridors for the transmission of genetic material between populations. Conserve Lake County promotes place-based ecology with its Conservation@Home program, which offers consultations, classes, and workshops designed to transition traditional bluegrass lawns into more eco-friendly landscapes based on the indigenous ecosystem that occupied the space before the industrial and agricultural revolutions of the nineteenth and twentieth centuries.

The Ranneys believe that the construction of conservation amenities such as trails is essential in the early stages of a development, to broadcast to prospective buyers that the developers are committed to open-space preservation. It is also important that residents feel an attachment to the land. Sustainable conservation-friendly activities such as boating, fishing, skating, hiking, and birdwatching help develop an ethic of land stewardship within the residents—who can then pass the ethic across the generations. The biophilic nature of the open prairie provides an ambience that is comfortable for residents and visitors alike. The conservation amenities at Prairie Crossing have also helped create community, offering residents an opportunity to enjoy nature with their neighbors, as 83 percent reported doing. The range of activities available, all a short walk from home—horseback riding, viewing farm animals, a fitness center, boating, swimming, fishing, birdwatching, hiking, ice-skating, and biking—is wider than even most luxury and prestige communities offer. And these activities provide an emotional connection to the land that golf courses, tennis courts, and swimming pools generally do not.

The physical structures that occupy the land are also important. At Prairie Crossing, the windmills and the working organic farm prominently symbolize the conservation community concept and mission, and provide daily reminders that people and their homes are a part of nature. The transplanted nineteenth-century buildings and the Midwestern architecture of the homes help reinforce a positive sense of place and community in a way that conventional construction often does not. The homes are equipped with the latest in energy-saving technology, which makes them 50 percent more energy efficient than most contemporary homes—an important contribution to conservation. The impact is significant; one-third of the nation's energy is used to heat buildings.

If Prairie Crossing's conservation agenda has a shortcoming, it is education, particularly regarding transportation and the problems associated with planting nonnative species. The development failed in its attempt to change residents' dependence on the automobile. The relatively high level of wealth in the community has cushioned most residents from high gasoline prices. Residents still appear to prefer the expediency of door-to-door transportation in their vehicles of choice, irrespective of energy costs. Few suburban communities have more transportation alternatives than Prairie Crossing. Two separate Metra rail lines, offering more comfort and cleaner facilities than Chicago Transit Authority trains, and a highly organized homeowners association with the convenience of a community email list still have not persuaded residents to use mass transit or carpool in large numbers. While residents clearly understand the value of planting natives (nearly 82 percent in my survey did so), they still tended to harbor the misconception that planting anything green is beneficial. More than 43 percent of the surveyed households reported planting nonnatives, and only 39 percent selected the 70/30 ratio of native meadow/turf for their property. While seemingly benign, garden and landscape plants can be major contributors to conservation problems. A total ban on chemical applications might also have been helpful. The Homeowners Association considered but rejected a ban as too difficult to enforce. The community discourages the use of chemicals, however, and the adoption of voluntary means has its own advantages. Coercion can breed discontent and can undermine community living. Social pressure and a desire to maintain the "perfect" lawn still has some influence at Prairie Crossing.

The development's greatest failure, however, has been in the area of socio-economic and racial diversity, a fact noted by the residents themselves in the annual Prairie Crossing Institute surveys. Prairie Crossing is overwhelmingly white, relatively well-to-do, and highly educated. A resident walking the community trails is not likely to encounter a lower-middle-class minority person unless he or she is visiting the Liberty Prairie Reserve and crossing over on the trails. (However, the development's policies do permit and encourage outsiders' use of their amenities, in contrast to most other private developments.) Prairie Crossing is 90 percent white, and only 2 percent black and 3 percent Hispanic. The median annual income for the development is nearly three times that of the state. The median income probably understates the wealth required to buy into Prairie Crossing due to the fact that some of the residents are retirees, who generally have high asset wealth but lower annual incomes. The development is essentially an enclave of educated white wealthy professionals. The "premium" required to preserve the open space excluded the lower middle class, and perhaps even some of the middle middle class, from the pool of prospective buyers. It also lends some support to Peter Huber's thesis that wealth is required to help save the environment.[6] George Ranney places the environmental premium at 14 percent of the purchase price of the home. The quality of the homes actually leads to a slightly higher premium, 17 percent, because the houses are "semi-custom" products. Ranney argues that the open space could have been reduced from 60 to 50 percent to accommodate an additional 150 homes.[7] Such a scenario would have boosted profits 12 percent and possibly lowered the prices of the homes, but probably not enough to substantively impact socioeconomic diversity. If the original "granny flat" plan had been implemented, the development would likely have exhibited greater diversity. The homeowners themselves defeated the plan, and also unsuccessfully opposed the construction of the village center near the train stations.[8] Cost-cutting could have reduced the prices of the homes; however, such measures would likely have resulted in a reduction in environmental quality, as Ranney conceded. A less custom housing product, slightly higher density, and careful site selection utilizing place-based ecology might have made the concept more viable across a range of incomes. The cost of preserving and restoring open space is significant, but it can be done in a way that maintains economic viability.

## The Developmental Process

Frank Martin, working for Shaw Homes, served as the developmental manager for Prairie Crossing from the outset in the late 1980s until July 1997, when he was hired away to play the same role in the Hidden Springs conservation development in Idaho. Martin actually lives in the communities he is building. What he sees on a day-to-day basis gives him a feel for how well the development is progressing. As he said, "my eyes are worth a thousand words." The "biggest challenge" at Prairie Crossing, he said, was educating the contractors, architects, landscapers, and designers regarding the novel conservation aspects of the development. In the late 1980s and early 1990s, green development was in its infancy, and the founding concepts of Prairie Crossing were "foreign" to most contractors. The planning stage took two years before the development team broke ground. It "took a lot of time to convince" contractors that the extra costs for the vertical construction (e.g., energy-efficiency features) would still keep the price of the homes within a marketable range. Two indispensable aspects of Prairie Crossing, in Martin's opinion, were the conservation easement and the agreement with the nearby landfill. The conservation easement was the development's "saving grace"; it provided the necessary guarantee to prospective buyers that the open space would never be developed. It also furnished a "premium on a square foot basis" that helped pay for the open-space preservation. The landfill agreement, which guaranteed that the owner of the disposal site would buy any home that had not sold after 180 days, also eased homebuyers' concerns about any potential negative impacts of being so close to the facility.[9]

Martin is in agreement with a number of the other principal actors in the Prairie Crossing development that the guiding principles supplied a firm foundation during the planning and design stages. He later employed a similar set of "core values and guiding principles" at Hidden Springs. The Prairie Crossing design team was "committed" to the principles and "did not cut corners" in pursuit of profits. Martin did note, however, that while they were cognizant that economics were important for the development to be successful, profits were not the dominant factor during the developmental process.[10]

Gaylord Donnelley and the Ranneys hired landscape architect Bill Johnson of Berkeley, California, to translate their green ideas to paper. (Martin later hired Johnson to work with him again on the Hidden Springs project.) Johnson initially envisioned the development as "a 'farm village'—a compact development surrounded by agriculture."[11] That vision then broadened "early in the game" into "a larger preservation effort," one that not only preserved the rural character of the land but involved a wider restoration of the lost indigenous ecosystem. Peter Schaudt of Chicago joined the landscape planning team in 1994 and stayed for five years. He integrated the various parts of the first phase of development and saw himself as "the vehicle between Bill Johnson's vision and the Ranneys' plan." He developed the designs for the village green, the farmers' market, and the hiking paths and trails. Calthorpe Associates, a Berkeley, California–based urban planning firm that specializes in transportation-oriented designs, planned and designed the Station Village and Square in 1996.[12]

To help prospective buyers conceptualize the native prairie landscape design, four initial-phase buyers were recruited to allow their land to "serve as demonstrations" for the alternative residential designs.[13] This helped promote the native planting concept and set the change-the-culture idea into motion. The prairie and wetlands restoration efforts were "expensive," but the development got the money back through open-space premiums on home prices and through green infrastructure savings.[14]

Martin mentioned that there were several things, in retrospect, that he wishes he had done differently at Prairie Crossing. The farm ultimately proved to be successful, both as an organic operation and as a marketing tool for the development. The developers themselves farmed the land for the first eight years, however, and that was a mistake. Farming is too specialized an enterprise. Martin now recommends "incentivizing" the farming operation from the beginning as a "stand-alone" business. "Developers shouldn't be farming," he argues. Farms can be profitable, but they need to be run efficiently by established farmers.[15]

To impact the community's racial and socioeconomic demographics, Martin recommends "diversification of product." More diversity in lot size, home size, and home design, he argued, would have increased minority ownership and lower-income occupancy. He recommends home sizes as low as 1,000 or 1,200 square feet and the inclusion of "granny flats." He employed these lessons at Hidden Springs, which offered far greater diversity in home construction. At Hidden Springs, approximately 24–30 homes (out of 800) were built with separate apartments over the garages, and home prices ranged from $130,000 to $1,000,000. It is pricing, Martin believes, that has made the goals of racial and economic diversity so difficult to achieve at Prairie Crossing.[16]

Lastly, Martin would have brought in the charter school earlier. The Prairie Crossing community is divided into two school districts. Some neighbors have children in different schools, and greater coordination regarding education would have better helped bind the community together.

Conservation development is very site specific. Both Michael Sands and Frank Martin recommend working with the land to minimize disruption to plant and animal communities. Martin used densification in the flat areas at Hidden Springs, where he was confronted with elevation differences of 900 feet, compared to only 30–40 feet at Prairie Crossing. This allowed him to reduce mass grading of the building sites, and also to hide the homes in valleys to protect the viewscape. At the Prairie Crossing site, the design options were more flexible. Homes were spread throughout the open space in clusters to help integrate the residents with nature. Substantial infrastructure cost savings can result from the narrowing of streets, the elimination of curbs and sewers, and the use of walking paths and trails instead of sidewalks. A landscape suitability analysis should be conducted as part of the design process to consider a wide range of factors, including soils, vegetation, wildlife, hydrology, geology, topography, climate, and placement of essential human infrastructure. Prairie Crossing was able to save and restore land by developing it. Other sites may be less suitable for development, depending on human needs and natural conditions.

Prairie Crossing was among the first conservation communities, and it has been an influential one. The next section explores second-generation conservation developments, the debt they owe to Prairie Crossing, and the innovations they have used to improve the policy model.

## Exporting the Conservation Community Model

Michael Sands served as the environmental manager of Prairie Crossing for the first fifteen years of the development. Energetic, experienced, and highly educated, Sands has invested considerable effort into advancing the conservation community model. He is a member of both formal and informal conservation policy networks, within which he frequently exchanges ideas and innovations. An important aspect of his job at the development was introducing visitors to the conservation community concept. Through the Liberty Prairie Foundation and the Sustainable Agriculture and Food Systems Funders, he speaks several times per year at conferences throughout the United States. The result of his efforts, and those of the Ranneys and Steve Apfelbaum, the development's chief eco-restorationist, has been the export of the policy model to dozens of states and every region of the country.

One of the most widely adopted elements of the Prairie Crossing development approach has been the incorporation of a set of guiding principles or a vision statement. Environmental protection requires knowledge, comprehension, and awareness of exactly what ecosystems, landscapes, or historical agricultural practices are being preserved and for what reasons. Many second-generation conservation communities have copied, and found value in, an explicit vision and a set of conservation goals for green development. Serenbe in Georgia, the

Galisteo Basin Preserve in New Mexico, Hidden Springs in Idaho, the Homestead Preserve in Virginia, Spring Island in South Carolina, and Tryon Farm in Indiana are among the many conservation communities that have adopted a values statement or set of principles that is substantially similar to Prairie Crossing's guiding principles.

Conserving open space requires a significant financial investment. The relatively high cost of preservation and the occasional difficulties in obtaining financial support can be an impediment for conservation development. Prairie Crossing initially experienced problems in obtaining capital due to the unproven nature of green development. Second-generation conservation developments have been innovative in their efforts to fund open-space preservation.

Inspired by Prairie Crossing, Tryon Farm's developers in Michigan City, Indiana, chose perhaps the most unusual path toward land preservation. Tryon Farm is actually a "land condominium." Individual homeowners each have a 1/150th interest in the communal property and do not own the land on which their structure is built.[17] Ed and Eve Noonan, husband-and-wife developers like the Ranneys, created a nonprofit land conservancy as a means of preserving 170 acres of woodlands, wetlands, and prairie pasture. The 120-acre communal property is owned by the conservancy, which provides a tax shelter for the residents. The homes exhibit considerable variability in both style and price, ranging from $125,000 small cottages to $460,000 spacious full-time residences (2006 dollars). The development shares many similarities with Prairie Crossing, including a natural wetlands sewage-treatment system, a working farm, close proximity to mass-transit rail, and communal buildings that offer community events.

At 677 acres and 359 homes, Prairie Crossing is a modest-sized conservation community, though it is the central element of a much grander vision—the 5,770-acre Liberty Prairie Reserve.[18] Conservation development is site dependent and can be viable in a wide range of economic and ecological circumstances. Several second-generation developments encompass more than 10,000 acres. The largest of these, the Santa Lucia Preserve in Monterey County, California, permanently protects 18,000 acres of oak woodland and savanna, clustering its 298 homes on 2,000 settled acres. The conservation easement is the most common and cost-effective method of open-space preservation for these large-scale developments. Creative financing and the use of conservation easements and property transfer fees have permitted second-generation green developments to save ecologically important landscapes on scales that far exceed that of Prairie Crossing. The Santa Lucia Preserve protects 90 percent of the community's 20,000 acres. The Galisteo

Basin Preserve in New Mexico protects 96 percent of its nearly 14,000 acres of semi-arid scrubland, and Spring Island in South Carolina permanently protects 1,200 of the community's 3,000 acres. The Homestead Preserve in Bath County, Virginia, has placed 10,000 of its 11,500 acres under the management of the Nature Conservancy, the largest and best-known land trust organization in the world.

Nestled in the Chattahoochee Hills of Fulton County, Georgia, little more than thirty miles from Atlanta, is Serenbe, a 1,000-acre mixed-use green development. Serenbe's developers, Steve and Marie Nygren, yet another husband-and-wife team, visited Prairie Crossing in the 1990s and decided that they needed to think on an even bigger scale. The Nygrens already owned 1,000 acres in the Chattahoochee Hill Country region, but Steve Nygren soon realized that "his pockets were not deep enough" to halt the outward spread of development from Atlanta. He formed a regional coalition of diverse interests seeking "balanced growth . . . that would provide homes for people to live in and at the same time protect the rural character they cherished." The result was a comprehensive land-use plan covering 40,000 acres in Fulton County and protecting 80 percent as green space.[19] The Serenbe conservation community was the first development approved under the new plan. Serenbe has shown that regional planning can work utilizing a land trust conservancy approach with the constructive input of conservation and business interests.

Serenbe (a spinoff of the words "be serene") clusters its homes in named hamlets based on themes. The development is being built in phases, and three hamlets have been built to date: Selborne (the arts), Grange (agriculture), and Mado (health and healing). The fourth will focus on education. The community has a nineteen-room inn and a central commercial district. Serenbe shares many attributes with Prairie Crossing. Walking paths connect the homes, almost all of which have agricultural or natural viewscapes. Thirty acres are devoted to an organic farm, which sells a diversity of fruits, vegetables, flowers, and herbs to a local community-supported agriculture program. Wastewater is treated naturally through bioretention and a wetlands complex. Much like Prairie Crossing, Serenbe has community buildings that make it possible to host events, weddings, conferences, and retreats.

Communication and education on all levels is essential to the success and spread of conservation development. Prairie Crossing's developers began educating prospective buyers with the initial sales pitch and continued the emphasis through early occupation and into maturity. Bundoran Farm in Albemarle County, Virginia, estimated that its development team "spent at least ten hours with each of the first prospective buyers before they began the purchasing pro-cess."[20] Sometimes developers may also need to reach out to neighbors and nearby communities to explain the value that green development can bring to local aesthetics, watersheds, and property values. Occasionally green developers may have to reassure the local environmental community about their commitment to conservation. Education extends far beyond buyers, residents, and neighbors. Financiers and local politicians also need assistance in understanding the policy model and its potential to bring both economic and ecological benefits to regional economies and landscapes. The success of Prairie Crossing prompted the Vil-lage of Grayslake to revise its zoning regulations; it now permits construction on even tiny lots, contingent upon the permanent preservation of contiguous open space.[21] Zoning codes in many jurisdictions have not kept pace with the evolution of green construction, and many developers have to patiently lobby for code alterations and special dispensations. Financing may be getting easier as the number of successful developments increases; however, green construc-tion is location specific, and market research is needed to tailor the design of the community to local needs. Spring Island in South Carolina, for example, added an Arnold Palmer–designed golf course in response to market demand to ensure economic viability. The addition did not significantly degrade the environmental properties of the development; it is still a certified Audubon Cooperative Sanc-tuary.[22] And phased development—Hidden Springs in Idaho was built in seven phases—can be helpful in difficult and competitive markets. In developments that require extensive restoration, such as Prairie Crossing, early emphasis on green amenities can reassure early prospective buyers of the developers' com-mitment to conservation and open-space preservation.

Chicagoland real-estate analyst Steve Hovany was highly critical of the de-cision to include a working farm in the design of Prairie Crossing, believing it would be a drain on the marketability of the development. The farm proved to be a success at Prairie Crossing, and several second-generation conservation developments have found similar success in farming the land. Bundoran Farm in Virginia pastures 300 head of cattle on 1,000 acres of protected grassland, con-tinuing a six-decade tradition of historical agricultural practices on the property. Two working apple orchards on 154 acres also provide the regional economy with locavore produce. Bundoran engages in environmental stewardship by using natural resource management practices and has earned Audubon International Gold Signature Sanctuary status. The sustainable agricultural practices contrib-ute to the health of the regional ecology. The farm is part of the Chesapeake Bay watershed, which has been subjected to significant chemical pollution from the use of both agricultural pesticides and suburban lawn fertilizers.[23]

Far from being a drain on the sales and marketability of green development, the inclusion of farming or ranching as a conservation amenity has spawned a new form of housing community: the "agrihood." An agrihood is a housing development that uses a working farm as the "central feature" of the community. At least one dozen farm-based communities have sprung up nationwide, offering residents fresh organic produce, tax breaks for the preservation of agricultural land, a smaller carbon footprint, and a rural ambience that is absent from most urban and suburban settings. Several new projects have recently secured financing in the wake of the 2008 real-estate bust, including Rancho Mission Viejo in Orange County, California; Bucking Horse in Fort Collins, Colorado; Prairie Commons in South Olathe, Kansas; Harvest in Northlake, Texas; and Skokomish Farms in Union, Washington. In 2012 the agrihood concept took hold on the island of Kauai in Hawaii. There, the Kukui'ula community grows flowers, fruits, and vegetables on a ten-acre farm that also offers traditional clubhouse, golf course, and health spa amenities.[24]

The key to a successful agriculture-based development is careful selection of the farmer. Prairie Crossing went through several before finding the proper fit with Sandhill Family Farms. Organic farming operations require detailed documentation and strict compliance with USDA regulations to maintain certification. And developers need to be committed to the project, which may take time to implement. In the words of Michael Sands, "Developers cannot just build and walk away."[25] Joseph Johnston, the developer of Agritopia, a 160-acre agrihood community in Gilbert, Arizona, offers similar cautions. "I'm not sure most developers have the patience to really see it through and make it work," he said. "You have to be an excellent grower but also good at customer relations, business projections and labor controls."[26] Farming-based housing communities can be profitable but require good planning and attention to business details. As a marketing tool, the farms are a net plus. If designed properly, they increase the value of the land and provide multiple benefits for their residents and the surrounding community.

Jackson Meadows in southeastern Minnesota has also closely followed Prairie Crossing's community model. In addition to preserving the same grassland ecosystem, the development employs a wetlands septic and wastewater treatment system. Jackson Meadows worked in partnership with adjacent landowners to add to its conservation lands, as Prairie Crossing's developers did in adding adjacent property to their affiliated land trust and connecting the property to the county forest preserve system with a co-funded underpass. Like the Ranneys, Jackson Meadows's developer, Harold Teasdale, selected building designs from the surrounding area. Marine on St. Croix is the oldest European settlement in Minnesota, and Teasdale used Scandinavian architectural designs to invoke the "old-world feel," just as the Ranneys relied on Midwestern designs at Prairie Crossing. Several other communities use conservation-friendly wastewater systems similar to the one that Applied Ecological Services pioneered at Prairie Crossing.[27]

Several conservation communities have built on and surpassed the educational conservation focus that Prairie Crossing established. Bundoran Farm, Serenbe, Spring Island, the Galisteo Basin Preserve, and Hidden Springs all fund and run environmental education centers/institutes, on-site naturalist programs, or museums based upon local heritage. Following Prairie Crossing's lead, Hidden Springs and Galisteo Basin fund their stewardship and educational programs through real-estate transfer fees. Bundoran Farm runs the Baldwin Center for Preservation Development from a "state-of-the-art green building" located on the community's property. The Santa Lucia Preserve set aside a $25 million endowment paid for by a dedicated portion of lot sales and is controlled by a 501(c)(3) nonprofit conservancy to not only safeguard the property and habitat but engage in environmental research.[28] Spring Island runs a nature center staffed by three full-time naturalists who manage the community's wildlife conservation program. These communities have taken Prairie Crossing's guiding principle of "lifelong learning and education" to a new level.

Prairie Crossing's use of the cluster housing design has been replicated virtually everywhere. It saves money in infrastructure costs, is often density neutral, and allows for larger blocks of preserved open space. In certain ecological circumstances, such as at Dewees Island in South Carolina, it may be more beneficial and less disruptive for wildlife if homes are dispersed rather than clustered. Use of topography, natural elements, and landscape features was not of great importance at Prairie Crossing. Ice age glaciers bulldozed the landscape flat, and the wetlands complex on the property is man-made. Numerous developments, however, have shown that careful site selection can enhance value and marketability by using the local topography to hide homes to protect the public viewshed and minimize disturbance while still building within "respectful proximity" to protected ecology.[29] Edward McMahon aptly describes the development process as "designing with nature in mind."[30] For example, the Galisteo Basin Preserve and Hidden Springs hide buildings in valleys so that construction does not dominate the landscape.

Careful site selection at the Santa Lucia Preserve also protected aesthetic views-
heds—almost none of the homes can be seen from other homes or from roadways.

The Serenbe community outside Atlanta proved to be successful in creating a thriving village center. Originally inspired by Prairie Crossing, Serenbe's
developers included some live/work units and created a town center far more
aesthetically pleasing and economically functional than Prairie Crossing's limited condominium-based village and square. Serenbe's effort more closely ap-
proximates a bustling center of commerce, with bakeshops, restaurants, grocers,
boutiques, art galleries, and an inn that more completely integrates the town with
the outside economy. Conservation communities in general tend toward higher-
end construction, though some, such as Tryon Farm in Indiana, do offer a full
range of homes, from small cottages to large residences. More mixed use, live/
work units, granny flats, and a wide range of construction, including condominiums and apartments, would extend the conservation community experience to
a wider economic demographic.

## Lessons Learned

Prairie Crossing represents something new in urban public policy, possibly the
first comprehensive conservation community that attempted to use free-market
principles to restore a relatively sizeable acreage of a largely extirpated ecosystem,
the Midwestern prairie grassland. All ambitious new policies experience growing
pains, and Prairie Crossing was no different. What lessons can be learned from
the Prairie Crossing development experience?

In designing Prairie Crossing, the Ranneys built on and borrowed from many
other practitioners, and that is to their credit. Realistically, ideas are often social products of their time. Very few ideas can be claimed to be genuinely novel
creations of sole individuals. Newton and Leibniz co-discovered the calculus at
roughly the same time. Darwin and Wallace did the same with natural selection.
In crafting their version of the conservation community model, the Ranneys rediscovered the cluster housing design, built on Frederick Law Olmsted's ideas,
borrowed the concept of a policy institute from Seaside, and incorporated many
aspects of New Urbanism into their customized homes. The one design feature of
Prairie Crossing that does appear to be new is the environmental-enhancement
element expressed in the first guiding principle. Environmental protection is intuitive, can often be subsidized by government through conservation easements,
and has an established political pedigree extending back at least a couple of cen-

turies. Today, many conservation communities protect valued natural areas. No others appear to have engaged in the relatively large-scale restoration that Prairie Crossing has.[31] The cost of restoration may be part of the reason.

Restoration adds an extra layer to the developmental process, and perhaps a measure of uncertainty. If George Ranney had added some homes and reduced the amount of space by 10 percent to increase profits, it would still have preserved several hundred acres of natural and agricultural land. But Ranney's retrospective critique represents a classic tradeoff between guiding principles. Conservation costs money, and for the conservation community to be a replicable model for future development, it must maintain economic viability. In developments requiring significant restoration, close attention needs to be paid to competing principles to maximize conservation and profitability. Given the untried nature of the enterprise, such scrutiny is to be expected. To further boost profits, George would have limited home designs and customization. Homebuyers were permitted to semi-customize the final product, providing that the changes were approved by an architectural committee. The process proved to be "too confusing, too time-consuming, and too expensive."[32]

In regard to conservation restoration, Michael Sands cautions future developers to "work with the landscape you have." At Prairie Crossing, the restoration efforts involved "minimal earth-moving." This strategy not only saved money, it saved species by minimizing disruption. Sands also cautions developers to pay close attention to local meteorological factors, particularly wind speed and direction. Excessive wave action at Lake Leopold has created chronic erosion and sedimentation problems that have cost the Homeowners Association $100,000 to contain. A simple 90-degree reorientation of the lake could have mitigated the problems. Interestingly, Sands stated that he would not have supported the building of the Prairie Crossing community, in spite of the ecosystem restoration efforts, without the nearby public transportation infrastructure (i.e., the two Metra trains linking the community to the greater region). He felt that complete automobile dependence would have canceled out the value of the restoration effort. He argues that too much focus has been placed on the conservation aspects of the development, and not enough on the transportation element. He cautions future developers to provide a firm "linkage and rationale for where you put communities." It is not enough to build a community with conservation value without sustainable transportation options, he argues.[33]

The Prairie Crossing guiding principles, a vision statement that was binding in a concrete way, provided long-term values for both the development and the community. Housing development needs to be guided by more than short-term shareholder profit, which often externalizes costs—traffic gridlock, pollution, global warming, fossil fuel consumption, and civic disengagement. The new town movement, Prairie Crossing, and second-generation conservation communities such as Serenbe, Tryon Farm, and Hidden Springs have shown that commitment to a vision beyond profits can generate public goods, profits, and a personal legacy that outlasts the developer.

Money, however, has influence, and profits do matter in a capitalistic society. The Ranneys are sensitive about the role that economic resources played in the building of the Prairie Crossing community. They shouldn't be, especially considering the era in which the property was fought over, purchased, planned, designed, and developed. In the 1980s, conservation developments were largely unheard of, and communication networks lacked the efficacy of the Internet. Revolutions may not be tweeted, but the Internet undoubtedly makes the dissemination of information and the communication of novel ideas easier. In 1987, wealth was an important component of this project; it provided patient money, a safe margin of time, and financial security for the developers to take a chance on a novel policy model. The new town developments in the 1960s and 1970s were no different. Patient money played a crucial role at Irvine, Columbia, and The Woodlands. Today, the conservation community is gaining traction in some markets, but as recently as a dozen years ago, Steve Nygren, the developer of Serenbe, was forced to "pledge our real-estate holdings in Atlanta, in addition to the land at Serenbe, as collateral to guarantee the development loans. We had a family meeting, when it became obvious this was our only choice if the development was to move forward, and I presented to Marie and the girls the situation we were in. I had their college funds in a safe account, but other than that, we would have to put the balance of our financial holding at stake."[34] Until the policy model takes hold in the real-estate industry, financing will continue to be important.

Prairie Crossing was largely unsuccessful in achieving its twin objectives of racial and economic diversity. In some ways the two goals are interrelated, though Columbia managed to reach an acceptable level of racial integration while failing to integrate economically. Michael Sands believes "in hindsight" that the goals would have been more achievable if the developers had done two things: (1) phase in the development over time to allow for changes during the permitting process, and (2) be more innovative by seeking a nonprofit partner to assist with housing affordability. More diversity in housing types in the original proposal, such as rental units and granny flats, would have made it easier to obtain permitting approval. Attempts to add those elements later led to opposition and failure. Both Prairie Crossing residents and Grayslake officials opposed the permit changes. Sands recommends that future developers work on a project in stages so that they can alter their plans if need be as building progresses. Locking in the permits early made it too difficult to modify plans and designs in response to market developments. Sands also suggested partnering with a nonprofit to expand housing affordability. Some buyers who purchased early with secondary mortgages provided by the Prairie Holdings Corporation "flipped" the houses for a profit as prices increased. Without a clause to prevent resale, some buyers were able to defeat the intent of the mortgage assistance program.[35]

On balance, however, Prairie Crossing has experienced far more successes than failures. The inclusion of sustainable agriculture in the policy model received its fair share of criticism at the beginning. Fine-tuning the farm business took a decade, but the farm at Prairie Crossing has proven to be a success, one that has been so widely copied that agriculturally based communities have become their own policy model spinoff.[36] The teaming of the farm with a nonprofit foundation also proved successful. Not only has the Liberty Prairie Foundation helped to export the policy model around the country, it has helped to foster the local organic farming industry by training and mentoring fledgling farmers.

Another successful innovative practice was the seller's tax. The revenue generated by a 0.5 percent tax on the sale of homes is used to fund the foundation, along with a partnership with the local landfill. The tax was initially somewhat risky; however, the technique has been successfully replicated elsewhere, most notably at Hidden Springs, in the tax-averse red state of Idaho. Prairie Crossing's use of conservation easements has also been adopted as the vehicle of choice to save relatively large parcels of land in very different political climates from Virginia to California.

Prairie Crossing's careful focus on infrastructure—the emphasis on conservation amenities rather than golf courses, clubhouses, and swimming pools—has saved the developers and the Homeowners Association a considerable amount of money. The Byron Colby Barn is self-financing; it hosts more than a hundred events a year and provides an additional revenue stream to the Liberty Prairie Foundation. By eliminating sewers, curbs, and sidewalks and narrowing the streets, the developers saved $1.375 million in infrastructure costs while also receiving the concomitant environmental benefits of using fewer resources and better water management. These savings are easily replicable.

Prairie Crossing's natural drainage system provides more than monetary and flood-mitigation benefits. The introduction of threatened and endangered fish species to the development's wetlands produced a demonstrable public good, acting as a source for downstream dissemination. As described in chapter three, a study conducted by U.S. Geological Survey scientists concluded that Prairie Crossing could serve as a model for increasing biodiversity in urban environments: "We suggest that well-designed storm water systems such as Prairie Crossing can play a role in biodiversity conservation, especially in urban landscapes that would support no aquatic diversity otherwise."[37] The Prairie Crossing drainage model is superior to conventional tile sewer systems on five levels: cost, water retention, human recreation, development aesthetics, and suitability for wildlife.

Prairie Crossing's emphasis on community, from sales through occupation and maturity, has been widely copied. It is important to be upfront with prospective buyers and explain the concept behind the development. My research showed that a genuine focus on community through organizations, events, social expectations, opportunities for involvement, and joint responsibility for common natural areas can produce positive behavioral changes. The culture of car convenience proved to be more resistant to change, though residents' utilization of mass transit is greater at Prairie Crossing than in the surrounding region. As Ann Forsyth notes in *Reforming Suburbia*, private-sector solutions have their limits.[38] Comprehensive government intervention will likely be required to undo nearly a century of suburban dependence on the automobile.

The Liberty Prairie Reserve represents the larger, grander vision for central Lake County. Prairie Crossing is perhaps the most well known parcel of land within the nearly 5,800-acre reserve, and it anchors the northwest corner. Gaylord Donnelley and George Sr. planted the seeds for the reserve when they moved to the area in the mid-1940s and immersed themselves in the community. The two families helped ground the reserve with their commitment to values and community, both the neighborhood and the larger village. The emphasis on community meant that the reserve's value element is greater than mere respect and aesthetic appreciation for the environment. The Donnelleys and Ranneys tried to do something unique and somewhat difficult: put a price tag on nature. Public goods—clean air and water, endangered ecosystems, cherished viewscapes, disappearing species—have long been considered valuable, but these benefits did not have concrete monetary value. Both Prairie Crossing and the Liberty Prairie Reserve have tried to measure their financial worth.

To create the reserve took personal and institutional patience and pragmatism. The principal players adopted long-term perspectives from relatively early on and instilled the organizations they created with that same institutional patience. Certainly, patient money helped make that perspective possible. However, Gaylord Donnelley, the principal investor, also led by example. The reserve is expanding incrementally, puzzle piece by puzzle piece, with an emphasis on core habitats, biotic corridors, and sensitive environments. This approach is important because Lake County is home to the most threatened and endangered species in the state.

Pragmatism frequently permeated the decision-making process. Green activists are often characterized as zealots who are not willing to compromise, radicals who would rather go down with the ship than cut a deal to get some, but not all, of what they want. For the Donnelleys and Ranneys, however, market viability was always an important consideration, though never paramount. Balance and tradeoffs between principles were common business practices. The guiding principles helped keep the developers grounded.

Today, the reserve is managed with businesslike efficiency and pragmatism, along with a sense of big-picture prioritization. The Illinois Route 53/120 expansion provides an example. Reserve stakeholders realized that intractable opposition to any expansion might lead to a loss of public support for the reserve. It seemed better to broker an agreement, one that considers important environmental values, and accept the glass as half full, rather than have no influence over the final product. The result was a four-lane limited-access parkway with a lower speed limit and use of native plantings. Another example involves tradeoffs between land preservation and sustainable agriculture. Land managers have observed that even organic farming methods can sometimes negatively impact high-quality natural areas through erosion, nutrient influx, and water quality problems, and have recommended that some operations be scaled back to protect the environment.[39]

Outreach to both the public and public institutions has proved fruitful. The reserve has continually sought to increase public access by creating new trails and new trail linkages. The 2013 master plan also calls for increased public safety measures and informational signage. The Ranneys could have limited Prairie Crossing's conservation amenities to residents, but they rejected the idea of privatizing nature. They split the cost of a trail underpass with local government and connected the community to the Oak Openings county preserve. The Liberty Prairie Foundation mentors and subsidizes organic farming startups, and the Liberty Prairie Conservancy, founded by Prairie Crossing resident Betsy Dietel, changed its name to Conserve Lake County to better reflect the group's expanded focus. In an attempt to reclaim the native environment one property at a time, the organization assists property owners in rewilding their private lands through Conservation@Home. This program shows promise and can be adapted to any climate or ecosystem. In 2011, Conserve Lake County met with large private landowners to discuss the reserve's future, and in March 2013, the organization held a public open house to allow people to review the draft master plan before its final release. Marketing of the reserve is essential to cultivate and maintain public support. People won't support what they don't know and understand as a benefit to themselves.

Reserve stakeholders have also reached out to government officials to establish a "shared vision" for the reserve.[40] This is essential for coordination of planning and policy and the sharing of resources and expertise. Nine government bodies have jurisdiction over reserve lands in some fashion. Coordination between organizations has also been important. The Liberty Prairie Foundation, Conserve Lake County, Openlands, Sandhill Family Farms, and the Prairie Crossing Farm Business Development Center have worked together and coordinated their efforts. Each of the organizations has focus, and they keep their institutional egos in check, which helps maximize the return on their collective efforts.

The most important element of the conservation community model is the committed developer. That commitment must be balanced between competing principles, particularly conservation and profits. As Barry Commoner argued nearly half a century ago, the narrow focus on profits has the potential to cause serious environmental degradation over the long term. Climate change, species extinction, exhaustion of finite resources, habitat destruction and fragmentation, air and water pollution, and loss of a sense of place and community are all exacerbated by sprawl's inefficiencies. Green development can mitigate and sometimes reverse these negative externalities, but it requires a commitment to build sustainably according to a set of values beyond the calculus of short-term gain. Studies have shown that homebuyers value, and are willing to pay for, green-space amenities; green development can be profitable. The biggest challenge for future green developers appears to be creating affordable low-income housing within the conservation community.

## Nature's Suburb: Seeking Sustainability in a Domesticated World

Peter Kareiva is the chief scientist for the Nature Conservancy, a member of the National Academy of Sciences, and a conservation iconoclast. This "inconvenient environmentalist" has ruffled feathers within the confines of the world's largest environmental organization. Unafraid of courting controversy, he has questioned whether halting deforestation in the Amazon is "even necessary."[41] Kareiva argues passionately that "conservation is losing the war to protect nature despite winning one of its hardest fought battles—the fight to create parks, game preserves, and wilderness areas."[42] Acknowledging the obvious pole-to-pole "domestication" of the planet, he maintains that "conservation cannot promise a return to pristine prehuman landscapes."[43] Instead, twenty-first-century conservation must change and adopt a new vision, one that is premised upon nature existing within the framework of modern human development, whether urban, industrial, or agricultural. Writing more than twenty years after the Ranneys helped set the conservation community concept in motion, Kareiva argues that integrating nature into human environments is the future of conservation: "Conservation should seek to support and inform the right kind of development—development by design, done with the importance of nature to thriving economies foremost in mind. And it will utilize the right kinds of technology to enhance the health and well-being of both human and non-human natures. Instead of scolding capitalism, conservationists should partner with corporations in a science-based effort to integrate the value of nature's benefits into their operations and cultures."[44] In crafting the conservation community concept, the Ranneys were a generation ahead of their time. They employed capitalism in an effort to integrate humans into nature using the best technology available, with a goal of preserving a prairie ecosystem lost in a century-long rush of national economic expansion. Though perhaps a bitter solution for many an environmentalist, an economic partnership with capitalistic forces may be the only way to save what remains of a largely domesticated planet.

The data on humans' impact upon the earth is sobering. Between 1981 and 2003, more than 23 percent of its surface area "likely experienced [a] decline in ecosystem function and productivity." Human degradation of the planet as measured by surface area was estimated in 1995 to be approximately 43 percent. Of the ice-free continental landmass, 83 percent is "directly influenced" by human activity and 75 percent is no longer "wild" using scientific criteria.[45]

Conservation communities are not going to reverse large-scale human-induced degradation. But on a planet that mankind has essentially already domesticated, or at least substantially altered, green development has a chance of reversing local small-scale damage. Green development can create connective wildlife corridors in urban environments, save or restore existing land of conservation value, and generate economic profits through free-market incentives. Conservation communities represent an alternative to business as usual, an opportunity to build in closer concert with the principles of nature and ecology. Environmental degradation need not be considered an inexorable consequence—a price to be paid—for progress. Indeed, conservation development uses the cutting edge of technology—everything from geothermal heating and cooling to green roofs to wastewater treatment. Green development has the potential to bring benefits beyond the physical boundaries of the community; it has the power to change cultural attitudes and behavior, integrate the citizen into nature, nudge people toward greater sustainability, create social capital, and encourage civic responsibility.

During the last twenty-five years, the conservation community has grown from a handful of developments to more than one hundred, in every region of the United States, including Hawaii, and nearly every type of ecosystem. The policy model, however, represents just a small fraction of homes built throughout the country. The future provides an opportunity to make a substantive impact. Two-thirds or more of the housing likely to exist in the year 2050 has yet to be built.[46] And green development does not have to be limited to single-family homes. The model can viably be applied to higher-density dwellings as well. Conservation can be democratized; it need not be the exclusive province of the rich.

Conservation development may be profitable as condominium construction. Market research has repeatedly shown that Americans are "willing to pay extra for parks, natural areas, and other open-space amenities."[47] Conservation-friendly design is also possible in commercial development. Corporate parks can easily incorporate native vegetation into their landscaping and grounds. Prairie Stone Business Park in Hoffman Estates, Illinois, is one such example. The 780-acre master-planned business park employs wetland and prairie restorations that are actively managed. Native prairie plants are burned, and one hundred acres of open space provides outdoor recreation for park workers and the at-large community. Prairie Stone is the corporate headquarters of Sears, Roebuck and Company, which moved there in 1994.

Flooding mitigation also does not need to be limited to the conventional retention pond (an excavated bluegrass depression devoid of native flora and biodiversity). For example, in suburban Glenview, twenty miles north of downtown Chicago, the village municipal center employs native prairie vegetation in its landscaping, which the village burns periodically. The Techny Basin Conservation Area in Glenview fulfills a dual function for the village; it provides flood control and also serves as habitat for wildlife. The 49-acre basin is planted in native grasses and forbs, including bluestems, switchgrass, and goldenrod, and at full capacity can hold 365 million gallons of water. The village also periodically burns the basin vegetation to stimulate growth and eliminate invasive species. The habitat attracts muskrat and a wide variety of waterfowl and grassland birds, including the prairie falcon and dickcissel, a species in serious decline. Glenview has shown that man-made structures, if designed with nature in mind, can also bring significant conservation benefits. The Evanston North Shore Bird Club schedules regular spring and fall birding trips at the Techny Basin because of the excellent birding it offers.

Glenview has a tradition of land preservation and restoration. Restored prairie fragments on the former Glenview Naval Air Station property preserve plants indigenous to the region on a permanently protected 32-acre tallgrass parcel. The Grove National Historic Landmark, maintained by the Glenview Park District, is a 135-acre oak savanna remnant that is home to the original 1856 Kennicott House. As Glenview shows, communities that are open to green construction and preservation have many opportunities to support conservation through both public initiatives and private development.

Exporting nature's suburb throughout America and integrating the citizen back into the outdoors can benefit both people and the environment. As William Cronon has argued, there is trouble with the commonly held view that nature or wilderness is where people are absent:

> The trouble with wilderness is . . . the illusion that we can somehow wipe clean the slate of our past and return to the tabula rasa that supposedly existed before we began to leave our marks on the world. . . . This, then, is the central paradox: wilderness embodies a dualistic vision in which the human is entirely outside the natural. If we allow ourselves to believe that nature, to be true, must also be wild, then our very presence in nature represents its fall. The place where we are is the place where nature is not.[48]

Returning nature to human environments enriches ecology, the economy, and the human spirit. Prairie Crossing and second-generation conservation communities offer a viable model for incorporating a measure of wildness into the daily human experience.

# PRAIRIE CROSSING TIMELINE

1833   The second Treaty of Chicago grants the land that is now Prairie
       Crossing to the United States

1848   The Illinois and Michigan Canal opens, linking the Great Lakes to the
       Mississippi River and the Gulf of Mexico

1857   The Wright Schoolhouse is built near Libertyville

1860   Chicago becomes the world's largest railroad center and livestock,
       lumber, and grain market

1885   The Byron Colby Barn is built in Lake County

1968   The Ranneys visit the Sea Ranch

1972   Vicky Ranney publishes a monograph, *Olmsted in Chicago*; the
       Heartland Development proposal for 3,000 homes on the Prairie
       Crossing land triggers intense community opposition, with Heartland
       subsequently filing a lawsuit

1976   Illinois passes conservation easement legislation

1977   Marshall Field starts land-preservation efforts in the area with a
       thirteen-acre conservation easement—the first easement under the
       conservation easement statute

1981   Robert Davis breaks ground in Seaside, Florida

1982   Davis creates the Seaside Institute, an inspiration for the Liberty Prairie
       Foundation

1986    The Heartland Agreement is reached and the lawsuit is settled; a group
        led by accomplished philanthropist Gaylord Donnelley purchases the
        Prairie Crossing property

1987    Gaylord Donnelley asks the Ranneys to craft a green development to
        preserve the "country feel" of the Prairie Crossing land; the Ranneys
        accept

1989    Gaylord and Dorothy Donnelley and George Ranney Jr. announce
        plans for the Liberty Prairie Reserve, with the support of the Lake
        County Forest Preserve District and Libertyville Township; the
        Donnelleys donate land to launch the reserve effort; construction of a
        new tollway is blocked

1990    Rare native prairie and fen is discovered on Donnelley property

1991    The first management plan for the Liberty Prairie Reserve is created

1992    Gaylord Donnelley dies; the Prairie Crossing guiding principles
        are adopted; the permitting process for the homes is initiated;
        an agreement is reached with the nearby landfill that includes a
        home value guarantee for buyers; the Ranneys first coin the phrase
        "conservation community"

1993    The Village of Grayslake approves the Prairie Crossing plans; the
        Liberty Prairie Foundation is established; Applied Ecological Services
        begins the prairie and wetlands restorations; home construction begins

1994    The Prairie Crossing Farm is the first organic-certified farm in Lake
        County; construction begins on the trails and underpass; the first
        residents begin moving into the development in November

1995    Michael Sands creates an important "founder" role as environmental
        team leader; Metra announces new commuter service at Prairie
        Crossing; Conserve Lake County is organized as the Liberty Prairie
        Conservancy land trust by resident Betsy Dietel

1996    The Byron Colby Barn and Wright Schoolhouse are moved to the
        property; the first rail station is built

1999    The Prairie Crossing Charter School opens; an expansion of the initial
        Prairie Crossing plans is approved

2000    The Liberty Prairie Reserve is named one of four "Last Chance
        Landscapes in U.S." by Scenic America

2002    Dorothy Ranney Donnelley dies

2004    The second rail station is built; construction begins on three new
        buildings for the charter school

2005    Prairie Crossing sells the last of its single-family homes; Station Square
        construction begins
2006    The Liberty Prairie Foundation launches the Farm Business
        Development Center
2007    The original Liberty Prairie Reserve Plan is completed
2011    The last condominiums in the Station Village are sold
2012    An agreement settles a fifty-year dispute over Illinois Route 53/120; a
        green-friendly expansion of the roadway is accepted
2014    The Prairie Crossing community marks its twenty-year anniversary;
        the value of Liberty Prairie Reserve public and private investments
        exceeds $100 million (private conservation easements donations top
        $33 million)

# NOTES

## Chapter One. Saving the Land by Developing It

1. Several earlier developments had significant conservation elements, including the Village Homes in Davis, California, and The Woodlands north of Houston, Texas. Prairie Crossing appears to be the first green development to incorporate the substantial restoration of a regionally extirpated ecosystem—the tallgrass prairie—and to employ a comprehensive conservation agenda.

2. Downs, *New Visions for Metropolitan America*, 7. Downs argues, "Homebuilders, realtors, advertisers, town governments, and local planning officials sing the praises of suburban life-styles and uncrowded, safe communities. This vision is now so strongly entrenched that it has become almost political suicide for elected officials to challenge any of the elements."

3. George and Vicky Ranney believe that they were the first to use the term "conservation community" for this kind of development. In 1992, during a discussion of how best to market Prairie Crossing, they combined the word "conservation," the first guiding principle of the development, with "community," the fourth guiding principle. George Ranney pers. comm., November 15, 2014.

4. Commoner, *The Closing Circle*, 299–300.

5. Judd and Swanstrom, *City Politics*, 270.

6. Postwar housing construction employed mass production techniques that "greatly intensified the environmental impact of homebuilding." See Rome, *The Bulldozer in the Countryside*, 3.

7. Burchell et al., *Sprawl Costs*, 71.

8. Ogden, *Letters from the West*, 55.

9. Wandersee and Schussler, "Toward a Theory of Plant Blindness," 3.

10. The presence of invasive species may increase the frequency of burns in a specific area, and burns are deliberately varied by season for each parcel to foster biodiversity and avoid homogeneity.

11. Helzer, *The Ecology and Management of Prairies*, 5.

12. Ibid., 5–6.

13. Cather, *My Ántonia*, 16.

14. See "Prairie and Foursquare," *Architectural Styles of America and Europe*, http://architecture styles.org/prairie/.

15. Byers and Mitchell, "Sprawl and Species with Limited Dispersal Abilities," 164.

16. For the impact of ecological fragmentation on biodiversity, see MacArthur and Wilson, *The Theory of Island Biogeography*. For sprawl's impact on species dispersal, see Byers and Mitchell, "Sprawl and Species with Limited Dispersal Abilities." For the impact of habitat fragmentation on predators and the concept of trophic cascades, see Eisenberg, *The Wolf's Tooth*.

17. Apfelbaum et al., "The Prairie Crossing Project."

18. Thomas E. Dahl and Gregory J. Allord, *History of Wetlands in the Conterminous U.S.*, U.S. Fish and Wildlife Service, National Wetlands Inventory, https://www.fws.gov/wetlands/ Documents/History-of-Wetlands-in-the-Conterminous-United-States.pdf.

19. A 2009 study by the USGS found that more than 40 percent of streams in the United States exhibited chloride levels that exceeded the federal criteria, which "can inhibit plant growth, impair reproduction, and reduce the diversity of organisms in streams." John Mullaney and Diane Noserale, "Chloride Found at Levels That Can Harm Aquatic Life in Urban Streams of the Northern U.S.—Winter Deicing a Major Source," U.S. Geological Survey, http://www.usgs.gov/newsroom/article.asp?ID=2307&from.

20. Thompson, "Overcoming Barriers to Ecologically Sensitive Land Management," 142.

21. See Thomas Hayden, "Could the Grass Be Greener?," *U.S. News & World Report*, May 16, 2005, 42.

22. Due to the processes of bioaccumulation and biomagnification, the concentration of chemicals can increase as they rise through the food chain. For the impact of lawn chemicals on the Arctic, see Cone, *Silent Snow*, 28–29.

23. DeStefano and Johnson, "Species That Benefit from Sprawl," 212.

24. Ash trees make up approximately 12 percent of Evanston's 33,000 trees. The emerald ash borer has spread throughout the entire city, and the cost of tree removal has so depleted city finances that there is not sufficient funding to replace the trees. The city is accepting donations for tree replacement. In 2012 the City of Evanston described the state of its ash tree population: "The unintended consequence of this plan is that those blocks designated to be planted with only ash trees are now being stripped of nearly all their trees. Some blocks have even been entirely cleared of all parkway trees." "Evanston's Emerald Ash Borer and Ash Tree Removal Update," March 28, 2012, http://www.cityofevanston.org/news/2012/03/evanstons -emerald-ash-borer-and-ash-tree-removal-update/.

25. Lockwood and McKinney, *Biotic Homogenization*, vii.

26. Lenart, "Liberty Prairie Conservancy Springs to Life in Reserve," 1.

27. Bartlett, *Urban Place*, 8.

28. John Elder and Robert Finch call the *Almanac* "one of the benchmark titles of the ecological movement"; *Nature Writing*, 376. Cramer, *Deep Environmental Politics*.

29. Quote from Aldo Leopold, "The Land Ethic," in *A Sand County Almanac*, 239.

30. George Ranney, pers. comm., June 15, 2005; "Guiding Principles for Prairie Crossing," http://www.prairiecrossing.com/pc/site/guiding-principles.html. Perhaps the most obvious cultural impact of sprawl is the resulting traffic gridlock. Depending on the study and the year, metropolitan Chicago invariably has the worst or second-worst road congestion in the nation. The economic costs are significant. Although Chicago relinquished its "worst in the nation" traffic gridlock ranking to Washington, D.C., in 2010, the region's rush-hour drivers still paid the "highest congestion penalty" in the country, averaging $1,568 in lost time and wasted motor fuel per year, according to an urban mobility study conducted by the Texas Transportation Institute at Texas A&M University. The study estimated that area drivers spent 367 million hours stuck in traffic, costing the region $8.2 billion. That adds up to a loss of 71 hours per commuter, or nearly 9 full workdays stuck in traffic per year. In 2010, Chicago also led the nation in costs to the trucking industry—31 million hours delayed in traffic at a cost of $2.3 billion. Nationally, the average commuter lost 34 hours to road congestion, costing an estimated $750 per person. Hilkevitch, "Chicago Area Falls to No. 2 for Worst Traffic Congestion." A considerable amount of research suggests that traffic gridlock and long commutes have a negative effect on both happiness and civic participation. One study concluded that commutes of longer than 45 minutes for just one marriage partner result in a 40 percent increase in the likelihood of divorce. Annie Lowrey, "Your Commute is Killing You," Slate.com, May 26, 2011, http://www.slate.com/articles/business/moneybox/2011/05/your_commute_is_killing_you.html. Excessive time behind the wheel also erodes social capital. Harvard political scientist Robert Putnam argues that long commutes are "demonstrably bad for community life." He found that the effect of commuting time as an influence on civic involvement is second only to education among demographic factors. The more time spent behind the wheel, the less time people spend attending meetings or church, or otherwise participating in public life. Putnam, *Bowling Alone*, 213.

31. Transit-oriented development is generally characterized by transit-stop access within a one-quarter- to one-half-mile radius of residential housing, the distance pedestrians are willing to walk.

32. "Public Transportation Usage among U.S. Workers: 2008 and 2009," October 2010, U.S. Census Bureau, American Community Survey Briefs, http://www.census.gov/prod/2010pubs/acsbr09-5.pdf.

33. For the benefits of exposure to nature for children and adults, see Louv, *Last Child in the Woods* and *The Nature Principle*. See also Wilson, *The Future of Life*, and Merchant, *Reinventing Eden*.

34. For scholarly criticism regarding sprawl's degradation of community aesthetics, see Duany et al., *Suburban Nation*; Dreier et al., *Place Matters*; Kunstler, *The Geography of Nowhere*; Jacobs, *The Death and Life of Great American Cities*; Schipper, *Disappearing Desert*; and Scully, *American Architecture and Urbanism*.

35. Vicky Ranney, pers. comm., September 19, 2008.

36. New Urbanism seeks to replicate in modern town design the great sense of place found in many old American towns, such as Scarsdale, New York, Alexandria, Virginia, and the Georgetown section of Washington, D.C. The goal is to re-create the pedestrian-friendly design, graceful architecture, and old-town ambience captured so well by those late nineteenth-

century and early twentieth-century towns that avoided modern demolition and urban redesign based on automobile convenience.

37. Blakely and Snyder, *Fortress America*; Hillery, "Definitions of Community."

38. The Prairie Crossing farmers' market, which played a strong role in helping forge community during the early years of the development, closed in 2012. Erin Cummisford of the Liberty Prairie Foundation described the decision to close the market as "difficult." The reason for the closure was that the organic food business had changed significantly since the farmers' market opened in 1996. In the early years, the market was a "novelty" for residents. Since then, the number of on-site farm businesses has grown, and residents have embraced the community-supported agriculture program, which provides them with multiple home-grown options. Competition from other markets in Grayslake, Libertyville, and Mundelein also made it more difficult to attract customers from outside the community. For these reasons, a shrinking customer base made the market unsustainable for the Liberty Prairie Foundation to operate.

39. See McKenzie, *Privatopia*, for the "culture of non-participation" in private government. See Blakely and Snyder, *Fortress America*, for the "lack of participation" in gated communities. See Reich, "Secession of the Successful," for the growing tendency of the affluent to "disengage themselves from their less favored fellows." See Putnam, *Bowling Alone*, 15–28, for non-participation as a "central crisis."

40. George Ranney, pers. comm., June 15, 2005.

41. Comparisons were made using survey questions obtained from the University of Michigan's American National Election Studies (ANES) database. Results were adjusted for the development's median cohorts in age, education, and income.

42. Chicago real-estate analyst Steve Hovany placed the Prairie Crossing "premium" at 20 percent; pers. comm., May 17, 2005. Developer George Ranney placed the cost somewhat lower, at 14 percent; pers. comm., September 6, 2005. This cost will vary greatly depending on local circumstances, property values, and the extent of ecological restoration. Significantly degraded lands, such as Prairie Crossing, will drive up the cost of the homes.

43. Surveys found single-family homes to be 90 percent white, 5 percent Asian, 3 percent Hispanic, and less than 3 percent black. The condominium complex was not yet finished at the time of the survey.

44. The reported median income was $127,500 in 2005 dollars.

45. Handley, "Experiment on the Prairie."

46. McMahon, *Conservation Communities*, viii.

47. For home values and acreage, see Tanaka, "Why Homes with Open Space Command Big Bucks." For infrastructure savings and the distribution of conservation communities, see McMahon, *Conservation Communities*, 32, 243.

## Chapter Two. Genesis of an Idea

1. Flannery, *The Eternal Frontier*, 340.

2. Ibid., 146–169, quote from 148. At the end of the Pleistocene, twenty genera of large mammals became extinct in just a few hundred years, which is a geological "blink of an eye." In all, thirty-three genera disappeared. See Manning, *Grassland*, 59. For the discovery of

mastodon bones in Lake County, see Pamela Cytrynbaum, "Fossil's a Find, No Bones about It," *Chicago Tribune*, September 12, 1995, http://articles.chicagotribune.com/1995-09-12/news/9509120085_1_mastodon-illinois-state-museum-prehistoric.

3. One normally polar-loving species, *Triglochin palustris*, better known as slender bog arrow-grass, managed to survive 12,000 years of climate change, the industrial and agricultural revolutions, and urban sprawl in a prairie wetland depression on Gaylord Donnelley's property one mile east of the Prairie Crossing development.

4. Flannery, *The Eternal Frontier*, 153; Apfelbaum, *Nature's Second Chance*, 13–27; Kay, "Ecosystems Then and Now," 84.

5. Cochrane and Iltis, *Atlas of the Wisconsin Prairie and Savanna Flora*, 21.

6. George Catlin is best known for his work as an artist and painter of Native American portraits in the era just before the invention of photography. He did, however, travel widely in the 1830s, both solo and as a contributing member to several expeditions, including one with William Clark. See Susanna Reich's biography *Painting the Wild Frontier* for details of his explorations. Quote from Cronon, *Nature's Metropolis*, 213. Manning, *Grassland*, 141.

7. Quote from Colbee C. Benton, an early nineteenth-century visitor to Chicago, as cited in Keating, *Chicagoland*, 23. See also ibid., 23–26, for a description of Potawatomi communities and Native American influence.

8. Cronon, *Nature's Metropolis*.

9. Miller, *City of the Century*.

10. Cronon, *Nature's Metropolis*, 120.

11. For the impact of the cast-steel plow, see Halberstadt, *The American Family Farm*, 18.

12. Jacques Marquette and Louis Joliet discovered the linkage between the two watersheds in 1673 and understood its economic potential.

13. Steve Apfelbaum, pers. comm., October 26, 2005. Apfelbaum is the president of Applied Ecological Services, the restoration company for the Prairie Crossing project.

14. For example, in Evanston, Illinois, lakefront beaches consist of sand that is trucked in annually and sculpted by heavy machinery; other shoreline areas use limestone blocks for erosion protection. Much of Chicago's lakefront is artificial fill, debris from the Great Chicago Fire of 1871. Jackson Park was a wetland swamp of natural grasses and forbs until it was artificially reconstructed for the 1893 Columbian Exhibition. The Grove in suburban Glenview is a 123-acre nature preserve and national historic landmark. Saved from development in the early 1970s by "frog and fern ladies," the property features the original 1856 Kennicott House, the former home of Robert Kennicott, founder of the Chicago Academy of Sciences and a scientific explorer and collector for the Smithsonian Institution. It is doubtful that Kennicott, who is buried on the property, would recognize the Grove today, even though it is a never-developed nature preserve. The indigenous oak savanna has been replaced by hardwood forest, often choked with exotic invasives, such as European buckthorn. As recently as the early twentieth century, visitors (many of whom recorded their presence by signing their name on a wall of the house, the earliest dating from the 1870s) could see cottonwoods and oaks lining the Des Plaines River from the front porch a mile away. Today, the I-294 overpass blocks the view of subdivisions and heavily wooded county forest preserve property that is mostly free of the prairie and oak-savanna biotic assemblages that once populated the area.

15. Stone (dir.), *Earth Days*.

16. Layzer, *The Environmental Case.*

17. "Biographical Note," *Guide to the Ryerson Family Papers 1803–1971,* http://www.lib.uchicago.edu/e/scrc/findingaids/view.php?eadid=ICU.SPCL.RYERSON.

18. John Husar, "Gaylord Donnelley Is Illinois 'Open Lands' Lord," *Chicago Tribune,* November 4, 1990, http://articles.chicagotribune.com/1990-11-04/sports/9004030706_1_scott-and-zelda-fitzgerald-ernest-hemingway-fishing.

19. George A. Ranney Jr., prepared remarks given on April 24, 1992, at Rockefeller Memorial Chapel, University of Chicago.

20. See David Lauderdale, "ACE Basin: A 'Last Great Place' Turns 25," *Island Packet,* http://www.islandpacket.com/static/news/ace/.

21. Husar, "Gaylord Donnelley Is Illinois 'Open Lands' Lord."

22. James Janega, "Dorothy Ranney Donnelley, 92; Conservationist Who Aided Many Causes," *Chicago Tribune,* February 6, 2002, http://articles.chicagotribune.com/2002-02-06/news/0202060335_1_nature-conservancy-libertyville-south-carolina-low-country.

23. Undated Openlands film interview recorded to DVD provided by Brad Leibov of the Liberty Prairie Foundation.

24. "About Us," Gaylord & Dorothy Donnelley Foundation, http://gddf.org/about.

25. The University of Chicago has since sold the easement to Libertyville Township.

26. Husar, "Gaylord Donnelley Is Illinois 'Open Lands' Lord."

27. An easement is a voluntary, legally enforceable contract between a landowner and a private land trust organization or a state government agency. In return for protecting the ecological, aesthetic, and agricultural integrity of the land in perpetuity, landowners receive valuable tax credits, some unused portions of which may be sold.

28. "Donnelley Wildlife Management Area," http://www.americantowns.com/sc/charleston/organization/donnelly-wildlife-management-area.

29. Vicky Post Ranney's great-grandfather George B. Post was one of America's leading nineteenth-century architects. He designed the New York Stock Exchange Building, the Wisconsin State Capitol, and the New York World Building, at twenty stories one of the country's first skyscrapers.

30. *The Sea Ranch: Concept and Covenant,* 5, http://www.tsra.org/photos/VIPBooklet.pdf.

31. Ibid., 4.

32. George Ranney speech to the Liberty Prairie Conservancy Annual Meeting, February 10, 2005, transcription by Linda Wiens.

33. My use of "bulldozing the countryside" is a play on *The Bulldozer in the Countryside,* the title of Adam Rome's history of suburbia and the environmental movement.

34. Vicky Ranney , pers. comm., September 19, 2008.

35. http://www.tsra.org/photos/VIPBooklet.pdf.

36. George Ranney speech, February 10, 2005.

37. Taking advantage of newly passed green legislation, Marshall Field and his wife, Jamee, created the state's first conservation easement in 1977 on property that would eventually become the Liberty Prairie Reserve. They preserved a 13-acre easement remnant consisting of oak savanna and prairie on Casey Road just east of Prairie Crossing.

38. Ranney, *Olmsted in Chicago,* 3.

39. Ibid., 7.

40. Ibid.

41. Jackson, *Crabgrass Frontier*, 79–81.

42. Hayden, *Building Suburbia*, 64.

43. Rybczynski, *A Clearing in the Distance*, 293.

44. Frantz and Collins, *Celebration, U.S.A.*, 43.

45. The Seaside Institute, http://seasideinstitute.org/what-we-do/, http://seasideinstitute .org/who-we-are/.

46. George Ranney speech, February 10, 2005.

47. *Liberty Prairie Reserve Master Plan*, available at "What We Do," Conserve Lake County, http://www.conservelakecounty.org/what-we-do/liberty-prairie-reserve.

48. "Lake County Plants & Animals," Lake County Forest Preserves, http://www.lcfpd.org/ lake-county-species/. See also Ryan and Grese, "Urban Volunteers and the Environment," 173.

49. Lenart, "Liberty Prairie Conservancy Springs to Life in Reserve," 1.

50. Ibid.

51. Husar, "Gaylord Donnelley Is Illinois 'Open Lands' Lord." Founded in 1963 as one of the nation's first urban conservation organizations, Openlands (originally called the Open Lands Project) is committed to protecting "the natural open spaces of northeastern Illinois and the surrounding region to ensure cleaner air and water, protect natural habitats and wildlife, and help balance and enrich" the lives of Chicagoans. The organization seeks to create a "vast network of land and water trails, tree-lined streets, and intimate public gardens within easy reach of every city dweller." Openlands has a strong presence in the area's public schools, offering educational outreach and volunteer programs for both children and adults. Among the organization's accomplishments are 55,000 protected acres of public land and waterways, landscape-scale restoration efforts such as the Illinois Prairie Path, the I & M Canal National Heritage Corridor, and the 19,000-acre Midewin National Tallgrass Prairie, the creation of the Openlands Lakeshore Preserve at Fort Sheridan in Lake County, and the establishment of the bi-state Hackmatack National Wildlife Refuge in McHenry County, Illinois, and Walworth County, Wisconsin. See http://www.openlands.org/.

52. The planning team for the Liberty Prairie Reserve Master Plan included Conserve Lake County; the Chicago Metropolitan Agency for Planning (CMAP); the Lake County Forest Preserve District; the Lake County Departments of Planning, Transportation, and Stormwater Management; the Liberty Prairie Foundation; Libertyville Township; the Illinois Department of Natural Resources; the Illinois Nature Preserves Commission; and Openlands. Several private landowners were consulted and represented throughout the process. For the master plan, see http://www.conservelakecounty.org/what-we-do/liberty-prairie-reserve.

53. Ibid.

54. James Kunstler calls the city "the unofficial capital of the 'environmental' movement." Kunstler, *The Geography of Nowhere*, 204.

55. Katherine H. Daniels and Edward J. Sullivan, *Oregon's 40-Year-Old Innovation*, American Planning Association, http://www.oregon.gov/LCD/docs/Oregons_40_year_old_innovation .pdf.

56. Cox, *War on the Dream*, 135.

57. Ibid., 136, 144.

58. Duany et al., *Suburban Nation*, 143, emphasis in the original.

59. Ibid., 143–144.

60. Kunstler, *The Geography of Nowhere*, 206.

61. See Nicki Sitko, "Urban Growth Boundaries: Economic Development Tool or Unwanted Interference?," April 21, 2005, University of Michigan, Taubman College of Architecture and Urban Planning, *Urban & Regional Planning Economic Development Handbook*, http://www.umich.edu/~econdev/urbanbound/.

62. "Master Planning History," Baltimore County Government, http://www.baltimorecountymd.gov/Agencies/planning/masterplanning/historyofmasterplanning.html.

63. Melanie Yanney, "Smart Zoning and Planning Protect Rural North County," April 12, 2011, Protecting North County Maryland, http://protectingnorthcountymd.wordpress.com/is-it-working/.

64. Ibid.

65. Melanie Yanney, "Muddled Master Plan Creates Rift in Community," May 3, 2011, Protecting North County Maryland, http://protectingnorthcountymd.wordpress.com/writers-choice/.

66. Ibid.

67. Ibid.

68. Layzer, *The Environmental Case*, 447–487.

69. Louv, *The Nature Principle*, 166.

70. http://www.prairiecrossing.com/pc/site/guiding-principles.html.

71. Vicky Ranney, pers. comm., October 28, 2014.

72. The island of Tobago, at the time a British possession, established the first forest preserve, in April 1776. The purpose was to protect mahogany trees from overlogging. Today the land is still protected as the Main Ridge Preserve. See Anderson, *Mahogany*, 90.

73. *The Prairie Enthusiasts: Conservation at Work*, http://www.theprairieenthusiasts.org/TPE%20Membership%20Brochure%202010.pdf.

74. George Ranney, pers. comm., October 24, 2014.

75. Vicky Ranney, pers. comm., October 28, 2014.

76. Ibid.

77. Rodkin, "Landed Gentry."

78. Vicky Ranney, pers. comm., October 28, 2014.

79. Michael Sands, pers. comm., October 8, 2014.

80. Vicky Ranney, pers. comm., October 28, 2014.

81. Ibid.

82. Linda Wiens, pers. comm., October 30, 2014.

83. "About Us," Liberty Prairie Foundation, http://libertyprairie.org/about-lpf/.

84. Ibid.

85. Quote from Michael Sands, as cited in Buntin and Pririe, *Unsprawl*, 174.

86. Brad Leibov, director of the Liberty Prairie Foundation, co-chairs the Fresh Taste Steering Committee; see http://www.freshtaste.org/.

87. Sustainable Agriculture and Food Systems Funders, http://www.safsf.org/.

88. Members of community-supported agriculture programs accept weekly deliveries of organic produce and free-range eggs. The cost of a Sandhill three-season vegetable share in 2014 was $915. There are five different share options to choose from: fruits, vegetables, meat, dairy, and eggs. The meat and dairy products come from Sandhill's Wisconsin operation. Prairie Crossing residents can pick up the produce directly from the farm, and Sandhill distributes produce to outside customers through a network of fifteen regional drop sites. Jennifer Miller, pers. comm., November 24, 2014.

89. Michael Sands, pers. comm., April 7, 2014.

90. Buntin and Pirie, *Unsprawl*, 175.

91. "Prairie Farm Corps," Liberty Prairie Foundation, http://libertyprairie.org/2013/12/17/prairie-farm-corps-2/.

92. Strachan Donnelley died in 2008. Laura Donnelley continues the conservation and education mission of her parents as president of the Gaylord and Dorothy Donnelley Foundation.

## Chapter Three. Sea of Suburbia

1. Jim Movatelli, "A History of Greenwashing: How Dirty Towels Impacted the Green Movement," *DailyFinance*, February 12, 2011, http://www.dailyfinance.com/2011/02/12/the-history-of-greenwashing-how-dirty-towels-impacted-the-green/; Swain, "On the Alert for Misleading Ads."

2. *Oxford English Dictionary*, s.v. "greenwash."

3. Chase, *In a Dark Wood*, 375–381.

4. Woodward, "A Sliver of Prairie Still Untamed." For endangered species eradication, see Gallagher, *The Grail Bird*, 122–123.

5. Nixon, while lacking personal conservation convictions, nevertheless signed the Clean Air Act and the Endangered Species Act and created the EPA. Eisenhower created the Arctic National Wildlife Refuge and believed in conservation to a degree that would be considered anathema in today's Republican Party. Teddy Roosevelt is the political father of conservation, having set aside more federally protected land than all other presidents combined. Prior to Reagan's election in 1980, House Democrats and Republicans exhibited average League of Conservation Voters scores of 54 and 37, a 17-point difference. Following Reagan's lead of less government, deregulation, local control, and general antipathy toward environmental protection—he declared himself a "Sagebrush Rebel" on the campaign trail—the League of Conservation Voters differential expanded fourfold by 2003, to 68 points, with the GOP registering only 14 points. The Senate did not fare much better, turning a 31-point differential into 57 points over the same time frame. For the calculation of LCV scores, see "Methodology," National Environmental Scorecard, League of Conservation Voters, http://scorecard.lcv.org/methodology.

6. "Sharp Divide between Republicans and Democrats on Energy and the Environment," January 27, 2012, http://pewresearch.org/databank/dailynumber/?NumberID=1418. Here is how Martha Marks, Illinois Republican and founder of Republicans for Environmental Protection, describes the Great Green Divide: "a Republican is *supposed* to be anti-environmental, and . . . if you care about protecting the environment you must be a Democrat." Marks, "The Green Old Party."

7. Brewer, *Conservancy*, 1.

8. Ibid., 11.

9. Lakoff, "Why It Matters How We Frame the Environment," 71.

10. Lakoff, *Moral Politics*, chap. 5.

11. George Lakoff, "What Conservatives Really Want," *George Lakoff* (blog), February 19, 2011, http://georgelakoff.com/2011/02/19/what-conservatives-really-want/.

12. Lakoff, *Moral Politics*, chap. 6.

13. Hardin, "The Tragedy of the Commons."

14. Scientific debate is currently under way to add a new epoch, the Anthropocene, to the geological time scale to reflect the overwhelming impact humans have had on the planet. It has been argued that humans now have a greater impact on life than natural selection. Others have argued that the whole planet has effectively become "domesticated." See Kareiva et al., "Conservation in the Anthropocene."

15. Gottlieb, *Forcing the Spring*, 35.

16. Platt, *Land Use and Society*, 93.

17. Kostyack, "Habitat Conservation Planning."

18. George Ranney, pers. comm., June 15, 2005.

19. http://libertyprairie.org/2013/12/17/prairie-farm-corps-2/.

20. Vicky Ranney, pers. comm., June 15, 2005.

21. Steve Apfelbaum, pers. comm., October 26, 2005; Michael Sands, pers. comm., October 19, 2005; George Ranney, pers. comm., June 15, 2005.

22. Steve Apfelbaum, pers. comm., October 26, 2005. For water quality issues, see Glennon, *Water Follies*, 108–109, and Wilson, *The Future of Life*, 107.

23. "Introduction to StopGreenwash.org," Greenpeace, http://stopgreenwash.org.

24. Cox, *Environmental Communication and the Public Sphere*, 299.

25. Brewer, *Conservancy*, 1.

26. Ibid., 98.

27. Baskin, *A Plague of Rats and Rubbervines*, 257.

28. George Ranney, pers. comm., June 15, 2005.

29. Apfelbaum et al., "The Prairie Crossing Project," 34.

30. Ibid., 1–2.

31. Franko et al., *Developing Sustainable Planned Communities*, 206.

32. Apfelbaum et al., "The Prairie Crossing Project," 2–3.

33. Julie Sibbing of the National Wildlife Federation coined the term "wet deserts" to describe artificial ponds because of their lack of biological activity and diversity. See Barringer, "Fewer Marshes + More Man-Made Ponds = Increased Wetlands."

34. Michael Sands, pers. comm., October 19, 2005.

35. Opinion on the lake's size from Michael Sands, as cited in Buntin and Pirie, *Unsprawl*, 177.

36. Steve Apfelbaum, pers. comm., October 26, 2005.

37. Ibid.

38. Chicago Wilderness, *Summary Report*, 8, 38.

39. Steve Apfelbaum, pers. comm., October 26, 2005; Michael Sands, pers. comm., October 19, 2005.

40. Michael Sands, pers. comm., October 19, 2005.

41. I participated in an ENSBC birdwatching event there on April 3, 2004.

42. Steve Apfelbaum, pers. comm., October 26, 2005; Michael Sands, pers. comm., October 19, 2005.

43. "Fifth of All Bird Species Are on Extinction Path, Survey Finds," http://www.nbcnews.com/id/8058650/#.VWyCqWdFD4g.

44. Brewer, *Conservancy*, 50. For habitat loss and its effect on biodiversity, see Baskin, *A Plague of Rats and Rubbervines*, 79, and Chase, *In a Dark Wood*, 79–80.

45. Applied Ecological Services, *2005 Assessment of the Prairie Crossing Prairie Plantings*, 9.

46. Steve Apfelbaum, pers. comm., August 16, 2013.

47. Quote from Baskin, *A Plague of Rats and Rubbervines*, 139. For prairie ecosystem loss, see Babbitt, *Cities in the Wilderness*.

48. Buntin and Pirie, *Unsprawl*, 177.

49. Michael Sands, pers. comm., October 19, 2005.

50. Schaeffer et al., "Use of a Stormwater Retention System for Conservation of Regionally Endangered Fishes."

51. Ibid.

52. Proponents of sprawl such as Wendell Cox, author of *War on the Dream*, frequently argue that sprawl is not an environmental problem because it represents only 2.6 percent of land use in America, according to the 2000 U.S. Census. Sprawl's ecological footprint is far greater than the acreage it occupies. The cumulative environmental impact of sprawl and the industries that support it—unsustainable agricultural practices, oil and mineral extraction, military and transportation infrastructure, industrial forestry, materials for consumer products—and the effects of pollution and global warming have literally transformed not only the United States but also many other regions of the world. Spacious homes require stuff to fill them. The post–World War II revolution in consumer durables and throwaway products has had devastating consequences around the world, affecting everything from the tar sands in Canada to rubber plantations in Indonesia to tropical timber exploitation in Latin America to the immense garbage patches in the Pacific Ocean. American suburban lifestyles impact far more global space than the 2.6 percent figure cited by Cox. For Cox's argument, see *War on the Dream*, 71. For the ecological impact of American lifestyles on the tropics, see Tucker, *Insatiable Appetite*, and Anderson, *Mahogany*. For the impact of American cars on the Canadian boreal forest, see Nikiforuk, *Tar Sands*. For the impact of America's plastic on the Pacific Ocean, see Freinkel, *Plastic*, 115–116, 129–130, 136, 274.

53. Quammen, *Song of the Dodo*, 409, 436.

54. Weidensaul, *Living on the Wind*, 355.

55. The equation $S = cA^z$ defines the relationship between species $(S)$ and a given area $(A)$ of land. The equation is derived from induction, the collection of field data from diverse organisms and ecosystems throughout the world. The variables $c$ and $z$ are constants that actually vary according to specific ecological circumstances. Each taxonomic group and geographic region will have its own $c$, such as one for frogs in Borneo and another for prairie plants in a quadrat of Illinois grassland. The exponent $z$ represents the degree to which an ecosystem landscape causes the number of species to decrease with decreasing area; it is the slope of

the species-area curve. The greater the impact of area on species numbers, the higher the value for z. The carrying capacities of ecosystems vary widely from the tropics to the poles. The resulting species-area curve describes the correlation between species and area within a series of tracts of habitat. See MacArthur and Wilson, *The Theory of Island Biogeography*. For an informative layman's discussion of the concepts, see Quammen, *Song of the Dodo*, 385–447.

56. Quammen, *Song of the Dodo*, 385.

57. Different environments and ecosystems have different constants based on empirical examination of carrying capacities.

58. This problem is particularly important for the bobolink, which requires large tracts of relatively undisturbed grassland habitat. Small parcels cannot support viable populations.

59. MacArthur and Wilson, *The Theory of Island Biogeography*, 4.

60. F. W. Preston, "The Canonical Distribution of Commonness and Rarity: Part II," *Ecology* 43, no. 3 (1962): 410–432, as cited in Adams, *The Future of the Wild*, 11.

61. "Global Ecosystem Services Revalued at US$125–145 Trillion per Year," Chartered Institute of Ecology and Environmental Management, http://www.cieem.net/news/184/global-ecosystem-services-revalued-at-us125-145-trillion-per-year.

62. Michael Sands, pers. comm., October 19, 2005.

63. Babbitt, *Cities in the Wilderness*, 113.

64. See *Liberty Prairie Reserve Master Plan*, 3, http://www.conservelakecounty.org/what-we-do/liberty-prairie-reserve.

65. Ibid., 31.

66. Ibid., 11.

67. Chicago Wilderness, *Summary Report*, 9.

68. Steve Apfelbaum, pers. comm., August 16, 2013.

69. Steve Apfelbaum, pers. comm., October 26, 2005; Michael Sands, pers. comm., October 19, 2005.

70. Steve Hovany, pers. comm., May 17, 2005.

71. Michael Sands, pers. comm., October 19, 2005.

72. Manning, *Grassland*, 3; Babbitt, *Cities in the Wilderness*, 100.

73. Gore, *Earth in the Balance*, 183; Wilson, *The Future of Life*, 105–112.

74. "Green Landscaping: Greenacres," U.S. Environmental Protection Agency, http://www.epa.gov/greenacres/nativeplants/factsht.html.

75. Steve Apfelbaum, pers. comm., August 16, 2013.

76. Chicago Wilderness, *Summary Report*, 8.


## Chapter Four. Changing the Culture

1. Merchant, *Reinventing Eden*, 3, 7.

2. Unidentified resident, pers. comm., October 19, 2005.

3. Michael Sands, pers. comm., October 19, 2005.

4. Construction of the condominiums and town square was completed in 2007.

5. Michael Sands, pers. comm., October 19, 2005; George Ranney, pers. comm., September 6, 2005; Vicky Ranney pers. comm., September 6, 2005.

6. Michael Sands, pers. comm., October 19, 2005.

7. Baskin, *A Plague of Rats and Rubbervines*, 79; Baskin, "Curbing Undesirable Invaders"; Burdick, *Out of Eden*, 95; Wilson, *The Diversity of Life*, 254.

8. Pimentel et al., "Environmental and Economic Costs of Nonindigenous Species in the United States," 53; Baskin, *A Plague of Rats and Rubbervines*, 4.

9. Ibid., 127–130, quote from 127.

10. Michael Sands, pers. comm., October 19, 2005.

11. Michael Sands, 2009 PowerPoint presentation to Prairie Crossing Homeowners Association.

12. For limitations of public access, see Blakely and Snyder, *Fortress America*, and McKenzie, *Privatopia*. Information on Prairie Crossing public access comes from George Ranney and Michael Sands, pers. comm., September 6, 2005, and October 19, 2005..

13. Michael Sands, pers. comm., October 19, 2005.

14. Here is an influential summary of the rational choice perspective on human behavior: "All human behavior can be viewed as involving participants who maximize their utility from a stable set of preferences and accumulate an optimal amount of information and other inputs from a variety of markets." Becker, *The Economic Approach to Human Behavior*, 14.

15. Kahn, "The Tyranny of Small Decisions."

16. I used an ordinal scale instrument of "very active," "active," "occasional," "inactive," "non-participant" for the following questions: (1) How would you describe your level of environmental activism prior to moving into Prairie Crossing? and (2) How would you describe your level of environmental activism after moving into Prairie Crossing? The categories were coded from 1 (very active) to 5 (non-participant), and each category was defined using example activities to guide resident selection.

17. John Breen, pers. comm., November 25, 2005. Breen is currently a board member but no longer president.

18. Baskin, *A Plague of Rats and Rubbervines*, 117.

19. Ibid., 222, 119.

20. John Breen, pers. comm., November 25, 2005.

21. Forsyth, *Reforming Suburbia*, 267, 273.

22. Thompson, "Overcoming Barriers to Ecologically Sensitive Land Management," 141.

23. Rothman, *The Greening of America?*, vii.

24. Erin Cummisford, pers. comm., November 24, 2014.

25. Michael Sands, pers. comm., October 19, 2005.

26. Buntin and Pirie, *Unsprawl*, 164.

27. Ibid., 166.

28. Edwards, *The Sustainability Revolution*, 42.

29. Buntin and Pirie, *Unsprawl*, 167.

30. McMahon, *Conservation Communities*, 31–33.

31. Ibid., 33.

32. Ibid.

33. Buntin and Pirie, *Unsprawl*, 168.

34. In 2013, the last full year for which data is available, thirteen homes sold, representing 3.6

percent of the subdivision. In 2014, listings ranged from $475,000 for a four-bedroom, four-bath 3,170-square-foot home to $259,000 for a three-bedroom, two-bath 1,767-square-foot home. Home prices were obtained from the Carton Team, realtors affiliated with @properties, who specialize in selling Prairie Crossing homes. See http://prairiecrossinghomes.com.

35. Buntin and Pirie, *Unsprawl*, 169.

36. Ibid.

37. Mooney, "Your Neighbors May Be Turning You into an Environmentalist."

38. Ibid.

## Chapter Five. A Geography of Somewhere

1. Blakely and Snyder, *Fortress America*, 148–152; Duany et al., *Suburban Nation*, 130, 153; Reich, "Secession of the Successful," 14.

2. McKenzie, *Privatopia*, 79.

3. http://www.prairiecrossing.com/pc/site/guiding-principles.html.

4. McKenzie, *Privatopia*, 80–81, 84.

5. McKenzie, "Trouble in Privatopia," 192. For pervasive community problems in CID living, see Guberman, "Home Is Where the Heart Is."

6. McKenzie, "Trouble in Privatopia," 195.

7. McKenzie, *Beyond Privatopia*, 16–17, 78–79, quotes from 79, 78.

8. Income data comes from the Prairie Crossing resident survey, as measured in 2006 dollars.

9. The word "ecotopia" in this context is a spinoff of *Privatopia*, the title of McKenzie's book. Vicky Ranney has never used the word and dislikes the use of it to describe Prairie Crossing. The intent of using it here is to emphasize the environmental components of the private government model.

10. "Survey: Americans Like Their Community Associations," NewsUSA, http://www.newsusa.com/articles/article/survey-americans-like-their-community-associations.aspx.

11. Zogby conducted polling on community living in 2005, 2007, 2009, and 2012. Data on future living is reported from the 2005 poll only. For the most recent (2012) version of the report on poll results, see *Who Should Judge Community Association Success? The Residents Who Live in Community Associations!*, Community Associations Institute, http://www.caionline.org/info/research/Documents/national_homeowner_research.pdf.

12. Ibid.; data on future living is taken only from the 2005 Zogby poll.

13. Duany et al., *Suburban Nation*, 159.

14. Ibid., 209, 264, 81–82.

15. Frantz and Collins, *Celebration, U.S.A.*, 57.

16. Rodkin, "Landed Gentry," 14.

17. Vicky Ranney, pers. comm., September 6, 2005.

18. George Ranney, pers. comm., September 6, 2005.

19. Putnam, *Bowling Alone*, 275; Webber, "Order in Diversity"; Blakely and Snyder, *Fortress America*, 32.

20. Putnam, *Bowling Alone*, 275; Webber, "Order in Diversity"; Malcolm Gladwell, "Small Change: Why the Revolution Will Not Be Tweeted," *New Yorker*, October 4, 2010, http://

www.newyorker.com/magazine/2010/10/04/small-change-malcolm-gladwell. For the limits of social media in generating social advocacy, see Cox, *Environmental Communication and the Public Sphere*, 197.

21. Blakely and Snyder, *Fortress America*, 32; Hillery, "Definitions of Community."

22. Principal Maria Sanborn, pers. comm., November 18, 2005.

23. Blakely and Snyder, *Fortress America*, 132–133.

24. "Our Story," Conserve Lake County, http://www.conservelakecounty.org/who-we-are/our-story; "Lake County Vision for Land Preservation," http://www.conservelakecounty.org/what-we-do/land-preservation/countrywide-vision-for-open-space.

25. Sarah Surroz, pers. comm., August 28, 2014.

26. Blakely and Snyder, *Fortress America*, 178–179.

27. Ibid., 130–131.

28. Ibid. On p. 179 Blakely and Snyder ask: "How would you describe the level of involvement of residents in association-sponsored activities other than governance (i.e., social or charitable events)?" The choices they give are: "Very active," "Somewhat active," or "Not very active." Three new questions: (1) How often would you say that you socialize with your neighbors? Choices: One or more times per week, Once per month, Several times per year, Once a year, or Never; (2) Would you consider moving into a conservation-oriented community again? Choices: Yes, No, or Maybe; (3) Which of the following related conservation activities have you participated in at Prairie Crossing (select all that apply): Walking or biking on community trails, Birdwatching, Boating on lake or ponds, Ice-skating on lake or ponds, Horseback riding, Planting native plants on property, Cultivating organic garden, Volunteering on farm, Taking children to farm, Other: write-in.

29. Forsyth, *Reforming Suburbia*, 1.

30. Ibid., 18, 20, 23.

31. Schumpeter, "The Father of Fracking," *Economist*, April 3, 2013, http://www.economist.com/news/business/21582482-few-businesspeople-have-done-much-change-world-george-mitchell-father.

32. Forsyth, *Reforming Suburbia*, 11.

33. Ibid., 174.

34. McHarg, *Design with Nature*, 2, 5.

35. "He bought into the whole thing." Forsyth, *Reforming Suburbia*, 174.

36. McHarg and Steiner, *To Heal the Earth*, 325.

37. Forsyth, *Reforming Suburbia*, 11, 175.

38. Ibid., 203.

39. Ibid., 202–203, 207.

40. Ibid., 12, 107.

41. Ibid., 107–160.

42. Ibid., 143, 145.

43. Ibid., 99, 100.

44. Paul Goldberger, "Orange County: Tomorrowland—Wall to Wall," *New York Times*, December 11, 1988, cited ibid., 97.

45. Ibid., 89.

46. Ibid., 243, 259.

47. Population and acreage figures are from the 2010 U.S. Census. Household numbers are from the 2000 U.S. Census and are taken from Forsyth, *Reforming Suburbia*, 7. The Woodlands statistics are CDP (census designated-place).

48. Forsyth, *Reforming Suburbia*, 273.

49. The school serves Woodland District 50 and Fremont District 79.

50. The lottery is held once a year, in early March. Admittance forms are available both online and at the school office.

51. The school sponsors are Waste Management, Lightscape Outdoor Lighting, Southwest Windpower, Northwestern/Lake Forest Hospital, the Institute for Integrated Environmental Education, Maritek Energy Solutions, WRD Environmental, and Linden Group Health Services.

52. Vicky Ranney, personal comm., September 17, 2014; Maria Sanborn (former principal), personal comm., November 18, 2005; "About PCCS," Prairie Crossing Charter School, http://prairiecrossingcharterschool.org/about/. The current principal declined to talk to me because of the lawsuit.

53. The League of Conservation Voters, an environmental 501(c)(3) watchdog group, branded Republican Phil Crane one of its "Dirty Dozen"—those with the worst environmental voting records in Congress. Democrat Melissa Bean defeated and replaced Crane, in part on the basis of his poor environmental record. Bean went on to record LCV scores in the 1980s during her tenure. Joe Walsh, a tea party favorite, defeated Melissa Bean by less than 200 votes in the 2010 elections, only to be redistricted out of the district and then lose in 2012.

54. The current executive director of the school, Geoff Deigan, did not respond to repeated requests for an interview.

55. Frantz and Collins, *Celebration, U.S.A.*, 135–138, 252–254, 310 (quote), 319–320.

56. The school has won four state academic achievement awards, in 2004, 2005, 2009, and 2010, and received national recognition in 2012 for winning the Green Ribbon Award and again in 2013 for winning the Blue Ribbon Award. "Prairie Crossing Charter School among Top 50 School Districts in Illinois," Prairie Crossing Charter School, archived at http://patch.com/illinois/grayslake/prairie-crossing-charter-school-among-top-50-schools-illinois-0.

57. Lisa Black, "Woodland District Files Suit against Charter," *Chicago Tribune*, May 22, 2014, http://articles.chicagotribune.com/2014-05-22/news/ct-charter-school-lawsuit-met-20140522_1_prairie-crossing-charter-school-isbe-spokeswoman-state-aid.

58. "Prairie Crossing Executive Director: Letter Is Unfounded," Prairie Crossing Charter School, archived at http://patch.com/illinois/grayslake/prairie-crossing-executive-director-lawsuit-is-unfounded.

59. "For example, according to their Illinois District Report Card in 2013, with 6508 students enrolled, Woodland received $63,837,314 in local property tax and $474,761 in General State Aid, equaling approximately $9,882 per student. In contrast, Prairie Crossing received from the State's PCTC calculations approximately $9,620 per student for those who chose to attend PCCS over Woodland." Ibid. It should also be noted that Prairie Crossing receives outside funding from sponsors, donations, and auction sales.

60. Outreach Timeline 2009–2010, Prairie Crossing Charter School, http://www.isbe.net/foia/pdf/fy2010/apr10/10-324_doc.pdf.

61. Woodland attorney James Petrungaro argued in court proceedings that lack of school-provided transportation for at-risk students was a primary cause of lack of enrollment. He argued that many families did not have cars: "If I am a low income family, if I am a parent of a child from a low income family and lives in an apartment and I am having two, three jobs just to make ends meet, I don't have a car. My neighbors don't have cars." Petrungaro did not provide evidence for this assertion. National rates of car ownership show that 19 percent of African-Americans and 13.7 percent of Hispanics do not own cars, compared to 4.6 percent of whites. Since no study has been done at Prairie Crossing, it is hard to judge the merits of the transportation argument. If Woodland District 50 parents of at-risk students have car ownership rates similar to the national rates, it seems unlikely that that factor alone is responsible for racial enrollment disparities. It should also be noted that two train lines provide public transportation within walking distance of the school. *Board of Education Woodland District 50 v. Illinois State Charter School Commission, et al.*, Emergency Motion to Stay the Final Decision of the Illinois State Charter School Commission, filed June 6, 2014, Case No. 2014 CH 08573, https://www.dist50.net/ISCSC/Documents/Mtn%20Stay.pdf. For automobile ownership rates, see Alan Berube, Elizabeth Deakin, and Steve Raphael, "Socioeconomic Differences in Household Automobile Ownership Rates: Implications for Evacuation," June 2006, https://escholarship.org/uc/item/7bp4n2f6.

62. Black, "Woodland District Files Suit against Charter."

63. "A Textbook Case of Charter Skimming," *Diane Ravitch's Blog: A Site to Discuss Better Education for All*, http://dianeravitch.net/2014/05/26/a-textbook-case-of-charter-skilling/.

64. Here is the question I asked: "In researching the charter school at Prairie Crossing (PCCS), I came across your May 26, 2014, blog on skimming at the school. Is there anything you can tell me about how the school skims?" Pers. comm., October 2, 2014.

65. Diane Ravitch, pers. comm., October 2, 2014.

66. Diane Ravitch, pers. comm., October 3, 2014.

67. *Board of Education of Woodland Community Consolidated School District 50 v. Illinois State Charter School Commission, and Board of Directors of Prairie Crossing Charter School, and Illinois State Board of Education*, filed May 20, 2014, https://www.dist50.net/ISCSC/Documents/Complaint%20052014.pdf, 5.

68. On March 23, 2015, Judge Thomas Allen ruled that the Illinois Charter School Commission's five-year renewal of the school's charter was "clearly erroneous and is reversed." Allen's ruling was narrow, involving only one count: "that Woodland's complaints should have been considered in the state commission's decision to renew Prairie Crossing's charter for another five years." All three defendants in the case, the Illinois Board of Education, the Illinois Charter School Commission, and the Prairie Crossing Charter School, have appealed the ruling to the Illinois Appellate Court. No court hearing has been set as of June 15, 2015. The school remains open on appeal. Bookwalter, "Prairie Crossing Charter School's Future Uncertain"; Jeannie Nowaczewski, pers. comm., June 5, 2015.

69. Charter schools can be policy laboratories just as states are in our federal system. Massachusetts experimented with a market-based healthcare system that later became the model for Obamacare. The policy's effectiveness was tested on a smaller scale without subjecting our national system to possible large-scale failure. Charter schools can play the same role.

70. "Curriculum," Prairie Crossing Charter School, http://prairiecrossingcharterschool

.org/programs/curriculum. The North Central Regional Education Laboratory defines constructivism as "an approach to teaching and learning based on the premise that cognition (learning) is the result of 'mental construction.' In other words, students learn by fitting new information together with what they already know. Constructivists believe that learning is affected by the context in which an area is taught as well as by students' beliefs and attitudes." "Constructivist Teaching and Learning Models," Pathways to School Improvement, http://www.ncrel.org/sdrs/areas/issues/envrnmnt/drugfree/sa3const.htm.

71. http://www.prairiecrossing.com/pc/site/guiding-principles.html; Reich, "Secession of the Successful"; Duany et al., *Suburban Nation*, 46; Blakely and Snyder, *Fortress America*, 1.

72. Huber, *Hard Green*, 150, 185.

73. Steve Hovany, pers. comm., May 17, 2005; George Ranney, pers. comm., September 6, 2005.

74. George Ranney, pers. comm., September 6, 2005.

75. Jackson, *Crabgrass Frontier*, 84, 47.

76. Fishman, *Bourgeois Utopias*, 84.

77. Gonzalez, *Urban Sprawl, Global Warming, and the Empire of Capital*, 44.

78. Ibid., 59.

79. Judd and Swanstrom, *City Politics*, 268, 270.

80. Ibid., 272.


## Chapter Six. Civic Participation

1. McKenzie, *Privatopia*, 25, 131, 184; Blakely and Snyder, *Fortress America*, 35; Putnam, *Bowling Alone*, 15–28, quote from back of jacket.

2. American National Election Studies, *The ANES Guide to Public Opinion and Electoral Behavior*, http://electionstudies.org/nesguide/nesguide.htm.

3. McKenzie, *Privatopia*, 25.

4. The coattail effect refers to voters who, influenced by their support for the incumbent president, also vote for the candidates for Congress from the same political party.

5. Lake County Clerk Richard Carrison, pers. comm., March 1, 2006; Lake County Clerk Laura Hausmann, pers. comm., June 3, 2014.

6. Lake County Clerk Linda Hausmann, pers. comm., June 3, 2014.

7. For election data, see Election Results Archive, Office of the County Clerk, Lake County, http://countyclerk.lakecountyil.gov/ElectionInfo/Election-Results/Archive/Pages/default.aspx.

8. Ibid.

9. In 2006 Lake County began a new format of publishing election data, and it is no longer possible to perform similar reconstructions, which were done with the assistance of former clerk employee Richard Carrison.

10. "Voter Turnout 1948–2008," *ANES Guide to Public Opinion and Electoral Behavior*, http://www.electionstudies.org/nesguide/2ndtable/t6a_2_2.htm.

11. The scorecard used by the League of Conservation Voters "represents the consensus of experts from about 20 respected environmental and conservation organizations who selected

the key votes on which members of Congress should be scored. LCV scores votes on the most important issues of the year, including energy, global warming, public health, public lands and wildlife conservation, and spending for environmental programs. . . . Annual scores are based on a scale of 0 to 100 and calculated by dividing the number of pro-environment votes cast by the total number of votes scored. Lifetime scores are calculated in the same manner so that each vote counts equally. Note that lifetime scores are not the average of annual scores, which would assign different weights to votes since the total number of votes scored varies from year to year." "Methodology," National Environmental Scorecard, League of Conservation Voters, http://scorecard.lcv.org/methodology; League of Conservation Voters, National Environmental Scorecard Archive, http://scorecard.lcv.org/scorecard/archive.12. "LCV Names Rep Phil Crane to Dirty Dozen List," League of Conservation Voters press release, http://lcv-archive.pub30.convio.net/newsroom/press-releases/lcv-names-rep-phil-crane-to-dirty-dozen-list.html. Environmental Action and the League of Conservation Voters developed the original Dirty Dozen campaign in 1970. Resurrected by the LCV in 2004, the ad campaign has been extraordinarily effective. In the 2012 election, eleven of twelve targeted candidates suffered defeat.

13. http://scorecard.lcv.org/scorecard/archive.

14. "Summary & Observations: A Survey of Prairie Crossing Guiding Principles," unpublished report, February 2010.

15. The guiding principles proved to be valuable as a blueprint for the developers in the planning and developmental stages, and they also provide goals for the residents to aspire to. They are not, however, legally enforceable.

16. Vicky Ranney, pers. comm., November 13, 2014. For information on Michael Bond and Sandy Cole, see http://www.ilga.gov/senate/Senator.asp?MemberID=1339 and http://www.ilga.gov/house/rep.asp?MemberID=1350. For information on the Grayslake Village Board, see http://www.villageofgrayslake.com/index.aspx?nid=125.

17. Dunlap, "Developing a Suburb with Principles."

## Chapter Seven. Nature's Suburb

1. Cronon, *Changes in the Land*, 138. "Nature's Suburb," the title of this chapter, was coined by my mentor Dennis Judd of the University of Illinois at Chicago and plays off Cronon's *Nature's Metropolis*, his insightful exploration of Chicago's role in the nineteenth-century settlement of the West.

2. A recent study of subfossil leaves trapped in seventeenth-century milldam sediment has shown that Pennsylvania's forest composition and hydrology has changed dramatically since initial European contact. Elliot et al., "Subfossil Leaves Reveal a New Upland Hardwood Component of the Pre-European Piedmont Landscape," http://journals.plos.org/plosone/article?id=10.1371/journal.pone.0079317.

3. Steve Apfelbaum, pers. comm., October 26, 2005; Michael Sands, pers. comm., October 19, 2005.

4. George Ranney pers. comm., September 6, 2005; Michael Sands, pers. comm., October 19, 2005.

5. George Ranney pers. comm., September 6, 2005; Michael Sands, pers. comm., October 19, 2005.

6. Huber, *Hard Green*, 74.

7. George Ranney, pers. comm., September 6, 2005.

8. Michael Sands stated that Prairie Crossing attempted to permit granny flats on new homes built in the later stages of the development. Existing homeowners objected, and the Village of Grayslake also denied alteration of the building permits; pers. comm., April 7, 2014.

9. Frank Martin, pers. comm., November 8, 2014. The Prairie Crossing development team also helped design the landfill expansion that led to the agreement.

10. Ibid. For the Hidden Springs principles, see McMahon, *Conservation Communities*, 150.

11. Kane, "Prairie Flower," 11.

12. Ibid.

13. Ibid., 14.

14. Frank Martin, pers. comm., November 8, 2014.

15. Ibid.

16. However, Martin acknowledged that the terms of the Heartland Agreement somewhat limited the housing options. Ibid.

17. McMahon, *Conservation Communities*, 234.

18. Prairie Crossing is also part of the much larger Liberty Prairie Reserve, which legally protects 3,383 of 5,770 acres. The Liberty Prairie Foundation, Conserve Lake County, and other affiliated organizations are continually seeking to add to the protected acreage through conservation easement and land trust acquisition.

19. McMahon, *Conservation Communities*, 198–200.

20. Ibid., 129.

21. Dunlap, "Developing a Suburb with Principles."

22. McMahon, *Conservation Communities*, 213.

23. Layzer, *The Environmental Case*, 448.

24. Murphy, "Farm-to-Table Living Takes Root."

25. Michael Sands, pers. comm., October 19, 2005.

26. Murphy, "Farm-to-Table Living Takes Root."

27. McMahon, *Conservation Communities*, 174.

28. Ibid., 190.

29. Ibid., 85.

30. Ibid., 85–86, 89.

31. Michael Sands is not aware of any communities, McMahon's comprehensive examination of conservation communities did not report any, and as this book goes to press, I am not aware of any. See McMahon, *Conservation Communities*.

32. George Ranney, pers. comm., September 6, 2005.

33. Michael Sands, pers. comm., October 8, 2014, and October 19, 2005.

34. Louv, *The Nature Principle*, 223.

35. Michael Sands, pers. comm., April 7, 2014.

36. Murphy, "Farm-to-Table Living Takes Root."

37. Schaeffer et al., "Use of a Stormwater Retention System for Conservation of Regionally Endangered Fishes," 73.

38. Forsyth, *Reforming Suburbia*, 289.

39. *Liberty Prairie Reserve Master Plan*, 45, http://www.conservelakecounty.org/what-we-do/liberty-prairie-reserve.

40. *Liberty Prairie Reserve Master Plan: Summary Brochure*, 3, libertyprairie.org/wp-content/uploads/2013/12/lpr-master-plan-summary.pdf.

41. DeStefano and Johnson, "Species That Benefit from Sprawl," 212.

42. Ibid., 215.

43. Elizabeth Johnson and Michael Klemens, "The Impacts of Sprawl on Biodiversity," in *Nature in Fragments*, 45.

44. Kareiva et al., "Conservation in the Anthropocene."

45. For degradation in ecosystem function and productivity, see Bai et al., "Proxy Global Assessment of Land Degradation," and Daily, "Restoring Value to the World's Degraded Lands." For data on ice-free land surface alterations, see Sanderson et al., "The Human Footprint and the Last of the Wild," and Ellis and Ramankutt, "Putting People in the Map." Quotes from Hooke and Martín-Duque, "Land Transformation by Humans," 4.

46. McMahon, *Conservation Communities*, viii.

47. Ibid., 54.

48. Cronon, "The Trouble with Wilderness, or, Getting Back to the Wrong Nature," in *Uncommon Ground*, 69–90.

# BIBLIOGRAPHY

Adams, Jonathan S. *The Future of the Wild: Radical Conservation in a Crowded World*. Boston: Beacon Press, 2006.

Anderson, Jennifer L. *Mahogany: The Costs of Luxury in Early America*. Cambridge, Mass.: Harvard University Press, 2012.

Apfelbaum, Steve. *Nature's Second Chance: Restoring the Ecology of Stone Farm Prairie*. Boston: Beacon, 2009.

Apfelbaum, Steve I., John D. Eppich, Thomas H. Price, and Michael Sands. "The Prairie Crossing Project: Attaining Water Quality and Stormwater Management Goals in a Conservation Development." In Environmental Protection Agency, *Proceedings of a National Symposium: Using Ecological Restoration to Meet Clean Water Act Goals*, 33–38. [Chicago]: Northeastern Illinois Planning Commission, Natural Resources Department, 1995.

Applied Ecological Services. *2005 Assessment of the Prairie Crossing Prairie Plantings, Grayslake, Illinois*. Brodhead, Wisc.: Applied Ecological Services, 2005.

Babbitt, Bruce. *Cities in the Wilderness: A New Vision of Land Use in America*. Washington, D.C.: Island Press, 2005.

Bai, Z. G., D. L. Dent, L. Olsson, and M. E. Schaepman. "Proxy Global Assessment of Land Degradation." *Soil Use and Management* 24 (2008): 223–234.

Barlow, Maude, and Tony Clarke. *Blue Gold: The Fight to Stop the Corporate Theft of the World's Water*. New York: New Press, 2002.

Barringer, Felicity. "Fewer Marshes + More Man-Made Ponds = Increased Wetlands." *New York Times*, March 31, 2006.

Bartlett, Peggy F., ed. *Urban Place: Reconnecting with the Natural World*. Cambridge, Mass.: MIT Press, 2005.

Baskin, Yvonne. "Curbing Undesirable Invaders." *Bioscience* 46 (1996): 732–736.

————. *A Plague of Rats and Rubbervines: The Growing Threat of Species Invasions*. Washington, D.C.: Island Press, 2002.

Beach, Dana. *Coastal Sprawl: The Effects of Urban Design on Aquatic Ecosystems in the United States*. Arlington, Va.: Pew Oceans Commission, 2002.

Becker, Gary. *The Economic Approach to Human Behavior*. Chicago: University of Chicago Press, 1976.

Blakely, Edward J., and Mary Gail Snyder. *Fortress America: Gated Communities in the United States*. Washington, D.C.: Brookings Institution Press, 1999.

Bookwalter, Genevieve. "Prairie Crossing Charter School's Future Uncertain after Charter Pulled." *Chicago Tribune*, March 25, 2015.

Bormann, F. Herbert, Diana Balmori, and Gordon T. Geballe. *Redesigning the American Lawn: A Search for Environmental Harmony*. New Haven, Conn.: Yale University Press, 1993.

Bosso, Christopher J. *Environment, Inc.: From Grassroots to Beltway*. Lawrence: University Press of Kansas, 2005.

Brewer, Richard. *Conservancy: The Land Trust Movement in America*. Lebanon, N.H.: University Press of New England, 2003.

Brinkley, Douglas. *The Wilderness Warrior: Theodore Roosevelt and the Crusade for America*. New York: Harper Perennial, 2009.

Brugemann, Robert. *Sprawl: A Compact History*. Chicago: University of Chicago Press, 2005.

Buntin, Simmons B., and Ken Pirie. *Unsprawl: Remixing Spaces as Places*. Lexington, Ky.: Planetizen Press, 2013.

Burchell, Robert W., Anthony Downs, Barbara McCann, and Sahan Mukherji. *Sprawl Costs: Economic Impacts of Unchecked Development*. Washington, D.C.: Island Press, 2005.

Burdick, Alan. *Out of Eden: An Odyssey of Ecological Invasion*. New York: Farrar, Straus and Giroux, 2005.

Butler, Katy. "Winning Words." *Sierra*, July/August 2004, 54–64.

Byers, Diane L., and Joseph C. Mitchell. "Sprawl and Species with Limited Dispersal Abilities." In *Nature in Fragments: The Legacy of Sprawl*, edited by Elizabeth Johnson and Michael W. Klemens, 157–180. New York: Columbia University Press, 2005.

Calthorpe, Peter, and William Fulton. *The Regional City: Planning for the End of Sprawl*. Washington, D.C.: Island Press, 2001.

Carson, Rachel. *Silent Spring*. New York: Random House, 1962.

Cather, Willa. *My Ántonia*. New York: Barnes and Noble, 2003.

Chambers, Nicky, Craig Simmons, and Mathis Wackernagel. *Sharing Nature's Interests: Ecological Footprints as an Indicator of Sustainability*. London: Earthscan Publications, 2000.

Chase, Alston. *In a Dark Wood: The Fight over Forests and the Tyranny of Ecology*. New York: Houghton Mifflin, 1995.

————. *Playing God in Yellowstone: The Destruction of America's First National Park*. New York: Harcourt Brace and Co., 1986.

Chicago Wilderness. *The State of Our Chicago Wilderness: A Report Card on the Health of the Region's Ecosystems*. Chicago: Chicago Wilderness, 2006. http://c5.chicagowilderness.org/files/2213/3029/2620/cw_report_card_technical.pdf.

———. *Summary Report: The State of Our Chicago Wilderness*. Chicago: Chicago Wilderness, 2006. http://c5.chicagowilderness.org/files/2913/3054/8568/cw_report_card_summary.pdf.

Chu, Miyoko. *Songbird Journeys: Four Seasons in the Lives of Migratory Birds*. New York: Walker and Co., 2006.

Cochrane, Theodore, and Hugh Iltis. *Atlas of the Wisconsin Prairie and Savanna Flora*. Technical Bulletin No. 191. Madison, Wisc.: Department of Natural Resources, 2000.

Commoner, Barry. *The Closing Circle: Nature, Man, and Technology*. New York: Alfred A. Knopf, 1971.

Cone, Marla. *Silent Snow: The Slow Poisoning of the Arctic*. New York: Grove Press, 2005.

Cooper, Mary H. "Endangered Species Act: Is the Landmark Law in Need of Change?" *CQ Researcher* 15, no. 21 (2005): 493–516.

Cox, Robert. *Environmental Communication and the Public Sphere*. Thousand Oaks, Calif.: Sage Publications, 2013.

Cox, Wendell. *War on the Dream: How Anti-Sprawl Policy Threatens the Quality of Life*. Lincoln, Nebr.: iUniverse, 2006.

Cramer, Phillip. *Deep Environmental Politics: The Role of Radical Environmentalism in Crafting American Environmental Policy*. Westport, Conn.: Praeger, 1998.

Cronon, William. *Changes in the Land: Indians, Colonists, and the Ecology of New England*. New York: Farrar, Straus and Giroux, 2003.

———. *Nature's Metropolis: Chicago and the Great West*. New York: W. W. Norton, 1991.

———. *Uncommon Ground: Rethinking the Human Place in Nature*. New York: New York University Press, 1996.

Curtis, John T. "The Modification of Mid-Latitude Grasslands and Forests by Man." In *Man's Role in Changing the Face of the Earth*, edited by William L. Thomas Jr., 721–736. Chicago: University of Chicago Press, 1956.

Daily, Gretchen C. "Restoring Value to the World's Degraded Lands." *Science* 269, no. 5222 (1995): 350–354.

DeStefano, Stephen, and Elizabeth A. Johnson. "Species That Benefit from Sprawl." In *Nature in Fragments: The Legacy of Sprawl*, edited by Elizabeth Johnson and Michael W. Klemens, 206–236. New York: Columbia University Press, 2005.

Devine, Robert S. *Bush versus the Environment*. New York: Anchor Books, 2004.

Downs, Anthony. *New Visions for Metropolitan America*. Washington, D.C.: Brookings Institution, 1994.

Dreier, Peter, John Mollenkopf, and Todd Swanstrom. *Place Matters: Metropolitics for the Twenty-First Century*. Lawrence: University Press of Kansas, 2001.

Duany, Andres, Elizabeth Plater-Zyberk, and Jeff Speck. *Suburban Nation: The Rise of Sprawl and the Decline of the American Dream*. New York: North Point Press, 2001.

Dunlap, David W. "Developing a Suburb with Principles." *New York Times*, July 11, 1999.

Edwards, Andres R. *The Sustainability Revolution: Portrait of a Paradigm Shift*. Gabriela Island, B.C.: New Society, 2005.

Eisenberg, Cristina. *The Wolf's Tooth: Keystone Predators, Trophic Cascades, and Biodiversity*. Washington, D.C.: Island Press, 2010.

Elder, John, and Robert Finch. *Nature Writing: The Tradition in English*. New York: Norton Books, 2002.

Elliot, Sara J., Peter Wilf, Robert C. Walter, and Dorothy J. Merritts. "Subfossil Leaves Reveal a New Upland Hardwood Component of the Pre-European Piedmont Landscape, Lancaster County, Pennsylvania." *PLOS ONE* 8, no. 11 (2005): e79317.

Ellis, Erle C., and Navin Ramankutty. "Putting People in the Map: Anthropogenic Biomes of the World." *Frontiers in Ecology and the Environment* 6, no. 8 (2008): 439–447.

Fishman, Robert. *Bourgeois Utopias: The Rise and Fall of Suburbia*. New York: Basic Books, 1987.

Flannery, Tim. *The Eternal Frontier: An Ecological History of North America and Its Peoples*. New York: Atlantic Monthly Press, 2001.

Forsyth, Ann. *Reforming Suburbia: The Planned Communities of Irvine, Columbia, and The Woodlands*. Berkeley: University of California Press, 2005.

Franko, Richard, et al. *Developing Sustainable Planned Communities*. Chicago: Urban Land Institute, 2007.

Frantz, Douglas, and Catherine Collins. *Celebration, U.S.A.: Living in Disney's Brave New Town*. New York: Henry Holt and Co., 1999.

Freinkel, Susan. *Plastic: A Toxic Love Story*. Boston: Houghton Mifflin Harcourt, 2011.

Friedman, Thomas L. *Hot, Flat, and Crowded: Why We Need a Green Revolution—and How It Can Renew America*. New York: Farrar, Straus and Giroux, 2008.

Frug, Gerald E. *City Making: Building Communities without Building Walls*. Princeton, N.J.: Princeton University Press, 1999.

Frumkin, Howard. "The Health of Places, the Wealth of Evidence." In *Urban Place: Reconnecting with the Natural World*, edited by Peggy F. Bartlett, 253–270. Cambridge, Mass.: MIT Press, 2005.

Gallagher, Tim. *The Grail Bird: Hot on the Trail of the Ivory-Billed Woodpecker*. New York: Houghton Mifflin, 2005.

Glennon, Robert. *Water Follies: Groundwater Pumping and the Fate of Freshwater Rivers*. Washington, D.C.: Island Press, 2002.

Gonzalez, George A. *Urban Sprawl, Global Warming, and the Empire of Capital*. Albany, N.Y.: SUNY Press, 2009.

Gore, Albert. *Earth in the Balance: Ecology and the Human Spirit*. New York: Houghton Mifflin, 1992.

Gottlieb, Robert. *Forcing the Spring: The Transformation of the Environmental Movement*. Washington, D.C.: Island Press, 2005.

Guberman, Ross. "Home Is Where the Heart Is." *Legal Affairs*, November/December 2004. http://www.legalaffairs.org/issues/November-December-2004/feature_guberman_novdec04.msp.

Halberstadt, Hans. *The American Family Farm*. Norwalk, Conn.: MBI Publishing, 2003.

Handley, John. "Experiment on the Prairie: Transportation and Conservation Separate This Development from Rest of Suburbia." *Chicago Tribune*, September 29, 2002.

Hardin, Garrett. "The Tragedy of the Commons." *Science* 162 (1968): 1243–1248.

Hayden, Dolores. *Building Suburbia: Green Fields and Urban Growth, 1820–2000*. New York: Vintage Books, 2003.

Heclo, Hugh. "Issue Networks and Executive Establishment." In *The New American Political System*, edited by Anthony King, 87–124. Washington, D.C.: American Enterprise Institute, 1978.

Helzer, Chris. *The Ecology and Management of Prairies in the Central United States*. Iowa City: University of Iowa Press, 2010.

Hilkevitch, Jon. "Chicago Area Falls to No. 2 for Worst Traffic Congestion in U.S. but Is Still No. 1 for Costs to Drivers." *Chicago Tribune*, September 17, 2011.

Hillery, George A., Jr. "Definitions of Community: Areas of Agreement." *Rural Sociology* 20 (1955): 59–68.

Holmes, Hannah. *Suburban Safari: A Year on the Lawn*. New York: Bloomsbury, 2005.

Hooke, Roger LeB., and José F. Martín-Duque. "Land Transformation by Humans: A Review." *GSA Today* 22, no. 12 (2012): 4–10.

Hough, Michael. *Cities and Natural Process*. London: Routledge, 1995.

Huber, Peter. *Hard Green: Saving the Environment from the Environmentalists; A Conservative Manifesto*. New York: Basic Books, 1999.

Inouye, David W. "Biodiversity and Ecological Security." In *From Resource Scarcity to Ecological Security: Exploring New Limits to Growth*, edited by Dennis Pirages and Ken Cousins, 203–216. Cambridge, Mass.: MIT Press, 2005.

Jackson, Kenneth T. *Crabgrass Frontier: The Suburbanization of the United States*. New York: Oxford University Press, 1985.

Jacobs, Jane. *The Death and Life of Great American Cities*. New York: Random House, 1961.

Jansson, AnnMari, Monica Hammer, Carl Folke, and Robert Costanza, eds. *Investing in Natural Capital: The Ecological Economics Approach to Sustainability*. Washington, D.C.: Island Press, 1994.

Johnson, Elizabeth A., and Michael W. Klemens. *Nature in Fragments: The Legacy of Sprawl*. New York: Columbia University Press, 2005.

Judd, Dennis R., and Paul P. Kantor. *The Politics of Urban America: A Reader*. Boston: Allyn and Bacon, 1998.

Judd, Dennis R., and Todd Swanstrom. *City Politics: Private Power and Public Policy*. New York: Pearson Longman, 2004.

Kahn, Alfred E. "The Tyranny of Small Decisions: Market Failures, Imperfections, and the Limits of Economics." *Kyklos* 19 (1966): 23–47.

Kahn, Peter H., Jr. *The Human Relationship with Nature: Development and Culture*. Cambridge, Mass.: Harvard University Press, 1999.

Kane, Rene C. "Prairie Flower: An Ecologically Conscious Housing Development Begins to Mature West of Chicago." *Landscape Architecture*, October 2002, 4–15.

Kaplan, Rachel, and Stephen Kaplan. "Preference, Restoration, and Meaningful Action in the Context of Nearby Nature." In *Urban Place: Reconnecting with the Natural World*, edited by Peggy F. Bartlett, 271–298. Cambridge, Mass.: MIT Press, 2005.

Kareiva, Peter, Michelle Marvier, and Robert Lalasz. "Conservation in the Anthropocene: Beyond Solitude and Fragility." *Breakthrough Journal*, Winter 2012. http://thebreakthrough.org/index.php/journal/past-issues/issue-2/conservation-in-the-anthropocene.

Kay, Charles. "Ecosystems Then and Now: A Historical Ecological Approach to Ecosystem Management." In *Proceedings of the Fourth Prairie Conservation and Endangered Species*

*Workshop*, edited by Walter D. Willms and Johan F. Dormaar, 79–87. Edmonton: Curatorial Section, Provincial Museum of Alberta, 1996.

Keating, Ann Durkin. *Chicagoland: City and Suburbs in the Railroad Age*. Chicago: University of Chicago Press, 2005.

Kingdon, John. *Agendas, Alternatives, and Public Policies*. New York: Harper Collins, 1995.

Kostyack, John. "Habitat Conservation Planning: Time to Give Conservationists and Other Concerned Citizens a Seat at the Table." *Endangered Species Update* 14, no. 7–8 (1997): 51–55.

Kuhn, Thomas. *The Structure of Scientific Revolutions*. Chicago: University of Chicago Press 1962.

Kunstler, James. *The Geography of Nowhere*. New York: Simon and Schuster, 1993.

———. *The Long Emergency*. New York: Grove Press, 2005.

Lakoff, George. *Moral Politics: How Liberals and Conservatives Think*. Chicago: University of Chicago Press, 1996.

———. "Why It Matters How We Frame the Environment." *Environmental Communication* 4, no. 1 (March 2010): 70–81.

Layzer, Judith. *The Environmental Case*. Washington, D.C.: CQ Press, 2010.

Lenart, Claudia. "Liberty Prairie Conservancy Springs to Life in Reserve." *Grayslake Times*, October 21, 1994.

Leopold, Aldo. *A Sand County Almanac*. 1949. Reprint, New York: Ballantine Books, 1970.

Lockwood, Julie L., and Michael L. McKinney. *Biotic Homogenization*. New York: Kluwer Academy/Plenum, 2001.

Louv, Richard. *Last Child in the Woods*. Chapel Hill, N.C.: Algonquin Books, 2005.

———. *The Nature Principle: Reconnecting with Life in a Virtual Age*. Chapel Hill, N.C.: Algonquin Books, 2012.

Low, Tim. *Feral Future*. New York: Penguin Books, 1999.

Lowen, Sara. "The Tyranny of the Lawn." *American Heritage* 42, no. 5 (1991): 42–55.

MacArthur, Robert H., and Edward O. Wilson. *The Theory of Island Biogeography*. Princeton, N.J.: Princeton University Press, 1967.

Manning, Richard. *Against the Grain: How Agriculture Has Hijacked Civilization*. New York: North Point Press, 2004.

———. *Grassland: The History, Biology, Politics, and Promise of the American Prairie*. New York: Penguin Books, 1995.

Manzo, Lynne C., and Neil D. Weinstein. "Behavioral Commitment to Environmental Protection: A Study of Active and Nonactive Members of the Sierra Club." *Environment and Behavior* 19 (1987) 673–694.

Marks, Martha. "The Green Old Party." *Sierra*, July/August 2004. http://vault.sierraclub.org/sierra/200407/green.asp.

McHarg, Ian L. *Design with Nature*. Garden City, N.Y.: Natural History Press, 1969.

McHarg, Ian L., and Frederick R. Steiner, eds. *To Heal the Earth: Selected Writings of Ian L. McHarg*. Washington, D.C.: Island Press, 1998.

McKenzie, Evan. *Beyond Privatopia: Rethinking Residential Private Government*. Washington, D.C.: Urban Institute Press, 2011.

————. *Privatopia*. New Haven, Conn.: Yale University Press, 1994.

————. "Trouble in Privatopia." In *The Politics of Urban America: A Reader*, edited by Dennis R. Judd and Paul P. Kantor, 192–196. Boston: Allyn and Bacon, 1998.

McKenzie-Mohr, Doug. "Fostering Sustainable Behavior through Community-Based Social Marketing." *American Psychologist* 555, no. 5 (2000): 531–537.

McKenzie-Mohr, Doug, and William Smith. *Fostering Sustainable Behavior: An Introduction to Community-Based Social Marketing*. 2nd ed. Gabriola Island, B.C.: New Society, 1999.

McMahon, Edward T. *Conservation Communities: Creating Value with Nature, Open Space, and Agriculture*. Washington, D.C.: Urban Land Institute, 2010.

Merchant, Carol. *Reinventing Eden: The Fate of Nature in Western Culture*. New York: Routledge, 2003.

Miller, Donald. *City of the Century: The Epic of Chicago and the Making of America*. New York: Norton Books, 1991.

Mooney, Chris. "Your Neighbors May Be Turning You into an Environmentalist." *Washington Post*, June 8, 2015.

Moore, Robin C. "The Need for Nature: A Childhood Right." *Social Justice* 24, no. 3 (Fall 1997): 203–220.

Morris, Edmund. *Theodore Rex*. New York: Random House, 2001.

Murphy, Kate. "Farm-to-Table Living Takes Root." *New York Times*, March 12, 2014.

Myers, Nancy J., and Carolyn Raffensperger. *Precautionary Tools for Reshaping Environmental Policy*. Cambridge, Mass.: MIT Press, 2006.

Nikiforuk, Andrew. *Tar Sands: Dirty Oil and the Future of a Continent*. Vancouver, B.C.: Greystone Books, 2010.

Norton, Bryan G. *Sustainability: A Philosophy of Adaptive Ecosystem Management*. Chicago: University of Chicago Press, 2005.

Ogden, George W. *Letters from the West: Comprising a Tour through the Western Country, and a Residence of Two Summers in the States of Ohio and Kentucky*. New-Bedford, Mass.: Melcher and Rogers, 1823.

Openlands Project and the Illinois State Museum. *Prairies in the Prairie State: Midewin National Tallgrass Prairie*. Web exhibit, Openlands Project and the Illinois State Museum Society, 1999. http://exhibits.museum.state.il.us/exhibits/midewin.

Orfield, Myron. *Metropolitics: A Regional Agenda for Community and Stability*. Washington, D.C.: Brookings Institution Press, 1997.

Pearce, Fred. *When the Rivers Run Dry: Water—The Defining Crisis of the Twenty-First Century*. Boston: Beacon Press, 2006.

Peterson, Paul E. *The Price of Federalism*. Washington, D.C.: Brookings Institution, 1995.

Pimentel, David, Lori Lach, Rodolfo Zuniga, and Doug Morrison. "Environmental and Economic Costs of Nonindigenous Species in the United States." *Bioscience* 50, no. 1 (2000): 53–65.

Platt, Rutherford H. *Land Use and Society: Geography, Law, and Public Policy*. Washington, D.C.: Island Press, 1996.

Popelka, Bernice Benedict. *Saving Peacock Prairie: The Grassroots Campaign to Protect a Wild Urban Prairie*. Thiensville, Wisc.: Caritas Communications, 2010.

Popenoe, David. *Private Pleasure, Public Plight: Urban Development, Suburban Sprawl, and the Decline of Community.* New Brunswick, N.J.: Transaction Publishing, 2001.

Putnam, Robert D. *Bowling Alone: The Collapse and Revival of American Community.* New York: Simon and Schuster, 2000.

Quammen, David. *Song of the Dodo.* New York: Simon and Schuster, 1996.

Ranney, Victoria Post. *Olmsted in Chicago.* Chicago: R. R. Donnelley and Sons, 1972.

Rappaport, Bret. "Prairie Crossing: Opening a Space for Naturalistic Solutions." *Chicagoland Gardening,* September/October 1997, 17–20.

Reich, Robert. "Secession of the Successful." *New York Times Magazine,* January 20, 1991, 14–25.

Reich, Susanna. *Painting the Wild Frontier: The Art and Adventures of George Catlin.* New York: Clarion Books, 2008.

Reisner, Marc. *Cadillac Desert: The American West and Its Disappearing Water.* New York: Penguin Books, 1993.

Rodkin, Dennis. "The Good Earth: Prairie Crossing Is a Community Dedicated to the Idea That Developing Land Is the Best Way to Protect It." *Chicago Magazine,* February, 27, 1996, 27–29.

———. "Landed Gentry." *Chicago Magazine,* May 23, 1999, 10–15.

Rome, Adam. *The Bulldozer in the Countryside: Suburban Sprawl and the Rise of American Environmentalism.* New York: Cambridge University Press, 2001.

Rothman, Hal. *The Greening of America? Environmentalism in the United States since 1945.* Ft. Worth, Tex.: Harcourt Brace, 1998.

Rusk, Dean. *Cities without Suburbs.* Washington, D.C.: Woodrow Wilson Center Press, 1993.

Ryan, Robert, and Robert Grese. "Urban Volunteers and the Environment: Forest and Prairie Restoration." In *Urban Place: Reconnecting with the Natural World,* edited by Peggy F. Bartlett, 173–188. Cambridge, Mass.: MIT Press, 2005.

Rybczynski, Witold. *A Clearing in the Distance: Frederick Law Olmsted and America in the Nineteenth Century.* New York: Scribner, 1999.

Sanderson, Eric W., Malanding Jaiteh, Marc A. Levy, Kent H. Redford, Antoinette V. Wannebo, and Gillian Woolmer. "The Human Footprint and the Last of the Wild." *BioScience* 52, no. 10 (2002): 891–904.

Schaeffer, Jeffrey S., James K. Bland, and John Janssen. "Use of a Stormwater Retention System for Conservation of Regionally Endangered Fishes." *Fisheries* 37, no. 2 (February 2012): 66–75.

Schipper, Janine. *Disappearing Desert: The Growth of Phoenix and the Culture of Sprawl.* Norman: University of Oklahoma Press, 2006.

Schlosser, Eric. *Fast Food Nation: The Dark Side of the All-American Meal.* New York: Perennial, 2001.

Scully, Vincent. *American Architecture and Urbanism.* New York: Random House, 1969.

Shaiko, Ronald G. *Voices and Echoes for the Environment: Public Interest Representation in the 1990s and Beyond.* New York: Columbia University Press, 1999.

Steinberg, Ted. *American Green: The Obsessive Quest for the Perfect Lawn.* New York: W. W. Norton, 2006.

Stern, Paul C. "Psychology and the Science of Human-Environment Interactions." *American Psychologist* 55, no. 5 (2000): 523–530.

Stolzenburg, William. *Where the Wild Things Were: Life, Death, and Ecological Wreckage in a Land of Vanishing Predators.* New York: Bloomsbury, 2008.

Stone, Deborah. *Policy Paradox: The Art of Decision Making.* New York: W. W. Norton, 1997.

Stone, Robert (director). *Earth Days.* Boston: WGBH, 2010.

Sullivan, William C. "Forest, Savanna, City." In *Urban Place: Reconnecting with the Natural World,* ed. Peggy F. Bartlett, 237–252. Cambridge, Mass.: MIT Press, 2005.

Swain, Glenn. "On the Alert for Misleading Ads." *New York Times,* November, 16, 2011.

Switzer, Jacqueline Vaughn. *Environmental Politics: Domestic and Global Dimensions.* 4th ed. Belmont, Calif.: Wadsworth Publishing, 2004.

Switzer, Jacqueline Vaughn, and Gary Bryner. *Environmental Politics: Domestic and Global Dimensions.* 2nd ed. New York: St. Martin's Press, 1998.

Tanaka, Sanette. "Why Homes with Open Space Command Big Bucks." *Wall Street Journal,* May 3, 2013.

Thompson, Robert H. "Overcoming Barriers to Ecologically Sensitive Land Management." *Journal of Planning Education and Research* 24 (2004): 141–153.

Thompson, William J. "Land Matters." *Landscape Architecture,* October 2003, 3.

Tucker, Richard P. *Insatiable Appetite: The United States and the Ecological Degradation of the Tropical World.* Lanham, Md.: Rowman and Littlefield, 2007.

Vig, Norman J., and Michael E. Kraft. *Environmental Policy in the 1990s: Toward a New Agenda.* Washington, D.C.: CQ Press, 1997.

Walker, Jack L., Jr. *Mobilizing Interest Groups in America: Patrons, Professions, and Social Movements.* Ann Arbor: University of Michigan Press, 1991.

Wandersee, James H., and Elisabeth E. Schussler. "Toward a Theory of Plant Blindness." *Plant Science Bulletin* 47, no. 1 (2001): 2–9.

Webber, Melvin. "Order in Diversity: Community without Propinquity." In *Cities and Space: The Future Use of Urban Land,* edited by Lowdon Wingo Jr., 23–54. Baltimore: Johns Hopkins University Press, 1963.

Weidensaul, Scott. *Living on the Wind: Across the Hemisphere with Migratory Birds.* New York: North Point Press, 1999.

Wells, Nancy M., and Gary W. Evans. "Nearby Nature: A Buffer of Life Stress among Rural Children." *Environment and Behavior* 35 (2003): 311–330. .

Wilson, Edward O. *The Diversity of Life.* New York: W. W. Norton, 1992.

———. *The Future of Life.* New York: Alfred A. Knopf, 2002.

———. "What Is Nature Worth?" *Wilson Quarterly* 26, no. 1 (2002): 20–39.

Woodward, Richard B. "A Sliver of Prairie Still Untamed." *New York Times,* June 10, 2005.

# INDEX

Brand, Steward, 25
Breen, John, 85–87, 122
Bren, Donald, 109
Brewer, Richard, 53, 58, 59, 64
buildings. *See* construction of buildings; design of PC buildings
*Bulldozer in the Countryside, The* (Rome), 161n6
Bundoran Farm, VA, 142–144, 145
burns of native plants, 3–6, 21, 65–66, 162n10, *plate 11*
businesses at PC, 10
buyers of homes, motivations of, 80–81
Byron Colby Barn, 17, 44, 45, 47, 99, *plate 18*

Cadiz Township, WI, 70, 71
Calthorpe Associates, 139
Canada goose, 82
capitalism, conservation and, 75, 153–154
Carson, Rachel, 25
Cather, Willa, 8
Catlin, George, 22, 165n6
Celebration School, 112
*Changes in the Land* (Conron), 132
charter schools, 114, 177n69. *See also* Prairie Crossing Charter School
Chicago, IL, 23, 165n14; transit links from PC, 16, 34, 45, 136, 147
Chicago Wilderness, 63, 73, 76
*City Politics* (Judd and Swanstrom), 118
civil rights movement, 44–45
Clean Air Act, 54
*Closing Circle, The* (Commoner), 2–3, 25, 152
Cole, Sandy, 129–130
College of Lake County, 56
colonists, ecological effect of, 132
Columbia, MD, 105, 108–109
commercial developments, conservation-friendly, 154
common areas at PC, 58–59, 73–76, 78–79, 82, *plate 13*
Commoner, Barry, 2–3, 25, 152
common-interest developments, 95–97
community, sense of, 17–18, 44, 94–95, 100–105, 134
Community Associations Institute, 97
community participation: by Americans, 120, 130; and conservation behavior, 92–93; at

gated communities, 102–104, 120; at PC, 17–18, 99–100, 104–105, 135–136, 150
compass plant, 8, *plate 9*
conceptual development of PC, 49–50
condominiums at PC, 10, 92, 117, 119
Conron, William, 132
*Conservancy* (Brewer), 53, 58, 59, 64
conservation, environmental: and conservation communities, 83–89, 92–93 (*see also* conservation communities); Gaylord Donnelley as advocate, 26–28, 44; as guiding principle of PC, 43–44, 55–59, 146–147; market-based (*see* market-based environmental conservation); models of, 52–55; at PC, 11–15, 55–58, 60–76, 78–83, *plate 13*; by PC residents, 83–89, 102, 134; political views and, 52–54, 169nn5–6; of private land, 55; purpose of, 153
conservation activities, 83–89, 102, 134
conservation amenities, 80, 135–136, 149, 154
Conservation@Home, 38, 103, 135, 151–152
conservation communities, 3, 161n3; advocacy of, 134–135, 140; behavior of residents, 83–89, 92–93; benefits of, 153–154; developers, 80, 133–134, 147–148, 152; impediments to development, 141; PC as model, 19–20, 132–155, 140–146; satisfaction of PC residents, 102; second-generation, 140–146, 154; site selection, 145; water quality as motivation for, 57–58
conservation easements, 28, 58, 138, 141, 166n27, 166n37
Conservation Foundation, 103
Conservation Fund, 58
Conservation Research Institute, 91
"Conservative Environmental Manifesto" (Huber), 116, 137
Conserve Lake County: activities of, 38, 89, 103, 135, 151; goals of, 103, 151–152, 180n18; property owned by, 72, 73
constitutional organization of PC, 133–134
construction of buildings: green construction costs, 90–91, 140, 149; at PC, 45–46, 135
Countryside Landfill, 46
Cox, Wendell, 171n52
Crane, Phil, 124–125, 127–128, 176n53
criticism of PC, 74, 143, 164n42
Cronon, William, 155

cultural change as goal of PC, 16, 56, 77–93, 130–131
Cummisford, Erin, 164n38
cup plant, 8–9

Davis, Alexander Jackson, 31
Davis, Robert, 32, 33, 45
Deere, John, 23
Deigan, Geoff, 113, 114
demographics of PC, 19, 116–117, 137, 164n43
design of PC buildings, 9–10, 34, 45–46, 99.
    See also landscape design
Design with Nature (McHarg), 106–107
Des Plaines River, 24, 31; watershed, 12, 68
developers, role of, 80, 133–134, 147–148, 152
development of PC, 137–140
Dietel, Betsy, 72, 103, 151
diversity. See economic and racial diversity
Donnelley, Dorothy, 26–28, 37, 49
Donnelley, Gaylord: as conservation advocate, 26–28, 35–37, 44, 150, 151; support for PC, 45–46, 49, 50
Donnelley, Laura, 49, 49n92
Donnelley, Richard Robert, 26
Donnelley, Strachan, 49, 169n92
Donnelley-Depue Wildlife Area, 28
Donnelley family, 29–30, 35–37
Donnelley Wildlife Management Area, 28
Downing, Andrew Jackson, 31
Downs, Anthony, 161n2
drainage: farming's effect on, 12, 23–24, 60; stormwater at PC, 60, 61, 62, 75, 150
Duany, Andres, 32, 39, 98, 116
Ducks Unlimited, 27, 28, 35

easements, conservation, 28, 58, 138, 141, 166n27, 166n37
economic and racial diversity, 115–117; in Columbia, MD, 108–109; as guiding principle of PC, 44–45, 95, 115; housing patterns and, 116–118; at PC, 19, 116–117, 119, 136–137, 139, 148–149, 164n43
Economic Approach to Human Behavior, The (Becker), 173n14
economic viability of PC, 45–46, 74, 90–93, 151
ecosystems: carrying capacity, 69; economic value, 75; fires and, 5, 66; fragmentation, 11,

59, 69–70, 71, 76; at PC, 73–74; species-area effect, 69, 171–72n55
ecotopia, 96, 174n9
education of community: at PC, 45, 56, 87–89, 134, 136; second-generation conservation communities, 145
Edward L. Ryerson Conservation Area, 26
Ehrlich, Paul, 25
Eighth Congressional District, IL, 124–126, 127–128, 176n53
Eisenhower, Dwight, 169n5
elected positions held by PC residents, 129–130
election of 2004, participation of PC residents in, 123–125
emerald ash borer, 14, 162n24
energy conservation at PC, 45, 56, 89–90
environmental degradation, 75, 153–154, 181n45
environmental manager of PC, 133–134
environmental movement, 25–26
environmental premium, 116, 137
environmental protection. See conservation, environmental
Environmental Protection Agency, 76
Environmental Stewardship Committee, 86, 123
equilibrium theory for islands, 68–70
Ernest F. Hollings ACE Basin National Wildlife Refuge, 28
Ervin, Christine, 90
Eurasian water milfoil, 82
Evanston, IL, 14, 162n24, 165n14

farm-based communities, 144
Farm Business Development Center, 47, 48
farmers' markets, 74, 89, 164n38
farmhouse designs, 10, plates 8, 10, 17
farming: community-supported agriculture, 169n88; ecological effect of, 12, 23–24, 44, 64, 65; organic, 38, 42, 47–49, 144, 149
farmland preservation, 41
fertilizers: ecological effect of, 13, 14, 44, 79, 162n19, 162n22; use at PC, 79, 136
financing of conservation communities, 141, 143, 148
fire ecology, 3–6, 21, 65–66, 162n10
fish at PC, 12, 63, 66, 68, 150

*Fisheries* (journal), 66
Flannery, Tim, 21
flood control, 63, 66, 75–76, 154–155
forbs, 8–9
Forsyth, Ann, 87, 108–110, 111, 150
Foursquare design, 9–10
Fox River, 24, 72
fragmentation of ecosystems, 11, 59, 69–70, 71, 76
Fremont 79 (school district), 112
Fresh Taste, 47

Galisteo Basin Preserve, NM, 141–142, 145
garden plots, 56
gated communities, 102–104, 116, 120
Gaylord and Dorothy Donnelly Foundation, 27–28, 47
*Geography of Nowhere, The* (Kunstler), 17, 39, 94, 167n54
Gladwell, Malcolm, 101
Glasgow, Scotland, 107
Glenview, IL, 154–155, 165n14
Goldschmidt, Neil, 38
Gottlieb, Robert, 55
granny flats, 119, 137, 139, 180n8
grasses, lawn, 13, 14, 79, 162n19, 162n22. *See also* plants, native
grassland: biodiversity of, 65; flood control benefits of, 63, 66, 75–76; at PC, 4, 5, 7–9, 65; pre-colonization, 4, 5; preserves, 4, 52; remaining in U.S., 14, 44, 65, 75; root systems of, 66, 67
Grayslake, IL, 6, 35, 36, 62, 131, 143
great blue herons, 72, *plate 16*
Great Lakes, 24
Green County, WI, 70, 71
greenwashing, 51–52, 58, 61
guiding principles of PC, 43–46, 55–58, 128–129, 133, 179n15. *See also specific topics*
Gurnee, IL, 36

habitat: at Lake Aldo Leopold, 61; loss of, 11, 24, 64, 69–70, 71, 76; protection of, 36, 64, 72–73
healthy lifestyle, 16–17, 44
Heartland Agreement, 35
Heartland Development, 35, 49
herbicides, 12, 13, 24, 44, 79
Hidden Springs, ID, 137–140, 143, 145, 149

Homeowners Association, Prairie Crossing: bird boxes placed by, 7, 64, 100; burns of plants by, 3–6, 65–66, 162n10; conservation management by, 60–76, 78–83; developers, role of, 80; education of residents by, 88; invasive species policies, 81–82, 86; lawn care guidelines, 13, 79; participation of residents in, 80, 102–103, 121–123, 134; satisfaction with, 96, 97; surveys conducted by, 128–129
home ownership in U.S., 2
Homestead Preserve, VA, 142
homogenization, biological, 14
horse stables, *plate 12*
house sparrows, 81–82
housing at PC: color scheme, 57, 99; condominiums, 10, 92, 117, 119; designs, architectural, 9–10, 34, 45–46, 99; energy efficiency of, 56, 90, 136; environmental premium, 116, 137; number of homes, 1, 59, 141; photos of, *plates 1, 4–8, 13–15, 17*; placement of, 10, 74, 135, 145, 146; property values of, 91–92, 137, 173–74n34; tax on sales of, 46, 149
Hovany, Steve, 74, 116, 143, 164n42
Huber, Peter, 116, 137

ice age, 21–22
Illinois-Michigan Canal National Heritage Corridor, 28
Illinois Nature Preserves Commission, 73
Illinois River, wildlife refuge on, 28
income levels, housing and, 19, 116–118
Independence Grove, 36, 72
Inland Steel, 26, 45
Integrated Lakes Management, 78
invasive species: birds, 64, 76, 81–82; and burns, 9, 162n10; ecological impact of, 14, 81; at PC, 81–82, 86, 136
Irvine Company, 105–106
Irvine Ranch, CA, 105, 109–110
island biogeography, 68–71

Jackson Meadows, MN, 144–145
Jarvis, Ron, 130
John Deere plows, 23
Johnson, Bill, 138–139
Johnston, Joseph, 144
Jones, Lynne, 41
Judd, Dennis R., 118

JOHN SCOTT WATSON is a lecturer in the political science department of the University of Illinois, Chicago.

The University of Illinois Press
is a founding member of the
Association of American University Presses.

---

Composed in 11/14 Arno Pro
with Adrianna and Frontage display
by Jim Proefrock
at the University of Illinois Press
Jacket design by Jim Proefrock
Jacket photograph by Maryanne Natarajan
Manufactured by Cushing-Malloy, Inc.

University of Illinois Press
1325 South Oak Street
Champaign, IL 61820-6903
www.press.uillinois.edu